WONDERS OF IRELAND

Eric Newby and Diana Petry are also the authors of *Wonders of Britain* (1968) which describes 480 Wonders in England, Scotland and Wales

WONDERS OF IRELAND

A personal choice of 484

by Eric Newby and Diana Petry

Maps by John Flower

Stein and Day/*Publishers*/New York

First published in the United States of America by
Stein and Day/*Publishers* 1970

Library of Congress Catalog Card No. 74-104648

Printed in the United States of America
Stein and Day/*Publishers*/7 East 48 Street, New York, N.Y.
SBN 8128-1274-3

Photographs

KEY TO SOURCES

[1] *The Scenery and Antiquities of Ireland*

[2] *Excursions through Ireland*

[3] Diana Petry

[4] *Ireland: Its Scenery, Character, Etc.*

[5] Eric Newby

Contents

SECTION SEVEN

The Wonders

We would like to thank the Irish Tourist Boards for their help and advice, generously and unstintingly given, without which we would still be wallowing in their bogs.

Eric Newby and Diana Petry

Introduction

Wo·nder (wŭ–), n. Miracle, prodigy, strange or remarkable thing or specimen or performance or event.

The Concise Oxford Dictionary

By this definition, Ireland is one vast Wonder, but we have had to try to be selective otherwise this book would have run to twenty volumes instead of a modest one. On the whole we have not included Wonders in towns and cities, otherwise we would still be there.

Our choice of Wonders has been influenced, as it was when we were searching for the Wonders of Britain, by considerations that would not be acceptable to archaeologists, antiquaries or architects. Ours is a frankly romantic approach. To us it is not always the thing that is wonderful. Often it is its place in the landscape that makes it so, or the time of day at which one visits it. At sunrise and sunset even the lesser Wonders assume a majesty far above their station, but the Irish climate has a chameleon-like capacity for change, drenching everything in such a succession of sun, shade and water, that any time of day could be the right one.

The kinds and character of the Wonders of Ireland are legion: lonely islands, hidden loughs, huge precipitous cliffs, caverns, towers, abbeys, castles, churches, follies, industrial remains, tombs and memorials, great houses and demesnes, waterfalls, subterranean rivers, canals, cloud-capped mountains, passes, ancient woods, dolmens, crannogs, stone circles, cairns, earthworks, bridges, holy wells, crosses, Ogham stones, prehistoric cemeteries, places of pilgrimage. Go now, before they crumble away, fall over the cliffs, or get surrounded by impenetrable thickets of brambles, creepers and trees.

There is little commercialization. The Irish believe that their Wonders belong to the nation. Except for some on private property, and some with notices about this or that belonging to somebody or other and don't deface it, they DO belong to the nation. It is a case of finding them. They are all yours if you can. In this book we have given as clear directions as we can for getting to the Wonders we have chosen, but it still won't always be easy.

When you fail, as you most certainly will, ask locally, otherwise you may never find them at all. Whoever you ask will either: (a) talk to you for an hour about it;

(b) talk to you for two hours about something else altogether because they don't know where the thing is you want; (c) take you home and give you a cup of tea while they ask the neighbours; or (d) take you there personally because they have always wanted to see it themselves, and never have. Perhaps this is more than half the point. You look for wonders and find the Irish, who are the walking (and talking) Wonders of the World.

Don't expect perfect road signposting. How can there be when so many roads lead from nowhere to nowhere? Even where signs exist, they may abandon you after the first one and leave you to decide what to do at the next crossroads. Even the maps are not infallible, nor do they always show the place you want. Perhaps they call it by some other name, spell it some other way, or make up for leaving it out by putting in other Wonders which otherwise you would never have heard of at all.

Spellings! Irish is another language and even within its own framework there are numerous spellings for one place or personal name, added to which there are English translations—different again. The spelling we have used is the one said by the Irish Tourist Boards to be 'common usage'. Don't be surprised if it is not what's on the map or even on the signposts. There are several versions of 'common usage'.

As with pubs, there is not really such a thing as 'normal opening times' in Ireland. Many Wonders seem to be either permanently open or permanently closed. Where we are reasonably sure, we have given the times, or at least some indication of them. It is best to pay no attention to them, but check locally, and you can still be wrong.

Be relaxed. Ireland is essentially a relaxed land full of kind people who will tell you a thing is a mile away if you look tired, because they don't want you to feel daunted, as it really is six miles.

If a Wonder is on private land, don't just stalk on to it. Ask permission; it will always be granted. Many churches may be locked up. Don't despair. Just go to the nearest cottage, farm or schoolhouse if one is near, and ask there. They will know. Whether the bloke they send you to for the key is in, or has lent it to his brother in the next village, is another matter. Don't feel frustrated. Remember Ireland is Ireland, and come again next year.

As we found when we were working on *Wonders of Britain*, we are not by any means infallible, and we may have slipped up, although we have tried to be accurate. If you find us out, do write in and say so; we welcome correction.

The Authors

Notes

National Tourist Offices, for general literature and information:

London: **Irish Tourist Office**
Ireland House
150 New Bond Street, London, W1

Dublin: **Bord Failte Eireann**
(Irish Tourist Board)
Baggot Street Bridge
Dublin 2

London: **Northern Ireland Tourist Board**
11 Berkeley Street
London, W1

Belfast: **Northern Ireland Tourist Board**
10 Royal Avenue
Belfast BT1 1DQ

Each Wonder is given its National Grid reference immediately after its name (see the last page of the map section). The Eire $\frac{1}{2}''$ Ordnance Survey map series is common to the whole country; but in the case of Northern Ireland, as there is a Northern Ireland Ordnance Survey 1″ series, both map numbers have been given.

Section 1

Dublin

Meath

Louth

Monaghan

Cavan

Longford

Westmeath

[1]

Ben of Howth O 293368 (Eire ½″ Map 16)

At Howth, 9 miles north-east of Dublin. Grassy headland rising to 560 feet at the extremity of the long isthmus which forms the northern arm of Dublin Bay. Magnificent views from its southern side across the deep bay to Dublin and, still further south, to the Dun Laoghaire coast, while to the north is Ireland's Eye, a small, offshore islet with a deeply cleft rock at its tail. The best views are from the vicinity of Bailey's Lighthouse, facing southwards over impressive cliff scenery, and where the ditches and ramparts of an old promontory fort can still be traced. The views are particularly fine at night, when the far coasts are bands of brilliant lights. There are some good walks over the bracken-covered slopes of the headland.

Howth Castle demesne, overlooking the harbour from the north side of the headland, has beautiful gardens with very fine rhododendron walks, and half a mile of beech hedge, 30 feet high. (Gardens only open to the public; admission charge.)

[2]

Dunsoghly O 118431 (Eire ½″ Map 13)

Three and a half miles north-north-west of Finglas, to the right of the Dublin–Ashbourne road. Huge, remarkably well-preserved keep with square angle towers, rising through three storeys. Some of the massive roof and floor timbers are still in place. The north-eastern tower can be ascended by an interior stairway which leads to the battlements. Built in the 15th century by Sir Thomas Plunkett, Chief Justice to the King's Bench, the castle was finally besieged and taken over by Cromwell's troops. Exceptional views from the parapets of Howth to the north, of the Dublin countryside, and of planes landing and taking off from the airport a few miles to the east. (Key to tower from near-by house.)

By the side of the castle is a small, 16th century chapel whose doorway has remnants of carvings: on one side a Tudor rose and on the other, a fleur-de-lys. Above the doorway, carved on an encased tablet, are symbols of the Passion: the cross, nails, ladder, hammer, lash and pillar.

[3]

Hellfire Club O 114231 (Eire ½″ Map 16)

On the summit of Montpelier Hill, a 1271-foot overgrown height 8 miles south-south-west of Dublin. The ruins are of a building planned as a sporting lodge and built about 1720 by Speaker Conolly, from the stones of a near-by cairn. Not long after its construction, the roof was blown off in a violent storm, a calamity attributed by local people to the desecration of the cairn, which was an ancient burial site. In 1785 it was acquired by James Worsdale, the painter, and Richard Parsons, first Earl of Rosse, who bought it as a suitable rendezvous for the Hellfire Club whose meetings had hitherto been held in The Eagle Tavern, Dublin. Club members included lords and high ranking officers of the day, place of bad honour being given to an enormous black cat, which was said to preside over the drunken orgies. The Club, whose reputation was enhanced by local gossip, came to an end in the early 1840s, when many of its members were expelled from the country.

The shattered building, dangerously ruinous, dominates the surrounding country. The climb up is steep but worth it for the fine views on a clear day of Dublin and its great bay, and of the distant Mountains of Mourne.

The ruin can be reached from a gap in the high hedge on the Dublin–Glencree road, 1 mile north of the Kilakee car park and crossroads (view point). From here, a steep, straight track leads up through Forestry Commission conifers to the summit.

[4]

Joyce Museum O 258280 (Eire ½″ Map 16)

At Sandycove, 1 mile south-east of Dun Laoghaire harbour. Converted Martello tower standing on a rocky promontory above the boulder-strewn foreshore. This is the coastal tower in which James Joyce set the opening pages of *Ulysses,* where the three young men lived in the summer of 1904 – Stephen Dedalus (Kinch – a representation of Joyce himself), Buck Mulligan, and the Englishman, Haines:

'Do you pay rent for this tower?'
'Twelve quid,' Buck Mulligan said.
'To the secretary of state for war,' Stephen added over his shoulder.
They halted while Haines surveyed the tower and said at last:
'Rather bleak in wintertime, I should say. Martello you call it?'
'Billy Pitt had them built,' Buck Mulligan said, 'when the French were on the sea. But ours is the *omphalos* . . .'

The tower is now a museum of Joyce paraphernalia and some of his original manuscripts are there. From the top there are splendid views up and down the coast, over the foreshore where Joyce's young men used to swim, and of offshore Dalkey Island and the open sea. (Open May–October; admission charge.)

[5]

Killiney Hill O 260255 (Eire ½" Map 16)

South of Dublin, on the northern arm of Killiney Bay, between Dalkey and Killiney. Thickly wooded height rising nearly 500 feet above the coast road, and now preserved as a public park with some fine walks. On the summit is a tall obelisk mounted on a square, arched base, erected after the Great Frost in 1741. On the southern slope are some fragments of an ancient church and some grouped stones known as The Druid's Chair. Magnificent views of the very beautiful bay with its background of mountains, proudly compared locally with Naples Bay, which it does, indeed, resemble. To stress the image, there is a Sorrento Park and a Vico Road.

[6]

Lusk Church O 223550 (Eire ½" Map 13)

At Lusk, 5 miles north of Dublin, on the road to Skerries. Sixteenth century, square belfry tower of a demolished medieval church, standing within a small churchyard cramped at the back of the village. A unique feature is the 95-foot round tower of an earlier date, with a broken conical cap, which has been incorporated into one of the angles, the other three being occupied by more conventional turrets. Inside it, are some fine early tombs with armoured effigies, some of them elaborate. A 19th century Protestant church has been added to the existing belfry tower, but in spite of this, the effect, especially from behind or from a distance, is one of a battlemented, aggressive fortress. (Key from village shop behind the tower.)

[7]

Tully Crosses and Church O 235234 (Eire ½" Map 16)

Eight miles south-east of Dublin centre, just south of the village of Ballybrack. Reached by a turning off the Dublin–Bray road. The mutilated 13th century church, of which little remains but the chancel, stands in an old graveyard on an ancient site called Tulach nan Esboc (Hill of the Bishops), where there was once an early Christian monastery. One ancient cross, by the roadside, has been erected on a massive stone plinth in which steps have been cut leading up to it. It is inscribed as a memorial to James F. Grehan, 'who saved this Celtic cross in 1897'. A second cross is close to the edge of a field on the opposite side of the road. It is tall, very weathered, and has a fractured wheel. On one side can be distinguished the figure of a woman, who could be the Virgin; on the other, is an unidentifiable head.

MEATH

[8]

Balrath Cross O 000650 (Eire $\frac{1}{2}''$ Map 13)

At Balrath, which is on the main Dublin–Slane road, about 4 miles south-west of Duleek. A charming wayside *Pietà*, probably of the 16th or 17th century, set against the hedge. The original inscription in raised Gothic letters, commemorates a member of the Bathe family, and is a prayer for Ihoannis Broin. A later inscription in incised Roman capitals states that it was 'beautified in 1727 by Sir Andrew Aylmer and his wife'.

[9]

Bective Abbey N 858600 (Eire $\frac{1}{2}''$ Map 13)

Five miles south of Navan, on the river Boyne. Great, dark, grey stone ruin, founded in the 12th century for the Cistercians. Hugh de Lacy's torso was interred here, although later its ownership was disputed by St Thomas's Abbey, Dublin, which only had possession of the head and wanted the lot. A good deal of rebuilding took place until, after the Dissolution, the abbey was converted to a fortified dwelling. There remain the ruins of the original chapter house and church, parts of a later cloister, and the battlemented remnants of the fortified house.

[10]

Donaghmore Round Tower and Church N 878699 (Eire $\frac{1}{2}''$ Map 13)

One and a half miles north-north-east of Navan. A 100-foot-high round tower and the ruinous arch of a 16th century church stand together in a lovely setting on the west bank of the river Boyne, on the site of one of St Patrick's early churches. The tower has a Romanesque doorway 12 feet above the ground, with a crucifixion above it, and small carved stone heads on either side. A mile or so to the east are the remains of Dunmoe Castle, 16th century seat of one of the d'Arcy family, burnt out in the late 18th century. It looms grimly above the river which here flows swiftly between steep banks. It can be reached through a gate beside the adjacent farm. According to local legend, a tunnel used to lead from the vaults of the castle, under the Boyne, coming out again 100 yards or so from the south bank of the river. It may still be there, on the other hand it may not.

[11]

Dulane Church N 735788 (Eire ½″ Map 13)

Two miles north of Kells. Ruins of a pre-Romanesque church almost twice as long as it is wide, with a fine, early doorway spanned by a massive lintel over 7 feet long and nearly 2 feet high. A mile or two to the south-east, in an extensive wooded demesne with a lake, is Headfort House, an imposing mansion designed by Robert Adam. Purchased in the 17th century by a Cromwellian, Sir Thomas Taylor, the estate subsequently passed to his son, the first Earl of Bective. (See Hill of Lloyd under Kells.) It is now a preparatory school.

[12]

Fourknocks O 110621 (Eire ½″ Map 13)

Two miles west-north-west of the village of Naul, which is 6 miles west-south-west of Balbriggan. Reached from the main road by a signposted footpath along the edge of farm fields. A Bronze Age passage-grave is concealed beneath a prominent grass-grown mound. A long passage leads into the main, oval chamber, which has three flag-roofed side chambers. Many of the huge slabbed stones are decorated with spirals, zigzags, concentric circles and other geometric motifs. In the side chambers and the passage, the remains of over 60 burials were discovered, as well as grave goods which included stone beads, bone pins and a stone axe. (Key from near-by cottage.)

[13]

Hill of Ward N 736647 (Eire ½″ Map 13)

One mile east of Athboy, near the Trim–Oldcastle road. A three hundred and ninety-foot high grassy hill with four rings of ramparts, the contours of which are now somewhat blurred. This is the reputed site of the Palace of Tlachta, and was used for centuries as an important place of assembly. There are fine views from the summit. In 1649, the Cromwellian army encamped here. One mile to the west, at the small market town of Athboy, the Protestant parish church is worth a visit. A 15th century tomb topped by weathered effigies of an armoured knight and his lady, stands by the door.

Three miles north-east of Athboy are the ruins of 15th century Rathmore Castle and manorial church, standing in farm fields. The church, built by the Plunkett family, has some good sculptures and its fine tomb effigies include an elaborate one of Sir Christopher Plunkett and his wife, Katherine Preston.

[14]

Kells N 738757 (Eire $\frac{1}{2}''$ Map 13)

On the main Navan–Virginia road. An old, countrified town, the ancient Ceanannus Mor or Great Residence, in the wooded valley of the river Blackwater. A monastic settlement, probably of the 6th century, and inhabited in the 9th century by monks from Iona, it survived, with intervening disasters, until its dissolution in 1551.

The remains are concentrated in the vicinity of the Protestant parish church. Four of the five high crosses are in the graveyard. In various states of preservation, they are marvellously decorated with incidents from the Scriptures, and with hunting scenes and processions. The fifth cross, also richly sculpted, stands in the market place in the centre of the town. It was used in the 18th century as a gallows.

Beside the cemetery gate is a 90-foot round tower, its conical cap missing, but otherwise in perfect condition. Its top storey is lit by five small windows—unusual, because most of these towers have only four—said to face the five ancient roads to Kells. Outside the churchyard stands St Columcille's house, a small, 24-foot-long stone structure with immensely thick walls, thought to have been a church, as its design is similar to that of St Kevin's at Glendalough (q.v.). The doorway, which was 8 feet above the ground, has been blocked up and another opened at ground level. (Key from house in village street opposite the churchyard.)

The Book of Kells, a splendid, 8th century manuscript in Latin, can be seen in Trinity College Library, Dublin. Another Kells treasure, a beautiful crozier, is in the British Museum.

One and a half miles west-north-west of Kells, is the Hill of Lloyd, on which stands a 100-foot-high tower with a lantern-shaped top, erected in memory of Sir Thomas Taylor by his son, the first Earl of Bective, in 1791.

[15]

Loughcrew Hills Surrounding N 585775 (Eire $\frac{1}{2}''$ Map 13)

Three miles east-south-east of Oldcastle. An east-west ridge, extending nearly 4 miles and having three principal peaks: Slieve na Calliagh (Sliebh na Caillighe or the Hag's Mountain, or Carnbane East, 904 feet), Patrickstown (855 feet), and Carnbane West (824 feet). Spread across the three summits are something like 30 chambered cairns as well as tumuli, pillar stones, a ring fort, and scattered earth-

iney Hill, Co. Dublin *(Wonder No. 5)*

Ruined church and mote at Fore, Co. Westmeat
(Wonder No. 44

Swift Mausoleum, Co. Meath *(Wonder No. 18)*

Dunmoe Castle, Co. Me
(see under Donaghmore Round Tower and Chu
(Wonder No.

works—the impressive remains of a Bronze Age cemetery and one of Ireland's most remarkable sites.

The greatest concentration of cairns is on Slieve na Calliagh, the central peak, and on Carnbane West, a mile to the west. When mass excavations were carried out in 1865 by E. A. Conwell, much damage had already been caused by pillaging and neglect; later, in 1943, a single tomb was excavated.

The cairns, mostly of the passage-grave type, with entrance passages and corbelled side chambers, have been given identifying numbers by archaeologists. Cairn D on Carnbane West is the largest, with a diameter of 180 feet. Cairn T, on the summit of Slieve na Calliagh, has very large kerbstones, one of which is called the Hag's Chair because it has a hollowed-out, seat-like cavity at its top. It weighs about 10 tons. Within this tomb are 27 decorated stones; the designs on them including the spiral, rare in this region, more common at Newgrange (q.v.). The tombs were found to contain either bones or the ashes of cremation, and finds included vast quantities of objects such as bone pins, broken pottery sherds, stone beads, pieces of bone polished into blades, and ornamental plaques, mainly from the Bronze Age, although there were also some later Iron Age finds, such as glass and amber beads and bronze and iron rings.

The summits can be reached by turnings from the Oldcastle–Crossakeel road. One leads from the road to Carnbane West, another, about 1½ miles to the east, leads to Patrickstown; and from the north, a turning runs south-westwards to Carnbane East. All these small roads climb to a certain extent, but only reach the foot of the ridge. The ascent to the cairns must be made on foot over farmland and rough, grass-grown hills. The views from the top of the ridge over the great central plain across low foothills are magnificent. The burial ground, in what must have been lonely, archaic splendour, is very moving.

[16]

Newgrange O 017727 (Eire ½″ Map 13)

Seven miles west-south-west of Drogheda. One of the Boyne Valley tombs, and one of the most impressive of its kind not only in the British Isles, but in Western Europe. It dates back to about 2000 BC. The huge mound, on the highest part of a ridge above the river Boyne, and visible from a great distance, is surrounded by the remains of an enormous stone circle, 340 feet in diameter, and once consisting of 35 or more standing stones which encircled an area of two acres. Only 12 of the stones have survived and one of these is fallen. The mound, in reality a cairn 100 yards across and over 40 feet high, is composed of smooth pebbles, and was once splendidly encased in white quartz stones which have been collected during excavations, and will eventually be replaced, at least in part.

The great cairn is confined by kerbstones, many of them decorated, and varying in length from 5 to over 14 feet. The massive stone which originally covered the entrance mouth, now stands at its side. It is a remarkable piece of megalithic art, worked with bands of double spirals and lozenges.

The inner chamber and its three side chambers, are reached by a 65-foot passage which has, set back about 8 feet from the entrance, a curious 'roof-box'—an almost square space topped by a decorated stone—which has no discovered purpose but is thought to have been concerned with some tomb ritual.

The great central chamber is 20 feet high and is an impressive piece of corbelled vaulting, the diameter of the sides diminishing until, at the top, the roof is sealed by a single capstone. In the side chambers are flat, lipped stone basins which might have contained the remains of the aristocratic family for whom the tomb was supposedly built. Nobody knows. The fine ornamentation on many of the stones is still best seen by candle or torchlight, in spite of the electricity which has been installed, which detracts from the mystic wonder of a building so old and so secret. Opposite the site is a small museum. (Admission charge to tomb.)

Two more enormous mounds, Dowth and Knowth, as well as numerous smaller ones form, with Newgrange, a vast, prehistoric cemetery built within an area of 3 square miles contained in a great loop of the river Boyne.

Knowth may emerge as a monument even more startling than Newgrange. It is already proving to be one of the world's greatest wonders. Excavation has been going on since 1962 and a great chamber has been discovered, entered by a passage 114 feet long. Now yet another huge chamber, over 21 feet high, has been unearthed, with an entrance passage almost as long as the first, and many more, marvellously decorated stones. It may be a long time before the public can see this astonishing place. It is thought that the tombs were built by people who sailed up the Boyne more than 4,000 years ago. It is known where they interred their dead. Where they lived is still a mystery.

[17]

Slane Hill

N 960753 (Eire $\frac{1}{2}''$ Map 13)

Prominent hill, 529 feet high, dominating the village of Slane which is on the north bank of the Boyne, 8 miles west of Drogheda. Here, in the year 433, St Patrick lit the Paschal Fire in defiance of a decree by King Laoghaire. (Fires, Paschal or otherwise, presumably, are still banned, according to a small notice on the hill.)

On the summit stands a much ruined friary church with a tall, slim, turreted belfry tower, built about 1500 on the site of a still earlier church. A small graveyard of crosses and old, lopsided tombstones surrounds it. Beneath a stone slab is St Patrick's Well, where the water is said to rise and fall with the level of the Boyne floods.

Adjoining the church is the even more ruinous college, founded in 1512 by Sir Christopher Fleming and his wife, Elizabeth Stuckley, for four priests, four clerks and four choristers.

There are fine views from the hilltop.

[18]

Swift Mausoleum N 715488 (Eire ½″ Map 13)

At Castlerickard, near an old bridge over the river Blackwater, 8 miles south-west of Trim. A large, pyramidical, stone structure put up next to the church. It stands amid trees in the churchyard, somewhat cumbersome and mottled with age. Enclosed within a rough diamond shape cut in one side of it, is inscribed the solitary word 'Swifte'.

At Laracor, 6 miles to the north-east, the present Protestant church is built on the site of the one where Swift was incumbent, and the communion silver which he used is preserved there. Just north of Laracor, at Knightsbrook, is the small building known as Stella's House, named after Swift's Stella (Esther Johnson) who lived there with Mrs Dingley.

[19]

Tara N 915598 (Eire ½″ Map 13)

One mile west of the Dublin–Navan road; 6 miles south of Navan. Ancient seat and assembly place of the High Kings of Ireland dating from the 3rd century, although as a sanctuary and burial ground, its occupation goes back to 2,000 years BC. Here, in the 5th century, came St Patrick, on a mission to convert the pagan King Laoghaire. The not very good modern statue of the saint seems wrong in this very old place, empty now except for grazing sheep and cattle.

Here are the mounds and depressions, the ditches and ramparts of the burial grounds, forts, and lost palaces of the High Kings. All traces of the buildings, which were of timber, have long since vanished. There is not a lot to see, except in the contours of the land, but the atmosphere is powerful. With the aid of a chart it is easy to identify and to imagine the Fort of the Synods, the Fort of the Kings, Cormac's House, and the great banqueting hall—a huge, rectangular hollow enclosed by earthen ramparts—where one day it may be proved that 'the harp that once, through Tara's halls, the soul of music shed'—was more than romantic legend.

Excavations have revealed that the Mound of the Hostages, once thought to have been the place of interment of hostages brought to Tara in the 3rd century by Cormac Mac Airt, was, in fact, a 2000 BC passage-grave. In it were discovered the cremated remains of about 40 persons, and one skeleton of a boy wearing a necklace of bronze, amber and jet. There were also finds from later Bronze Age burials within the same mound: pottery, pins, beads and pendants. Here, too, on this ancient and mysterious hillside, where so much is still unknown, lie the bodies of the insurgents who died in the Battle of Tara, 1798, their grave marked by a stone—Lia Fail (The Stone of Destiny), an ancient upright stone marked with a cross, which was associated with prehistoric Tara. (Admission charge.)

[20]

Trim N 805564 (Eire ½″ Map 13)

On the Dublin–Athboy road, 7 miles south-east of Athboy. A market town on the river Boyne, one-time medieval stronghold of the English Pale and one of the oldest and most important ecclesiastical centres in Ireland. It is almost excessively rich in remains.

The dominating feature is the truly wonderful castle on the south bank of the river, the largest Anglo-Norman fortress in the country, its walls enclosing more than 3 acres. The great, square keep, with towers projecting from each of its four sides, dates from the early 13th century. The walls of the main building are over 11 feet thick and are pierced by arched apertures for windows and doorway, and contain within their thickness stairs and passages leading to other floors. The curtain walls are fortified with towers, the main one forming the gateway. In this gate-tower Richard II imprisoned the young Lord Gloucester and Prince Henry of Lancaster, later to be Henry V of England.

On a ridge opposite the castle, is the Yellow Steeple, part of an Augustinian abbey. The steeple – it is not yellow – a huge, shattered 125-foot 5-storey bell tower, was destroyed by fire in 1649 to prevent its capture by the Cromwellians. It is very dilapidated.

About ½ mile east of the town is the ruined Abbey of St Peter and St Paul, founded in 1206 by Simon de Rochfort, who was the first English Bishop of Meath. A gate in the hedge faces the ruins (signposted). This is the Echo Gate. If you call from it across the intervening fields, a perfect echo comes back from the abbey shell as if it were still inhabited.

The best view is from the bridge over the river, on the outskirts of the town. From here, the whole beautiful complex of medieval ruins can be seen, their outlines reflected with trees in the water.

[21]

Trimblestown Castle N 760576 (Eire ½″ Map 13)

Three miles west-north-west of Trim, above the north bank of the river Boyne.

Huge, turreted ruin above the river, once the seat of the Barnwall family—the Barons Trimblestown or Tremblestown. Although heavily manned and fortified, it was overpowered and captured during the Parliamentary wars. The approach is either from a gate opposite Trimblestown Stud, and then over fields; or a longer but very pleasant walk of about a mile along a track leading off the main road by the bridge where there is a weir.

LOUTH

[22]

Castleroche H 990116 (Eire ½" Map 8)

Six miles north-west of Dundalk, just south-east of the Castle Roche crossroads. Impressive, triangular-shaped ruin on an enormous bed of precipitous rocks below which cattle graze. Built in the 13th century by the Lady Rohesia de Verdon and her son, John, in a strategic position commanding a hill pass, as a defence against the Irish. There are remnants of the formidable curtain walls and towered gatehouse. One of the windows was known as Fuinneog an Mhurdair (The Murder Window), because the builder of the castle was subsequently thrown from it. Four and a half miles south-east, at Castletown, is the motte and bailey of Bertram de Verdon's castle, on the site of an early ring fort. The ruined folly on its summit was built in the 18th century by a Captain Byrne. The views are wonderful.

[23]

Charity Fathers Monastery J 145166 (Eire ½" Map 9)

At Omeath, on the southern outskirts of the town, overlooking the head of lovely Carlingford Lough. Open-air calvary and stations of the cross. Here are statues of Christ, the Virgin, and St John, brought secretly from France when their safety was threatened by persecutions, relics from Bethlehem and Calvary, replicas of the crucifixion nails, and soil from the various stations of the cross. Omeath is on the western side of the long, thumb-shaped peninsula, between Dundalk and the Newry river, and can be reached by the encircling coast road. But a far more exciting route is by the narrow mountain road which crosses the Cooley Mountains by way of Windy Gap, with splendid views of the wild, remote hills full of sheep, of Slieve Foye (1,935 feet), the beautiful lough, and the distant Mountains of Mourne.

[24]

Collon Catholic Church N 997817 (Eire ½″ Map 13)

At Collon, midway between Slane and Ardee. In the church is a charming monument to Dorcas (died 1876), daughter of the 10th Viscount Massereene. Carved in white marble, her effigy reclines on a tomb slab. She looks young and very beautiful.

A mile and a half to the north-west is Mount Oriel (810 feet), with a ring fort on its summit; and just over a mile further north, Mullaghash (740 feet), crowned by the remains of two ancient forts. These, and other near-by low, wooded hills, are all the more prominent because of the flat country around them, and they command fine views towards the sea.

[25]

Jumping Church N 975887 (Eire ½″ Map 13)

Two miles south-south-east of Ardee, in Kildemock. The ruined gable, all that remains of St Catherine's Church, stands 2 feet inside its original foundations. The prosaic explanation is that the movement was caused by a great storm in 1715, but according to local legend, the wall 'jumped' inwards to exclude the grave of a heretic who was buried there. There are some curious old gravestones and slabs in the churchyard, including one dated 1688 to William Orson and Sara, with a gruesome skull and crossbones cut on it.

[26]

Kilsaran Church O 058943 (Eire ½″ Map 13)

At Kilsaran, 2 miles south of Castlebellingham. The site of a preceptory of the Knights Templar. Catholic church built in 1866, with a very plain, rectangular nave and chancel, in sharp contrast to the highly decorative north porch, done in the then prevalent Gothic Revival style. A high, very slim, square tower rises from the castellated top of the porch, which is flanked by miniature corner spires. The top of the tower is ornamented with more needle-like spires and a cross. The pale grey of the belfry tower, and the quoins, painted in charcoal grey, combine to produce an elegant, fragile look. There are some good altar carvings. Pike-staff railings and neat, urn-topped entrance pillars enclose a drive-in edged with clipped box hedges and some nice clumps of cypress. It is all quite charming.

Half a mile to the south is the Greenmount, a prominent Norman mote. Here, during excavation, a piece of bronze with an inscription in Scandinavian runes was discovered.

[27]

King John's Castle J 190120 (Eire ½″ Map 9)

At Carlingford, on the southern shore of Carlingford Lough. Imposing ruin of a huge, D-shaped fortress high on great rocks above the harbour. It is thought to have been built by King John who came to Carlingford in 1210. A massive wall divided the structure into two halves, the western part consisting of a wide courtyard and gatehouse with only enough room for one horseman to pass at a time. A doorway in the basement below the eastern wall leads to the cliff edge.

[28]

Mellifont Abbey O 015780 (Eire ½″ Map 13)

Four and a half miles west-north-west of Drogheda. Fragmentary but important remains of Ireland's first Cistercian abbey in a wooded hollow on the banks of the tiny river Mattock, a tributary of the Boyne. Founded in the 12th century by St Malachy who, stopping at the abbey of Clairvaux on his way to Rome to secure papal permission for reforms, later brought monks trained at Clairvaux to Mellifont. Much of it is ruinous masonry and stumps of foundations, but the 14th century chapter house, a beautiful fragment of the arched, octagonal lavabo dating from the 13th century, and a short range of elegant, slim cloister columns, are in better shape. North of the approach to the abbey are the gaunt remains of a 15th century castle gatehouse.

[29]

Monasterboice O 043821 (Eire ½″ Map 13)

Three miles east of Collon; a mile west of the Drogheda–Dundalk road. Site of the monastery founded in the 6th century by St Buite, its ruins standing lonely amid fields. There remains the 100-foot-high, topless round tower, the remnants of two churches, an ancient sundial and, amid an array of tombstones, three wonderfully carved high crosses. The first to be seen on entering the graveyard is the Cross of Muiredach, 17 feet 8 inches high, one of the finest in the whole country. It is inscribed with the name Muiredach, an early 10th century abbot, and is carved with an astonishing wealth of scenes from the Scriptures. The West Cross reaches the imposing height of 21½ feet and is similarly carved, though it has weathered badly. The third cross – the North Cross – has been reconstructed and has great panels of spirals on it. (Key from the cottage next to the tower.)

[30]

Proleek Dolmen J 086119 (Eire ½″ Map 9)

At Ballymascanlan, 3½ miles north-east of Dundalk. Portal grave, otherwise known as The Giant's Load, situated about 100 feet up on the side of a low, wooded hill above a stream. The enormous granite capstone, weighing about 50 tons, is poised on one 6 foot and two 7 foot uprights. According to popular fancy, if pebbles tossed on to the capstone, which is some 13 feet from the ground, remain there, the thrower will be wed before the year's end.

The dolmen is reached by a signposted turning off the coast road. The lane leads to a stream, which is crossed by a wooden bridge, and on the far side of it, at the left of a steep approach to a farm, is a gate. Go through it and up steeply through trees to the site.

[31]

The Red Cave O 176843 (Eire ½″ Map 13)

On the south side of Clogher Head (205 feet). A huge cave on the seashore lost among the rock stacks and boulders and only possible to enter at low tide. It is so called because of the reddish fungus that grows over it, although local legend has it that here hid a party of fugitives from Cromwell's troops, their position given away by the barking of a dog. The troops reached the cave by boat and slaughtered the wretched fugitives on the spot, their blood staining the cave red.

It is best reached from Clogher Head Harbour, where a stone stile leads over the wall to the foreshore. A difficult scramble at sea level (low tide) leads from the harbour, round the Head to The Strand, a beach on the south side of the headland, a distance of just over a mile and a fine walk for any reason. The cave, difficult to find, is just over halfway round, a little to the south, the entrance flanked by a flat curtain of rock. Above it, the headland is grassgrown and sheer. (It is probably best to ask for help locally to find the cave.)

MONAGHAN

[32]

Castle Leslie H 726418 (Eire ½″ Map 8)

At Glaslough, 6 miles north-north-east of Monaghan town. On a mile-long, idyllic lough overhung thickly with trees and bushes. Graceful, 19th century,

Italianate mansion built on the site of a medieval keep, the home of the Leslie family who have lived here for 300 years. It stands in a fine, walled demesne of over 1,500 acres. To match its Italian style, a dolphin fountain was imported from Siena, and a Della Robbia fireplace; the cloister was copied from one by Michelangelo, and a shipload of ancient pilasters were brought here from Rome and built in. The grounds extend along the shores of the lough, where there is a bird sanctuary. The formal Italian garden is very beautiful. Some of the trees are among the tallest in Ireland, the Douglas, Sitka and Silver Firs exceeding the 150-foot mark. (Open to parties by prior arrangement; admission charge.)

[33]

Mannan Castle H 853074 (Eire $\frac{1}{2}''$ Map 8)

At Donaghmoyne, $2\frac{1}{2}$ miles north-north-east of Carrickmacross. An enormous mote and bailey on a low, wooded hilltop, with fragmentary remains of a medieval castle. This was the site of a manor granted to an Englishman, Peter Pepard, in 1193, after the conquest of the ancient territory of Oriel, of which Monaghan was a part. He built a castle on it, probably of wood, which was replaced in the 13th century by one of stone, erected by one of his descendants. Later, when the Irish regained the territory, it was abandoned altogether.

Except for the mote, which is of tremendous size, it is almost impossible to realize that a great castle stood here. Nothing remains of it but crumbling, overgrown walls. Even the hill itself is almost lost among numerous other small hills. Nothing disturbs the quiet, heavy, other-world atmosphere. The ruins can be reached from the roadway. About 30 yards to the north of an entrance with gateposts, is an old gateway. Go through it and up the track to the hilltop—an easy climb—muddy, but not too heavily overgrown.

CAVAN

[34]

Cloughoughter Castle H 358078 (Eire $\frac{1}{2}''$ Map 8)

Four miles north-west of Cavan. Thirteenth century, ruined circular tower, once a formidable fortress of the O Reilys and one of the finest of its kind. It stands on a small, lonely island in Lough Oughter, surrounded by a maze of channels and inlets formed by other islands and by spits of land across which straggle a few narrow roads. It is from this tangle of waterways that the river Erne finally extricates itself to flow southwards. Bishop Bedell (see Kilmore Cathedral) was imprisoned in the castle in

1641. Twelve years later it was captured by the Cromwellian army and reduced to ruins. It is best reached from the south-east, by a narrow road that runs northwards from the hamlet of Garthrattan.

[35]

Drumlane H 340122 (Eire $\frac{1}{2}''$ Map 8)

Four miles south-west of Belturbet. Reached by a lane leading south-eastwards from the village of Milltown. Remains of a 14th century church and a 45-foot round tower built on the site of an abbey founded by St Columcille. The ruinous arch is ornamented with small carved heads. The remains are fragmentary, but they stand in a wonderfully tranquil position on high ground banked between two small lakes—Drumlane and Derrybrick—in an area of gentle countryside full of countless small, secret expanses of water.

[36]

Kilmore Cathedral H 385037 (Eire $\frac{1}{2}''$ Map 8)

Three and a half miles west-south-west of Cavan. Modern, Protestant Cathedral of St Fethlimidh, built in the Gothic style, with high arched windows filled with vivid coloured glass. The fine, Irish-Romanesque doorway was brought from an old monastery which stood on Trinity Island in Lough Oughter, a few miles to the west. In the graveyard of the cathedral, which is on the opposite side of the road, is the ornate tomb of William Bedell, Protestant Bishop of Kilmore (1639–42) who, with Murtagh King, James Nangle, and Denis Sheridan, translated the Old Testament into Irish.

[37]

Knockbride Protestant Church H 659047 (Eire $\frac{1}{2}''$ Map 8)

Six miles south-east of Cootehill. Reached by an eastward turning from the main Cootehill–Bailieborough road at Canningstown. Small, aged church cramped in an even more aged-looking graveyard, thick with trees and old, forgotten tombs. A stone wall, almost obscured beneath a tangle of mosses and masking creepers, leads to another bit of the graveyard where there are more overgrown, sunken headstones lurching about in the high grass and weeds, and a few crosses. The surprise is the sudden view of a charming, very small lough below the broken wall, which seems to be so close that you feel you might have fallen in but for the barrier of the stones and undergrowth. There is nothing here of any historical, architectural or archaeological note, only the enchanted and immensely peaceful atmosphere of a lost corner.

[38]

Shannon Pot H 050318 (Eire ½″ Map 7)

About 4 miles south-south-west of Blacklion, which is on the Northern Ireland border. Shannon Pot—the source of the river Shannon—is a pool on the lower, boulder-strewn western slopes of the wild Cuilcagh Mountains, across which runs the Border. The only road linking this very remote part of Cavan with the rest of the county, starts at Swanlinbar, a one-time spa on the eastern side of the range. (A mile to the north of the town is Northern Ireland and the Customs posts.)

The mountain road, which is high and which virtually encircles the mountain tops, first swerves south-westwards from Swanlinbar, then climbs in a north-westerly direction through the Bellavally Gap, between the spectacular Cuilcagh Mountain (2,438 feet) to the north, and Benbrack (1,653 feet) to the south. Veering northwards, it passes a signpost pointing uphill, marked 'Source of the Shannon'. From this point, a rough climb of about half a mile leads to the pool.

The loop road is narrow but good, and well-surfaced. There are constant magnificent views of lonely mountain tops and of valleys almost lost to sight between steep enclosing slopes, while, visible to the north, are Loughs Macnean Upper and Lower, and the hills of Northern Ireland beyond.

LONGFORD

[39]

Carn Clonhugh N 190843 (Eire ½″ Map 12)

Six miles north-east of Newtownforbes. The highest point in the county (916 feet)—a somewhat bare hill with a prehistoric cairn on its summit. Here, in about the year 561, lived Muadan, with a religious community. He was visited by St Columcille who was, unaccountably, churlishly received and the saint was so incensed by his treatment that before he left, he put a curse on the place: 'that it would never be henceforth a home of clerics, but a den of wild beasts'. It is doubtful if any wild beasts have survived, but there are certainly no clerics there now. As late as the 17th century, the hill was also known as Carn Chairbre, after Cairbre, son of Niall of the Nine Hostages, who ruled that part of the country. Cairbre, too, fell foul of a saint—St Patrick—who dubbed him 'the foe of God'—a fearful insult.

In County Longford and the surrounding countryside, they have a phrase for a man of sharp sight: 'he could see a speck on the top of Carn Hill'. Anyone of average sight can see the fine views from the summit.

[40]

Mote of Granard N 328810 (Eire $\frac{1}{2}''$ Map 12)

At the south-west end of the town. Enormous and prominent mound with surrounding banks on high ground close to the church, and visible from far off. It is believed to be the site of the royal palace of Cairbre, son of Niall of the Nine Hostages. Strongly fortified and used as a defence about 1200 by the Anglo-Normans. A large statue of St Patrick now crowns the summit, placed there in 1932 to commemorate the 15th centenary of his coming to Ireland.

About a mile to the north-west, the main road cuts across a long, defensive earthwork known as Black Pig's Race, part of a rampart dug to block the gap between Loughs Sheelin and Gowna, probably pre-dating the Anglo-Normans, though no doubt put to good use by them. (See also Black Pig's Dyke, and the Doon of Drumsna.)

[41]

Richmond Harbour N 063760 (Eire $\frac{1}{2}''$ Map 12)

At Cloondara, 4 miles west of Longford. Three bridges, one of old stone and arched, are grouped at an idyllic, almost forgotten corner, spanning the river Camlin and the disused Royal Canal, which here joins the Shannon. Tall, old, pale grey stone warehouses stand idle along the banks of the stream, and remains of decrepit great waterwheels lie about. Beyond the warehouses, on the opposite side of the road, is a huge, derelict lock, weeds spreading across its motionless water. Above it, stands the fragmentary remains of an old, very small abbey. There is talk of the warehouses being opened again. Perhaps they will be. But now it is as if nothing ever could have been different, or will ever be changed.

[42]

Tubberpatrick Cemetery N 200942 (Eire $\frac{1}{2}''$ Map 12)

Two and a half miles north-north-east of Ballinamuck, west of the Drumlish-Arvagh road. Old, lonely cemetery amid farm fields. It contains a memorial to General George Blake, Commander-in-Chief of the Irish Insurgent battalions who joined with the French to fight the English at the Battle of Ballinamuck in 1798, and who was subsequently executed. There is also a memorial there to Gunner Magee, who loaded his guns with old, broken pots and pans when his ammunition was exhausted. In the village of Ballinamuck, the battle is commemorated by a fine statue of a pikeman holding a fractured pike-shaft.

[43]

Baronston House N 327626 (Eire $\frac{1}{2}''$ Map 12)

Two miles north-east of Ballynacargy where, just beyond the crossroads, is a gated drive. A church (Kilbixy Church) stands almost next to it, though hard to see behind an almost impenetrable wall of high trees. This is the entrance to the demesne of Baronston House, deserted and massively overgrown like the fairy wood conjured up around the Sleeping Beauty. Unlike the story, there is no palace within, although once there was a fine mansion.

In the 16th century the lands were in the hands of the Piers family, who built a fine house there, but the family died out, and it fell into ruin. Later the estate was taken over by the Malones, who rebuilt the mansion, but in the early 1920s it was accidentally destroyed by fire. This time the demesne was bought by the Land Commission, who bulldozed the remnants of the house and the land was given to the various tenants. Only the mote remains and a few stumps of unrecognizable masonry. In the tangle of high weeds is a small family graveyard, a few subsided tombstones marking the graves in the grass-grown, bumpy ground. Beneath the house there must once have been an extensive network of tunnels and cellars because, according to local farmers, their cattle fall into them now and again. Once there was a lake, and one of the Malones built an artificial island in it. Now most of the lake has been drained and the island is about 200 yards inland, near the north shore. It is nothing more than a mass of stones with a few trees on top. It is a strange scene of melancholy dilapidation. The silence can almost be felt.

Kilbixy Church originally stood in the estate grounds. It was built by Lord Sunderlin, a relative of the Malone family, in 1798. It was regarded as one of the finest examples of Georgian architecture in the country. Now it is dreadfully ruined. In 1962 the roof collapsed. Only a few days before, a service had been conducted there with a congregation of over a hundred people. They were lucky that the vibration of the organ music and the singing did not bring the walls down about their ears. By this time there were only seven families in the parish, and it was decided to brick off one end of the church and use this only. It was pleasantly rebuilt in semi-modern style, using some of the original pews, centuries old. (Key to the church from the sexton, whose cottage is on the main road to Ballynacargy, about 100 yards south of the church.)

Just inside the church gate is St Brigid's Hospital, or The Leper House. Mass burial in lime was normal for lepers in the Middle Ages, and skulls and other remains have been found in the adjacent field, with traces of lime on them.

Much of the Baronston estate and a considerable area to the south of it, was the site of the medieval village of Kilbixy, an Anglo-Norman citadel of considerable importance. 'There were twelve burgesses in their scarlet gowns, a mayor or sovereign, with other officers suitable to so great a port.' In 1430 the town was plundered and burnt by O Neill and the Irish. Nothing at all remains of it.

[44]

Fore N 515704 (Eire $\frac{1}{2}$" Map 16)

Three miles east of Castlepollard. Small, secluded village in an idyllic valley surrounded by lumpy hills. Has been variously known as Foure, Fowre, Fobhair and Baile Fobhair (Town of the Spring). Once a noted monastic centre, founded in the 7th century by St Fechin who died there some years later. There is a fine concentration of antiquities, as well as strange phenomena attributed to the Saint. His monastery was reputedly built in the middle of a quaking bog.

In an ancient graveyard high above the road, are the remains, partly reconstructed, of St Fechin's Church. The massive lintel stone with an inscribed cross in a circle on it, weighs over $2\frac{1}{2}$ tons. According to legend, the workmen were quite unable to lift it and St Fechin, using his miraculous powers, wafted it up into position. Pieces of an ancient cross found in the churchyard have been reassembled and erected there.

Near the churchyard is the Anchorite's Cell, a small, crumbling watchtower with oratory attached, where Patrick Beglen, one of the last anchorites in Ireland, lived in the early 17th century in conditions so cramped that he was known as 'The Holy Man in the Stone'. After his death the structure became the mausoleum of the Greville-Nugent family.

Lying low to the north of the village are the impressive remains of 13th century Fore Abbey, with a strongly fortified look. In its grounds is a ruinous, circular pigeon house.

Phenomena attributed to the influence of St Fechin include a stream flowing uphill to feed a now ruined mill; an ash tree only bearing three branches in honour of the Blessed Trinity; and a holy well whose water cannot be brought to the boil. Near the foot of Ben Fore (713 feet), is a huge earthen mound, thought to be part of an Anglo-Norman fortification. There are still traces of the walls which once surrounded medieval Fore. (Keys of St Fechin's Church and Fore Abbey from local post office.)

[45]

Jealous Wall N 419477 (Eire $\frac{1}{2}$" Map 12)

At Belvedere, $1\frac{1}{2}$ miles south of Lynn, on the north-eastern shore of Lough Ennell. Great, ivy-grown, ruinous Gothic wall built by Barradotte on the instruction of the then Lord Belvedere to shut out the sight of his Lordship's brother, whom he accused of being a paramour of Lady Belvedere. Her Ladyship was locked in her room and the wall effectively shut off from her sight her brother-in-law's mansion a few hundred yards away. No chance then to wave signals to him from her window. Belvedere House, the Earl's fishing lodge, has remained in the hands of the same family and its gardens, which are very beautiful, are opened once a year to the public; otherwise, they can be visited by previous arrangement. (His home was a large castle, now vanished, situated a few miles away.) The near-by mansion, belonging to the Earl's philandering brother, is now in ruins and stands, decaying picturesquely in desolate parkland beside the lough.

[46]

Lilliput House N 375445 (Eire ½" Map 12)

On the south-western shore of lovely Lough Ennell, 2 miles east of Castletown Geoghegan. Small, ruined house amid trees above the grassy verges of the lake, thought to be the house after which Swift named his Lilliputians in *Gulliver's Travels*, and where he was probably a visitor. Facing it, out in the lough, is a tiny island with a statue on it of the Goddess of Plenty, known locally as The White Lady. To the left is the island of Cro-Inis (Hut Island) where the great King Malachy (947–1022) died. A mile or two to the north, near the shores of the lough, is Dun na Sciath (Fort of the Shields), a large mound marking the site of one of the King's castles. Lilliput House can be reached by the narrow lane which runs from the southern end of the lough, along its western shore to Dysart. A gated track leads through woods to the house.

[47]

Lough Derravaragh Surrounding N 440660 (Eire ½" Map 12)

South-west of Castlepollard, the road to Mullingar running across its narrow, southern extremity. A beautiful lough, about 6 miles long, with wooded shores overlooked at the south-western end by the hill of Knockross (567 feet) and, facing it at the south-eastern end, by Knockeyon (710 feet), from whose summit there are romantic views.

Here was set the tragic story of the four Children of Lir, changed by a jealous stepmother into swans for 900 years, the first 300 of which they were compelled to spend on Lough Derravaragh. Their fate was even more miserable because they retained their human senses and could mourn their wretched lot down the centuries. But they were gifted with magical singing voices and the unearthly sweetness of their songs brought joy to all who heard them. The fearful spell ended with the coming of Christianity, and the children were converted by St Mochaomhog, although because they were then of a very great age, they died soon after. The wicked stepmother was punished by being changed into a dreadful flying demon. (See also Fair Head, and Inishglora and Inishkeera.)

On the slopes of Knockeyon are the scant remains of St Eyen's chapel. One mile east of the village of Crookedwood, which is at the southern end of the lough, is ruined Taghmon Church, a 15th century manorial church named after the 6th century St Munna (otherwise Munnu, Finnu or Fintan). It has a tall, fortified tower and a ruinous nave (key from cottage opposite).

[48]

Manorial Church N 450416 (Eire $\frac{1}{2}''$ Map 12)

One mile north-west of Rochfortbridge, reached from a side road west of the main Rochfortbridge–Mullingar road. Much ruined small church, ivy-grown and closely hemmed in by yews, a more recent stone wall enclosing the original graveyard of sunken stones and wildly overgrown mounds. Within the dilapidated nave, where weeds sprout thickly, lies a broken and weathered tomb slab carved with the effigy of a knight in armour, thought to be that of 16th century Sir John Tyrrel. A castle mound with scraps of masonry near the edge of the field is all that is left of the seat of the Tyrrel family, demolished in Cromwellian times. To reach the ruined, very lonely church, cross the farm fields alongside the castle site, and then a fast-running stream, roughly bridged by tree trunks set low in its banks—a distance of some 400 yards.

[49]

The Pinnacle N 114475 (Eire $\frac{1}{2}''$ Map 12)

Two miles east-north-east of Glassan. Tall obelisk on a 337-foot hill, erected in 1769 and said to mark the centre of Ireland. Three miles north-north-east, is Auburn, with the ruined residence of Oliver Goldsmith. Here he first went to school, and it is this region which he described in 'The Deserted Village'. Three miles south-south-west of the obelisk is the melancholy, romantic ruin of 19th century Moydrum Castle, built by the 1st Baron Castlemaine and destroyed during the Troubles.

Another 'centre of Ireland' is a few miles away. It is on an offshore island immediately opposite the Hodson Bay Hotel, which is on the western (Roscommon) shore of Lough Ree, 4 miles north-north-east of Athlone. The spot is marked by a stunted pillar stone. There is nothing unique about having more than one centre. England also has two at least (see *Wonders of Britain*).

[50]

Tullynally Castle N 445707 (Eire ½" Map 12)

One and a quarter miles north-west of the village of Castlepollard. The seat of the Earls of Longford, until 1961 known as Pakenham Hall; now the residence of Mr Thomas Pakenham. It is frequently referred to in the memoirs of Maria Edgeworth, 18th century novelist, whose father was a regular house guest. Originally a 17th century garrison house, it was domesticised in the Georgian period and, in the early 19th century, given its present flamboyant Gothic appearance by Francis Johnston. From the imposing, turreted gatehouse, a long drive leads through lush parkland and fine trees to the castellated, many-chimneyed mansion. It has a splendid banqueting hall, and a collection of Irish silver. There is a museum in the castle kitchen. The 18th century park and pleasure grounds are bespattered with statuary, and have a grotto and other rustic embellishments. There are immense walled gardens and peach houses. (Open to the public Saturdays, p.m.; April-September; admission charge.)

Section 2

Offaly

Laois

Kildare

Wicklow

Carlow

Kilkenny

Wexford

Waterford

Monasterboice, Co. Louth
(Wonder No. 29)

Powerscourt Waterfall,
Co. Wicklow
(Wonder No. 90)

Glendalough,
Co. Wicklow
(Wonder No. 84)

[51]

Astronomical Telescope N 053045 (Eire $\frac{1}{2}$" Map 15)

Midway between Roscrea and Cloghan, in the grounds of Birr Castle. The Great Telescope, invented by the 3rd Earl of Rosse (1800–67), who was a noted astronomer of his day, stands in the centre of the park. At the time it was built and for some 70 years after, it was the largest in the world. The reflector is in the Science Museum in London. There remain the walls and the tube—an impressive hulk—surrounded in spring by a mass of daffodils. The Earl also discovered the Spiral Nebulae. The 4th Earl (1840–1929) too, was an astronomer; and his brother invented the steam turbine. The beautiful grounds of Birr Castle, with an ornamental lake and arboretum, are famous for their fine display of trees and flowering shrubs, and for the box hedges which are around 200 years old and 34 feet high—claimed to be the tallest in the world. (Admission charge, grounds only.)

[52]

Castle Bernard Cross N 197056 (Eire $\frac{1}{2}$" Map 15)

One mile north-east of Kinnitty, at the foot of the Slieve Bloom Mountains. The castle, an ornate 19th century castellated mansion, is the property of the Department of Lands (Forestry Division), and used for research purposes. On its grassy terrace stands the high shaft of an ancient cross carved with a series of biblical scenes which, though faint, can be seen to represent the Fall of Adam and Eve, and the Crucifixion. The site on which the castle is built was once occupied by a monastery founded in the 6th century by St Finan, patron and abbot of Kinnitty, and a pupil of St Brendan of Clonfert. The stable buildings contain fragments of the monastery, and the cross shaft is thought to be one of its relics.

From Kinnitty, a narrow but good road leads east-south-east to Forelacka Glen, a county beauty spot south of the Camcor river, where the stream falls in miniature cascades over a stony bed. The road winds picturesquely across the mountains, through miles of peat bog filled in summer with the white mops of bog cotton, to join the north-south mountain road between Clonaslee in the north, and Coolrain and Castletown in the south.

[53]

Clonfinlough Stone N 043297 (Eire $\frac{1}{2}$" Map 15)

Two and a half miles east of Clonmacnoise (q.v.). A massive, flattish limestone boulder embedded in the earth, originally measuring about 10 feet long and 8 feet broad, and profusely covered with incised crosses and what appear to be stylized human figures. One of the most ancient of Irish monuments, its markings resemble the rock carvings discovered in eastern and central France, and in Galicia in Spain, suggesting some form of link between the various peoples. In addition to elongated crosses, some of them resembling the Greek letter phi (Φ), there are numerous well-defined cup marks and deeply hollowed footprints. The symbols are thought to record a great Neolithic battle.

The stone can be reached from the Roman Catholic church at Clonfinlough, which stands on a small loop road south of the Clonmacnoise–Athlone road. A narrow track leads back behind the church. At its far end, cross two fields over rising ground to where the stone lies recumbent in the grass.

[54]

Clonmacnoise N 010306 (Eire $\frac{1}{2}''$ Map 15)

Six miles west-south-west of Ballynahown, on the east bank of the river Shannon, here a wide, reed-edged loop of tranquil water. An ancient monastic site founded in the 6th century by St Ciaran, which swelled to a great community as its fame as a seat of learning and culture spread. It achieved its greatest power in medieval times. Attacked in turn by the Vikings, the Anglo-Normans and the English, decline set in during the 12th century, but it was only in the 16th century that it was finally brought to ultimate destruction by the English troops.

The impact of the ruins, set on rising ground above the river, is still powerful: the ruined cathedral and seven other ecclesiastical buildings, two round towers, three high crosses—one, the marvellously carved Cross of the Scriptures erected in the 10th century. The Nun's Church, situated to the west of the new cemetery, was built in the 10th century and restored in the 12th by Dervorgilla, wife of Tiernan O Rourke, Prince of Breifne. It is a splendid example of Irish Romanesque architecture and still retains some of its beautiful stone carvings. A causeway has recently been built near O Rourke's tower, and on the faces of its stepped walls have been set the remains of more than 200 grave slabs recovered from the site, bearing inscriptions and crosses dating from the 8th century.

[55]

Clonony Castle N 055204 (Eire $\frac{1}{2}''$ Map 15)

Three miles north-west of Cloghan. Remains of a great 16th century castle partly surrounded by a castellated stone wall pierced by a high, broken entrance arch. The massive square tower is wonderfully impressive from the road, though ruinous and overgrown with creepers. The inside has been remorselessly defaced over the years with senseless graffiti and visitors are none too careful where they leave their refuse, which is a great shame. It is still a fine place. Beside the ruined tower, on uneven ground by a tree, is a recumbent limestone slab marking the graves of two cousins of Anne Boleyn—Elizabeth and Mary—the inscription bearing their names still readable despite weathering and defilement. It is in this district that Anne Boleyn, daughter of the Earl of Wiltshire and Ormonde, is said by some people to have been born. But there is no real evidence of where the event took place, and what there is, is highly controversial.

[56]

Pietà, Kilcormac Church N 182140 (Eire ½″ Map 15)

In the small town of Kilcormac, which is on the main road between Tullamore and Birr. The church possesses a finely made 16th century *Pietà*, carved in wood and set above the altar. Before the Reformation it belonged to the church at Ballyboy, an adjacent village. To keep it safe during Penal Times, it was buried for over 60 years in a bog.

[57]

Rahan Churches N 258254 (Eire ½″ Map 15)

Five miles west of Tullamore, between the Grand Canal and the Tullamore river. Site of one of the earliest Christian monasteries, believed to have been founded by Bishop Camelacus, but more certainly associated with the 7th century Abbot, St Carthach. The great earthworks close to the site are prehistoric, possibly of a 3,000-year-old settlement.

Three churches remain, one of which is used as the present Protestant parish church. The other two are roofless ruins. One is small and primitive, with a Romanesque door added. The other, a larger 12th century Romanesque church, has a fine carved doorway, a round window elaborately decorated, and carvings of heads on the chancel arch.

The walk along the tow-path of the Grand Canal from Rahan to Tullamore is delightful. Above its banks, about 3 miles west of Tullamore, are the emaciated ruins of Ballycowan Castle, once a grand 16–17th century mansion with tall, imposing chimneys. Now sadly shattered, it is almost inaccessible because of the heavy tangle of thorny undergrowth and bushy banks. On the outskirts of Tullamore itself is the distillery of Irish Mist liqueur, decoratively built on the canal banks. (Visitors welcome, preferably by previous appointment.)

[58]

St Manchan's Shrine N 180298 (Eire ½″ Map 15)

Three miles west-south-west of Ballycumber, in Boher Roman Catholic church, which stands on a narrow loop road on the south of the road to Clonmacnoise. The shrine or reliquary is a finely made box of yew wood, intricately decorated, and bearing ten slim metal figures, possibly the Apostles, since there are spaces where two of the figures are missing. The box was made in the 12th century and is thought to be of the same workmanship as the famous Cross of Cong, now in the National Museum in Dublin.

LAOIS

[59]

Coolbanagher Church N 525043 (Eire ½″ Map 16)

South of the village of Emo; 5 miles south of Portarlington. A signposted turning off the main Portlaoise–Kildare road leads northwards to it. Beautiful Georgian Protestant church built by James Gandon, one of the finest architects to work in Ireland. (He also built the Custom House, the Four Courts, the King's Inn, and part of the Bank of Ireland, in Dublin.) The church was built to replace the previous thatched church which was burnt down in 1779. With its slim grey and white tower, surmounted by a narrow, sophisticated steeple, it is the epitome of elegance and dignity. Although some of the fine interior work has been lost, the gallery, the boxed pews, and the arched windows and niches, are Georgian architecture at its best. Great efforts are being made to restore it faithfully.

[60]

Killeshin Church S 672778 (Eire ½″ Map 19)

Three miles west of Carlow. Ruined 11th century church, all that has survived of a now vanished town. It has a magnificent Romanesque doorway with a high, pointed arch, embellished with intricate designs and carvings of heads. In the graveyard is one of the oldest decorated fonts in Ireland, weathered and bulbous, set on an octagonal base.

[61]

Lea Castle N 573121 (Eire ½″ Map 16)

Two miles east-south-east of Portarlington, on the river Barrow. Reached through a farmyard. Overgrown ruins of a powerful 13th century fortress of Maurice Fitzgerald, 2nd Baron of Offaly, deteriorating picturesquely on the banks of a charming, tranquil reach of the river which comes suddenly into sight as you cross the farmyard stile. The castle was dismantled in 1650 by Cromwellian forces. A maze of shattered masonry and grass-grown humps are all that remain of the parapeted wall, the entrance gateway and the great walled courtyard which extended almost to the water's edge. The massive towered keep still stands, broken and draped with creepers, but singularly impressive; one of its corner towers—still fairly complete—has an external diameter of about 30 feet. An idyllic site, its charm enhanced by the close proximity of the silver, winding river, and faintly mysterious now that greenery is disguising the broken stones.

[62]

Portarlington N 544126 (Eire $\frac{1}{2}$" Map 16)

Attractive small 18th century town on the river Barrow. Its new buildings lack the elegance of the old, some of which still happily survive in the older quarter. Under William III, the town and estates were given to the Huguenot, Marquis de Ruvigny, Earl of Galway, who brought Huguenot refugees to settle there. The 'French Church', dedicated to St Paul, was built in 1851 to replace the earlier church built by the Marquis. It is notable for its unusually wide nave and the gallery extending across its entire width, intended for the nobility of the time. The graves and tombs of the French settlers are confined to one section of the graveyard.

To the north of the town, and dominating it and the whole surrounding countryside, is the enormous white-painted tower of Ireland's first turf-fed Power Station. Quantities of cut turf, transported from the great Derrylea Bog near by, are stacked up beside it like some prehistoric rampart.

[63]

Rock of Dunamase S 525983 (Eire $\frac{1}{2}$" Map 16)

Three miles east of Portlaoise, on the north side of the road to Stradbally. Great, 200-foot-high, craggy grass-grown rock, on which stands a fantastic assortment of crumbling masonry—gaunt stumps of keeps, broken walls, defaced arches, devastated courtyards—the dramatic remnants of a once indomitable fortress of the powerful O More clan. This was their chief seat until its destruction in the 17th century by Cromwellian forces. In spite of intense mutilation, from a distance the vast fortress looks singularly complete, as if some nobility might still be sheltering there; even at close quarters, its shattered fortifications still give an impression of great strength.

There are splendid views from the rocky summit over the woods and plains, and southwards to Timahoe, whose round tower (q.v.) can be seen on the skyline.

[64]

St Fintan's Tree S 370952 (Eire ½″ Map 15)

Just over 1 mile east-north-east of Mountrath, by the side of the main road, overlooked by an old cemetery. Enormous sycamore tree in one of whose gnarled lower branches is a well which, even in a rainless season, never dries out. The whole trunk and the heavy branch in which the water lies like a small, dark and shallow pool, are thickly stuck over with coins embedded in the wood by pilgrims. Near by, at Cloneagh, the present church stands on the site of a monastery founded in the early 7th century by St Fintan, to whose miraculous powers the well is attributed.

[65]

Steam and Early Transport Museum S 573964 (Eire ½″ Map 16)

At Stradbally, 7 miles south-east of Portlaoise. The first of its kind in Ireland, set up by the Irish Steam Preservation Society in co-operation with the Midland Motor Museum. The exhibits, which date from the 1850s to the 1950s, are housed in a massive, barnlike, sculptor's workshop bought for the purpose, and already in need of enlargement. They include engines loaned, bought, or rescued from disintegration, drawings, photographs, prints and other miscellany. All the models are beautifully cared for and in perfect working order, and include some fine, shining specimens: a 1906 Jackson Dogcart; a 1913 Humberette; a 1904 Humber motor-tricycle with a basketwork trailer for lady friend, believed to be the only one of its kind in existence; an 1880 Merryweather horse-drawn fire engine with enormous brass funnel and red water buckets on the side platforms; and steam tractors, beam engines, pumping engines, a steam roller, and some fine racing motors. (Entrance charge.) Close to the exhibition building, in Stradbally village, visitors can see a narrow-gauge locomotive made in 1895 for the Guinness Brewery in Dublin, for the transport of passengers and goods in and out of the Brewery. It was donated by the Guinness Company to the Irish Steam Preservation Society. An annual Steam Rally, when everything of the period takes to the road, is held at Stradbally during the first weekend in August.

[66]

Timahoe Round Tower S 535902 (Eire ½″ Map 16)

At Timahoe, 5 miles south of Stradbally. Fine tower, almost 100 feet high, marking the site of the 6th century monastery of St Mochua. Its walls are mostly 4 feet thick.

The cone at the top leans nearly 2 feet out of alignment. A unique feature is its remarkably fine 12th century Romanesque doorway, set 17 feet above the ground. It is decorated with arches, adapted to the thickness of the wall. The capitals, though worn, show carvings of bearded men with interlaced hair.

KILDARE

[67]

Castledermot S 783849 (Eire ½″ Map 16)

A village 9 miles south-east of Athy; south of Moone Abbey (q.v.) on the Kilcullen–Carlow road. The site of an important monastery whose remains include a fine round tower, two 9-10th century high crosses, one of them bearing a carved crucifixion and intricately decorated with spiral designs; a 'Swearing Stone'—a worn, granite slab with an hour-glass-shaped hole in the middle, the subject of much early superstition; and some ancient grave slabs, some of them shaped like bolsters. Of the old church nothing remains but the remarkable 12th century doorway and its surrounding arched stonework. It has been erected in front of the new church, like a free-standing, second doorway to it. The new building is simple and dignified, and its own doorway follows closely the style of the beautiful, ruined one. On the opposite side of the road are the ruins of a fine 13th century Franciscan friary (key from adjoining house), with some interesting old carved tomb chests and grave slabs.

[68]

Castletown House N 990344 (Eire ½″ Map 16)

At Celbridge, 12 miles west of Dublin. One of the finest and largest Georgian houses in Ireland. Built for William Conolly, Speaker of the House of Commons in Dublin from 1711–28, and designed for him by Alessandro Galilei, who designed the new façade for the church of St John-in-Lateran in Rome. Begun in 1722, its handsome central block linked by curving colonnades to flanking wings, it was the earliest of Ireland's great Palladian houses. The Irish Georgian Society took possession in 1967, and have installed their headquarters there, proceeding steadily with the extensive and expensive work of restoration to combat years of neglect. Many of the rooms—there were originally 100, and what look like miles of corridors—are now open to the public. They include the magnificent main hall and staircase with plasterwork by Francini, the Italian stuccodore; the Red Drawing Room; the Print Room, a fantasy concocted by Lady Louisa Conolly, who decorated it herself with prints stuck on the wall (the plan to which she worked is on display); and the enormous and staggeringly ornate Long Gallery, decorated in the Pompeian manner by Reily, a pupil of Sir Joshua Reynolds. (Conducted tours; admission charge.)

The Conolly Mausoleum, which is a dismal, dark, disused church, reroofed to protect the huge monument it contains, is virtually lost in an old, overgrown churchyard at the opposite end of the village, and deserves better treatment. Conolly would certainly have thought so. The enormous white marble monument to the Speaker and his wife, both reclining on a tomb chest flanked by marble columns, is railed off behind a length of very beautiful wrought ironwork with a gate in it. The monument has proved too massive to be housed in the local church, and evidently too expensive to be moved elsewhere. This last, almost forgotten resting place of Speaker Conolly and his wife, is a sad fall from grace.

The key of the mausoleum can be borrowed from Celbridge rectory; the key of the churchyard from one of the cottages opposite the churchyard wall—a cumbersome and often frustrating way of gaining entry.

[69]

Conolly's Folly N 957364 (Eire ½″ Map 16)

Two and a half miles north-west of Castletown House (q.v.); ½ mile south of the main Dublin–Maynooth road, by a side turning. An imposing 140-foot structure set up by Speaker Conolly's widow in 1740, ostensibly to create employment after a hard winter. In fact, it closes very effectively a 2½-mile vista from Castletown House, from whose upper floors it can be seen—an elegant shape on the skyline, flanked by trees.

It stands in a field, close to the road, the tall, tapering obelisk mounted on a double row of deep arches which, in turn, are crowned with orbs and urns and pineapples on pediments. One of Mrs Conolly's sisters, who took a somewhat carping view of the whole affair, wrote: 'My sister is building an obleix to answer a vistow at the bake of Castletown House; it will cost her three or four hundred pounds at least, but I believe more—I really wonder how she can dow so much, and live as she duse'.

[70]

Dominican Church S 684941 (Eire ½″ Map 16)

At Athy, on a lovely reach of the river Barrow. An unusual and beautifully situated modern church, built in 1963–5. It is pentagon-shaped, with high, fly-away arms, all made of concrete. It can accommodate over 600 persons. The imaginative

Conolly's Folly, Co. Kilda
(Wonder No. 6

Dan Donnelly's footprints,
Donnelly's Hollow, Co. Kildare *(Wonder No. 71)*

interior planning and the raked floor emphasize the simple yet wonderfully impressive high altar. The bright stained glass of the long, slim windows, and of the stations of the cross, are by the Irish artist, George Campbell, adding height and light and a quality of other-worldliness.

[71]

Donnelly's Hollow N 810115 (Eire $\frac{1}{2}''$ Map 16)

Two and a half miles north-west of Kilcullen, beside the secondary road which runs north-westwards from Kilcullen to join the main Kildare–Naas road at the eastern end of the Curragh.

The deep hollow, 100 yards across, on this vast, open plain, which is covered with dips and hillocks, clumps of trees and grazing sheep, was the scene of many prize fights by the Irish bare-fist boxing champion, Dan Donnelly. The obelisk at its centre, which can be seen from the roadside, bears the legend that he was Champion of Ireland, and began his ring career by beating Tom Hall before 20,000 fans in 1814, leaving the ring in the 14th round crying foul. Here, too, a year later, he beat the English champion, George Cooper. Afterwards Donnelly went off to England and challenged all comers, beating the Englishman, Tom Oliver, in a 34-round fight.

A long line of deep footprints, alleged to be those of the fighter walking out of the ring, lead from the centre of the hollow and up its slope to the top, preserved by being trodden in by visitors. At Kilcullen, the Hideout Bar has Donnelly's mummified arm. It was so long that it was said that he could button his knee-breeches without stooping.

[72]

Dun Aillinne Hill Fort and Cairn N 820078 (Eire $\frac{1}{2}''$ Map 16)

Two miles south-west of Kilcullen, on the wooded summit of Knockaillinne (600 feet). Ancient fort, once a royal seat and residence of the Kings of Leinster (see Hill of Allen). A great, circular earthwork, rising in some places to 15 feet, with a diameter of 450 yards, it encloses an area of some 20 acres. Within the earth ramparts is a fosse or prehistoric ditch about 6 feet deep and 45 feet wide. The Iron Age cairn at the summit has been much defaced by quarrying; its contours are blurred and it only stands a few feet high. The way to it is by a gated entrance from the main road, then across fields and up to the hilltop.

Half a mile south-west, on the east side of the road on the way to Old Kilcullen, are all that remains of an early monastic settlement—the stump of a round tower and two crosses.

[73]

Grand Canal N 812253 (Eire ½″ Map 16)

At Robertstown, a charming village at the foot of a wooded slope. The village is at a junction of the Grand Canal, beside a bridge and faces, across flat, marshy ground, an immense skyscape pierced by tall trees. On the canal banks are old warehouses, and the huge, barrack-like block of the Grand Canal Hotel, opened in 1803 in the prosperous days of the waterways, when the village was the hub of the water transport system (see Leinster Aqueduct). Not only were tons of merchandise shipped down the canal, but thousands of passengers came, first by the old passage boats, then by smart fly-boats, to stay at the lavish new hotel, which had been built, including furniture, at a total cost of £7,492—a fortune in those days.

Now Robertstown is a quiet place, the canal is used by pleasure boats, and the hotel is a hotel in name only. The village reverts to something like its old hustle and bustle for one fortnight each year in August, when the Grand Canal Festa is held there. Then the hotel comes into its own again. It is used for colourful ceremonies, exhibitions (canal history among them), and there are candle-lit banquets. Anyone can go over the hotel, where a permanent waterways museum is planned to open from May–September. When closed, the key can be borrowed from the caretaker in the village.

[74]

Hill of Allen N 760205 (Eire ½″ Map 16)

Eight miles north-north-east of Kildare. Prominent hill rising 676 feet from the flattish surrounding countryside, famed as one of the three residences of the Kings of Leinster. (The others were at Naas, and Dun Aillinne (q.v.), and straight lines drawn between them form an equilateral triangle with sides 9 miles long.) Here, too, lived Fionn Mac Cumhaill, often referred to as Finn Mac Coul, 3rd century hero of many of the Irish legends. On a small mound at the summit, known as Fionn's Chair, a battlemented obelisk, visible for miles around, was erected in 1859 by Sir Gerald Aylmer of Donadea Castle, with various inscriptions in Latin carved on it. It is possible to ascend the tower by means of an inner spiral stairway. The names of the workmen who built the tower can still be traced at the bottom of the steps. There are remarkable views from the top of it.

The hill can be climbed easily from a narrow path which leads off the Kildare–Allen road just south of where it crosses the Allen–Rathangan road.

[75]

Jigginstown Castle N 880190 (Eire $\frac{1}{2}''$ Map 16)

One mile south-west of Naas, beside the road to Kildare. Enormous, overgrown shell of a great brick building begun in 1632 by Thomas Wentworth—'Black Tom'—Earl of Strafford. If completed, it would have been the largest unfortified residence in Ireland. It measures 390 feet long and 120 feet broad, and beneath it is an immense vaulted crypt of fine workmanship. Planned by the Earl as a vast and really impressive country residence at which he hoped to entertain his royal master, Charles I, it was, of necessity—unfortunately for the Earl—abandoned. In 1641, the Earl was beheaded in London. Now in a dangerously ruinous condition, authorities have put up 'no entry' notices, but even devastation has not destroyed its palatial appearance. It can be seen perfectly well without going in; in fact it can hardly be missed, as its great length lines the roadside.

[76]

Leinster Aqueduct N 885255 (Eire $\frac{1}{2}''$ Map 16)

Three miles north-north-west of Naas; $\frac{1}{2}$ mile west of Sallins. Secluded, picturesque aqueduct, 400 feet long, with seven arches, which carries the Grand Canal (q.v.) 30 feet above the river Liffey, here narrow and very beautiful between wooded banks. Five of the arches span the river; the other two are on the left bank and farmers drive their cattle through them. The aqueduct was built in 1783 by Richard Evans, who replaced General Tarrant as resident engineer. In those days the canal was a busy and prosperous commercial waterway. Now it is part of a tranquil, pastoral scene.

[77]

Long Stone of Punchestown N 918165 (Eire $\frac{1}{2}''$ Map 16)

Two and a half miles south-east of Naas, to the north of the Punchestown race-course. A great, tapering, enigmatic monolith of weathered Wicklow granite, standing in a corn field. In 1931 it collapsed to the ground and was found to be 23 feet long and to weigh 9 tons. Re-erected in 1934, it now measures 19$\frac{1}{2}$ feet above ground. It is thought to date from the early Bronze Age, as did the small burial cyst found at its base.

[78]

Moone Abbey S 798927 (Eire $\frac{1}{2}''$ Map 16)

Five miles north of Castledermot; 2$\frac{1}{2}$ miles south-south-west of Ballitore. Site of a

6th century Columban monastery. Within the fragmentary ruins—all that remain of the abbey—stands St Columcille's Cross, a truly magnificent, slim and elegant high cross, $17\frac{1}{2}$ feet tall, painstakingly restored in the 19th century. It is carved with 51 panels showing scenes from the Scriptures: the Fall of Man, the Sacrifice of Isaac, the Flight into Egypt, the Miracle of the Loaves and Fishes, and many more, all of them marvellously evocative. A fine front panel shows the 12 Apostles ranged in three tiers of four—little squat men cramped together to fit the space precisely. A copy of the cross was exhibited at the New York World Fair, 1964–5. The ruins and the great cross adjoin a farm, and can be reached from the road by a signposted stone stile alongside the farmyard. It is a strange yet curiously suitable place for so beautiful a monument.

Half a mile to the north, at Timolin, just inside the door of the Protestant church, is the impressive 14th century carved stone effigy of an armoured knight recumbent on a great stone tomb chest. (Key of church from near-by cottage.)

[**79**]

Mote of Ardscull S 730973 (Eire $\frac{1}{2}''$ Map 16)

Four miles north-east of Athy. Huge artificial mound, 55 feet high, of the type erected in the 12th century by Anglo-Norman invaders. The castle which occupied the flat top was constructed of wood, and probably protected by a stout palisade ringing the edge of the platform. Foundations of mortared buildings discovered on this platform were of late medieval date. The mound, surrounded by a stone wall, is densely covered with great trees beneath which gloomy, narrow tracks twist muddily to the top. Near here, Edward Bruce's army defeated a much greater English force in 1315.

In front of the mound, on an immaculately trimmed grass verge behind the main road, is a monument inscribed: '1903 Gordon Bennet Race'. The stone was erected by the Irish Veteran and Vintage Car Club to commemorate the 4th Gordon Bennet race held on July 2nd, 1903, the first ever to be run over a closed circuit. The winner was the famous Belgian racing driver, Camille Jenatzy, who covered the 327·5 miles in a 60 h.p. Mercedes racing car at an average speed of 49·2 m.p.h. A map of the circuit, the names of the contestants, and a picture of the winning car are all engraved on the stone.

[**80**]

St Brigid's Cathedral N 725126 (Eire $\frac{1}{2}''$ Map 16)

On the outskirts of Kildare. Reconstructed church, squat cruciform in shape, with a powerful central tower. It is on the site of an early wooden church founded by

St Brigid and St Conleth, whose shrines were carried off by invading Danes in the 9th century. In 1600 both town and cathedral were utterly devastated, and the building remained so until the late 19th century, when the laborious work of reconstruction began. In the handsome, unplastered interior, stand some fine ancient stone tomb chests with recumbent effigies, one of Fitzgerald of Lackagh, 1575; another, an effigy of a bishop, is thought to be that of John of Taunton, 1233–58. Also preserved is an ancient stone font and some finely carved stones.

In the churchyard is one of Ireland's tallest round towers, rising to 108 feet with more recent stepped battlements, and a door 15 feet from the ground. In the graveyard are all that remains of St Brigid's Fire House and Kitchen. On the wall near the entrance gate, the Arms of the Bishopric of Kildare, carved in granite and discovered broken into three pieces, have been erected. (Key of church from adjacent house.) On the opposite side of the road a signposted minor road leads to St Brigid's shrine and well.

[81]

St Patrick's College Museum N 934375 (Eire ½″ Map 16)

At Maynooth, a charming small town on the banks of the Royal Canal. Museum in the vast grounds of the seminary, with a fine collection of ecclesiastical relics, historical documents, and a section devoted to science. There are some beautiful chalices of the 15th century and later times, some of them richly chased; vestments worn during Penal Times, and some singularly fine ones from Irish colleges abroad made by ladies-in-waiting to Marie Antoinette, and one given by Elizabeth, Empress of Austria, in cloth-of-gold. A mutilated figure of Christ carved in wood is one of the few such images surviving from the 12th century.

In the scientific section is an induction coil made by Yeates and used by Marconi when he experimented in Ireland in 1898 (see Rathlin Island); also inventions used by Dr Nicholas Callan (1799–1864) such as his Horse-Shoe Machine, and some of his original electro-magnets and coils, and the Maynooth Battery, which led to his discovery of galvanized iron. The college itself, a very handsome building, is set in the midst of splendid, ornamental grounds. Both college and grounds can be visited during the summer from mid-June to mid-September, when the students are away.

Outside the college stands the massive ruins of Geraldine Castle on the site of a 12th century Fitzgerald stronghold. The castle was fortified in the 16th century by 'Silken Thomas' Fitzgerald, to withstand the English.

[82]

Baltinglass Abbey and Hill Fort

S 885892 (Eire $\frac{1}{2}''$ Map 16)

At Baltinglass, a charming town on the Blessington–Tullow road, in the midst of beautiful, wooded hills. The abbey was the second of the great Cistercian houses of Ireland, and a daughter house of Mellifont (q.v.). The ruins stand to the north of the village, reached through the grounds of the parish church. There are impressive remains of the fine 12th century nave and chancel, and of two notable monuments. One is the inscribed tomb slab of James Grace, formerly Lord Kilerige, decorated with a Celtic cross in the ancient strap-work style, surrounded by symbols of the Passion – the crown of thorns, the scourges, ropes, hammer and nails, the 30 pieces of silver, and the soldiers' dice. The second monument is a granite mausoleum of the Stratford family, Lords of Baltinglass, built in 1832 in the Egyptian style and topped by a stone pyramid. The personal monument of John Stratford, Baron Baltinglass, who was created in 1777 Earl of Aldborough of the Palatinate of Upper Ormonde and Viscount Amiens, has been removed to the south transept of the new church. On a wooded height above the town is a great cross, illuminated in winter.

The mountain beyond, known locally as The Pinnacle (1,258 feet), is crowned by a large passage-grave cairn decorated with white quartz stones and surrounded by a double kerb of stones up to 8 feet high. It was excavated in 1934 and its five chambers found to contain a large basin stone, fragments of bone, pottery, a polished stone axe and a flint javelin.

The entire hill-top cairn is contained within the great oval Iron Age fort of Rathcoran, whose double rampart and ditch follow the contours of the mountain top. An exhausting climb; you need to be booted and spurred against the undergrowth and nettles, but the tremendous views are inspiring.

[83]

Castleruddery Stone Circle

S 920942 (Eire $\frac{1}{2}''$ Map 16)

Five and three-quarter miles north-east of Baltinglass, at Lower Castleruddery. Twenty-nine stones forming a circle 100 feet in diameter, surrounded by a 15-foot-wide sloping bank. The two colossal portal stones are in white quartz; one rectangular recumbent stone has a line of holes along it. Only a few of the great stones are still standing and many of them are broken and fragments lie within as well as outside the circle. Vandalism over a long period, and now neglect have mutilated a fine monument, now overgrown to such an extent that some of the boulders are moss-covered and practically submerged in a tangle of grass and undergrowth. It still has the power to astonish. The way to it is signposted through a farm field.

[84]

Glendalough Surrounding T 126968 (Eire $\frac{1}{2}''$ Map 16)

The Valley of the Two Lakes, in magnificent, wooded hill country a mile west of Laragh, which is on the main Dublin–Rathdrum road. Great monastic settlement and centre of learning from the days of the hermit, St Kevin, who was born in 498, and eventually became its abbot. Here came thousands of students from all over the western world to study. Plundered in the 9th and 10th centuries by Danes and Irishmen, it revived during the 11th and 12th centuries, when some of its finest churches were built. It was finally burnt by the English in the 14th century, and its great buildings fell into ruin.

Spread over a vast area of mountain, river and lake, which form an enchanting, romantic setting, there are three main groups of ruins. In the lower group, situated east of the Lower Lake is the Deer Stone, hollowed like a baptismal font and claimed by legend to be the stone where a young doe shed her milk to feed two orphaned babies; St Saviour's Priory, a ruined 11th century church with some fine, carved capitals; and Trinity Church, on the opposite side of the river, said to have been the Church of St Mocherog, friend of St Kevin.

The central group lies between the river bridge and the Lower Lake. It includes the great, arched gateway, entrance to the ecclesiastical 'city'; the round tower, 110 feet high with a conical cap; the cathedral, with its magnificent doorway and massive lintel, the most imposing church in the valley, dedicated to SS Peter and Paul; St Kevin's Cross, 11 feet high, an unadorned granite pillar with an unpierced circle; the 12th century Priests' House, and the remains of three other churches—St Kevin's, St Kieran's and St Mary's.

The upper group is in the vicinity of the bridge that crosses the river to the east of the beautiful Upper Lake, and is reached by the 'Green Road' that borders the south side of both river and lakes. It consists of five crosses; St Kevin's Cell, the remains of a stone structure reached by a woodland path to its site on a rocky promontory overlooking the Upper Lake; the Righfeart Church, with a massive, chiselled granite doorway; the Rock Church (Teampall Na Skellig) on a steep ledge beneath the cliff; and St Kevin's Bed on the south side of the Upper Lake, where a bare rock, hollowed at the top, rises over 30 feet from the water. These last two can be reached by boat, and St Kevin's Bed ascended from the lake by ladder.

On the western side of the bridge can be seen the remains of a stone fort, about 67 feet in diameter, with 10-foot-thick walls, built after the style of Staigue Fort (q.v.).

The whole remarkable city of ruins, set in a beautiful, mountain-ringed valley is wonderfully moving. It is as widely visited now as it was in its powerful days, but nothing can touch its serene loveliness. A day is hardly enough to spend there.

[85]

Glenmalure Surrounding T 060955 (Eire $\frac{1}{2}''$ Map 16)

Deep mountain gorge drained by the Avonbeg river, the course of the valley followed by a splendid road beginning at Ballinaclash, which is 2 miles south-west of Rathdrum. The road winds between great conifer slopes, and then deeper into the mountains, until it peters out at Baravere Ford where a high lacey waterfall threads its way down the bare rock face, under the shadow of Lugnaquillia (3,039 feet), highest of the Wicklow Mountains. This magnificent valley is a fine starting place for climbing the mountain. In the glen, a great stone boulder by the wayside commemorates, on one side the Wicklow chief, O Byrne, who defied the English in the 16th century, and on the other, Michael Dwyer, leader of the 1798 rebellion (see Michael Dwyer's Cottage).

[86]

Meeting of the Waters T 190834 (Eire $\frac{1}{2}''$ Map 19)

Three miles north of Avoca. Confluence of the rivers Avonbeg and Avonmore, joining here in a wide, tranquil stream, and spanned by a fine old stone bridge. High above, sprouting from the thickly wooded heights, is turreted Castle Howard. A river-side park edges the water. Here is preserved the skeleton of an old tree beneath whose branches Thomas Moore, in 1807, composed the poem 'The Meeting of the Waters'. (It is also claimed that he composed the same piece in the grounds of Rathfarnham Abbey.) Pubs, cafés and souvenir shops on the road above cater briskly for visitors, but fail to destroy the beauty of the scene. Nonetheless, early morning is the best time to go.

Two miles south of Avoca, at Woodenbridge, is the confluence of the rivers Avoca and Aughrim (The Gold Mine river), forming a second, completely uncommercialized 'Meeting of the Waters', which can be seen glinting amid trees from the road, high above. Croaghan Kinsella (1,987 feet), the mountain at the head of the Gold Mine river, is where, in 1796, the discovery of a gold nugget led to a 'gold rush'. As much as 2,600 ounces of gold were found in 3 months. A bit of panning still goes on, though with little success.

[87]

Michael Dwyer's Cottage S 968913 (Eire $\frac{1}{2}''$ Map 16)

At Derrynamuck, 8 miles south-east of Dunlavin, from where a road runs into the wild and lovely Glen of Imail, through which flows the river Slaney. Michael Dwyer, leader of the Wicklow resistance in the 1798 Rising (see Glenmalure), was born in the glen, and used it as a hideout when on the run from the Redcoats. The humble cottage is isolated in the midst of remote and beautiful, wooded slopes, a perfect district in which to lie low. It is set out as Dwyer might have used it, with bench and rush-seated chair, iron cooking pots hanging over the fireplace. Here, in 1799, he was trapped by the British troops. He escaped, but one of his four companions, Samuel MacAllister, was killed.

The cottage is signposted through a farmyard, where a long, steepish lane ascends into the quiet hills beyond the farm outbuildings.

[88]

Mount Usher Gardens T 272970 (Eire $\frac{1}{2}''$ Map 16)

On the southern outskirts of Ashford, in the valley of the river Vartry. Privately owned botanic gardens laid out informally along the banks of the river, the Wicklow hills on the skyline. The fine collection of trees and shrubs, many of them rare specimens, have been collected from New Zealand, China, Japan, Tasmania, America, Africa and the Himalayas. A splendid array of flowers, shrubs and creepers ornament the river walks and rustic bridges. It is charming to walk there at almost any time except, perhaps, the depths of winter. There is also a collection of horse-drawn carriages. (Admission charge to gardens and/or carriage collection.)

[89]

The Piper's Stones N 930032 (Eire $\frac{1}{2}''$ Map 16)

One and a half miles south of Hollywood, 200 yards east of the secondary road to Baltinglass. Known also as the Athgraney Stone Circle. It is one of the finest of such monuments in the district. It consists of 14 huge granite boulders and one outlying stone, on a grassy slope where sheep graze. Some of the stones are boulders, others are pillars, varying in height from 2 to 6 feet; a few are now recumbent. According to legend, the outlying stone was the piper and the circle represented the dancers, all of them caught in the act of merry-making and petrified on the spot for violating the Sabbath.

[90]

Powerscourt Waterfall O 206121 (Eire $\frac{1}{2}''$ Map 16)

In the Deer Park of the enormous Powerscourt demesne, which extends over 14,000 acres. The waterfall is $2\frac{1}{2}$ miles south of Enniskerry. The Dargle river, rising in the foothills of the great Tonduff South Mountain (2,107 feet), and not far from the source of Dublin's great river, the Liffey, here pitches 400 feet over a narrowly confined precipice to pour in a beautiful, shimmering fall, dropping sheer into a deep pool in the boulder-strewn glen below. It is one of the highest, single-leap falls in Britain or Ireland, and one of the most beautiful. (Admission charge.)

Powerscourt gardens, on a scale and grandeur rarely seen, are landscaped and terraced to take full advantage of the skyline of the Wicklow Hills and the unmistakable shape of the Sugar Loaf Mountain. They are indeed very splendid. (Admission charge to gardens; the house is not open to the public.)

[91]

St Kevin's Reformatory O 142180 (Eire $\frac{1}{2}''$ Map 16)

Five miles west-north-west of Enniskerry, in the hills at the head of the beautiful Glencree valley. The Reformatory was one of a series of barracks built to guard the Military Road, which was built immediately after the 1798 Rebellion. (There is another, in a very ruinous state, at the head of the entrance to Glenmalure (q.v.). It was in use as a barracks until 1825. In 1859, the buildings were employed as a Roman Catholic Boys' Reformatory. It was finally abandoned in September 1940, although briefly used between 1945–7 as a shelter for children war refugees. Now it is again disused and stands, a huge great shell, windows gaping, surrounded by weeds. Alongside it is the simple, dignified church of St Kevin, from which the reformatory took its name.

Below, where steep, tree-hung paths and rough-cut steps lead down to the Glencree river, the water froths in cascades over the stony bed. On the bank, under a rock shelf thickly masked with trees, there is a grotto. Near-by, on the Enniskerry road, is the German war cemetery, set out against the background of encircling mountains. Here are buried Germans who were shipwrecked on the Irish coast during the first and second world wars, and members of air crews who crashed on Irish soil.

[92]

Tenants' Monument N 980146 (Eire $\frac{1}{2}''$ Map 16)

At Blessington. A monument of silver-grey granite built by the tenantry on the Wicklow, Kildare and Kilkenny Estates of the Marquis of Downshire, as a mark of respect and gratitude, and erected on the coming of age of the Earl of Hillsborough in 1865. It takes the form of an ornamental drinking fountain with a lion's head, and is inscribed: 'The water supplied at the cost of a kind and generous LANDLORD for the benefit of his attached and loyal tenants'.

In the churchyard is St Mark's Cross, a huge grey granite cross, ringed at the top but not pierced, moved to its present position to prevent its destruction from flooding by the Liffey hydro-electric scheme.

[93]

The Wicklow Gap O 068010 (Eire $\frac{1}{2}''$ Map 16)

Fine mountain pass running from Glendalough (q.v.) to the village of Hollywood, and most picturesque and dramatic when traversed in that direction (south-east to north-west). It is a magnificent, scenic route across the mountains, where cascades of a dozen foaming streams rush over a bed of great strewn rocks, to descend into the Vale of Glendalough and its lakes, and the Avonmore river. The road follows the course of the old Pilgrims' route across the moors to Glendalough. Where it passes Lough Nahanagan, about 3 miles north-west of the Abbey ruins, between the lake and the road are traces of St Kevin's Road, granite-paved and overgrown.

At its western end, the pass traverses wild, desolate, grudging country, with huge forbidding rock faces and the countless folds of distant hills. There are deep peat ridges and bogs full of bog cotton, and sheep graze on the lonely moors.

CARLOW

[94]

Adelaide Memorial Church S 820599 (Eire $\frac{1}{2}''$ Map 19)

At Myshall, 2 miles north of the Corrabut Gap, below the foothills of Mount Leinster in the Blackstair Mountains. Beautiful and impeccably kept silver-grey stone church with a high, decorated tower and fine doors. It is surrounded with neat curves of grass and splendid trees. Built by Duguid of Dover (1827–1913), who was a local landowner. A monument commemorating his mother, Adelaide, stands on a stepped pedestal within the church. It is a large white marble statue representing Innocence by Thomas Farrell, RHA, of Dublin.

From the village of Myshall, a secondary road runs south, then eastwards, through the Corrabut Gap and over the Blackstair Mountains to Bunclody. It is worth taking for the fine views.

[95]

Browne's Hill Dolmen S 755768 (Eire $\frac{1}{2}''$ Map 19)

Two miles east of Carlow, at Kernanstown, in the estate surrounding 18th century Browne's Hill House (the house is not open to the public; roads criss-cross the estate). The dolmen is an enormous, single-chambered grave with a colossal granite capstone, claimed to be the largest in Europe. It measures 20 feet square, 5 feet thick, and is estimated to weigh at least 100 tons. It rests, at one end, on two recumbent slabs, and the other, on three 6-foot upright pillar stones. This incredible monster stands, often inaccessibly because of the crops, in the middle of a very large cornfield. (Ask permission from the farmer to view it at close quarters.)

[96]

St Laserian's Cathedral S 646650 (Eire $\frac{1}{2}''$ Map 19)

At Oldleighlin, 2 miles west of Leighlinbridge. The site of an early monastic settlement. The 'cathedral', an enormous church for so small a village, incorporates some of the medieval features of an earlier church. Some fine, high arches, and short ranges of delicate columns have been exposed, with 13th and 15th century details. There is an ancient font, and a great stone tomb chest bearing a coat of arms and an inscription.

[97]

St Mullin's Churches S 729380 (Eire $\frac{1}{2}''$ Map 19)

Between Graiguenamanagh and New Ross, in the valley of the river Barrow. Remains of the monastery of St Moling, founded in the 7th century and still a place of pilgrimage. The ruins, which include the fragmentary remains of several churches and oratories, a decorated high cross, the stump of a round tower, and St Moling's well—a hollow containing broken grinding stones—all stand within an immense graveyard surrounding the present parish church. It is a most attractive site, where one of the tributaries joins the main stream of the river. Beside it is a great, grass-covered mound within a deep fosse, probably the site of an early castle.

KILKENNY

[98]

The Cantwell Fada S 592452 (Eire $\frac{1}{2}''$ Map 19)

In ruined Kilfane Church, $2\frac{1}{2}$ miles north-north-east of Thomastown. The roofless church, originally dedicated to St Paan, has a castellated presbytery, and there are traces of consecration crosses. The remarkable effigy, carved in stone, possibly from a tomb slab, has been set upright against an inner wall. It represents a member of the local Cantwell family, probably Thomas Cantwell, who died about 1320. Known as The Cantwell Fada—or The Long Cantwell—on account of its extraordinary height—just over 8 feet—it is a truly splendid figure of a mail-clad knight with crossed legs, carrying a great, elongated, triangular shield with armourial carvings on it.

[99]

Clara Castle S 574578 (Eire $\frac{1}{2}''$ Map 19)

Six miles east-north-east of Kilkenny, in quiet farming country at the edge of the mountains. Fifteenth century fortified residence of the Shortall family, inhabited until early in the 20th century. It has a huge, six-storey tower with arrow-slit windows, enclosed on the north side by a walled courtyard. The massive oak timbers of the three lower floors remain in position, although the floors themselves have disappeared. The 4th floor is vaulted over. There are secret chambers and a 'murder hole'. (Key from cottage opposite.)

[100]

Dunmore Cave S 515650 (Eire $\frac{1}{2}''$ Map 19)

Five miles north of Kilkenny. Huge, natural limestone cave with passages and several chambers, one of which contains 'The Market Cross', an enormous stalagmite, christened in the way that such formations are, for its shape. The way down to the cave is through undergrowth, then descending steeply by boulder-strewn, muddy and slippery tracks to the cave mouth. It is all very deep, dark, dank and dirty, and the air is chilly. Here, according to Irish records, 1,000 people were massacred in the year 928 by Viking invaders. Bones have been found there, though whether from those days or later, is a matter for speculation.

As a concession to commercialization—there is no other—the authorities have fixed hefty iron railings in a series of descending 'stairways', to which you can cling on the steep way down to the cave mouth. Beyond this, the visibility is nil. You need a strong torch, old clothes, non-slip shoes and, unless you are an experienced caver or go with companions, for proper and safe exploration it is better to ask somebody in the village to act as guide. Preliminary inquiries could be made at the local pub. To reach the railed tracks which lead down to the cave, walk up a longish and, by comparison, domestic footpath which is signposted from the main road.

[101]

Gowran Church S 638535 (Eire $\frac{1}{2}''$ Map 19)

In Gowran village, which is 7 miles east-south-east of Kilkenny. The Collegiate Church of St Mary, founded in the 12th century, is a fine memorial to past splendours.

The existing remains – the roofless nave, the aisle and the lower part of the tower – date from the 13th century, and have been incorporated into the present parish church forming, with some later alterations, one of the finest interiors in the country.

Here are buried members of the powerful Butler family – the Earls of Ormonde. Some splendid monuments include great, carved tomb chests with effigies of knights in armour, some bearing the Butler Arms, and the effigy of a lady wearing a medieval, horned headdress, probably the wife of one of the Butlers. An altar tomb under the massive tower bears a figure in the vestments of a priest. The Latin inscription, translated, reads: 'Ralph, known as Julianus, while he lived was kind and generous to those in need', followed by the date of his death – March, 1253. This is one of the oldest inscribed monuments in Ireland. An ogham stone stands in the chancel. (If locked, the church key can be obtained from the caretaker in the village.)

[102]

Graiguenamanagh Abbey S 710442 (Eire ½″ Map 19)

At Graiguenamanagh, a pleasant small market town of old, narrow streets, on a loop of the beautiful river Barrow. The abbey, a great Cistercian foundation of the early 13th century, fell into the hands of the powerful Butler Lords – Earls of Ormonde – after the Dissolution, and it was not until the beginning of the 19th century that, with little funds for wholesale restoration, rough repairs were carried out and the abbey brought back into use as a parish church. It has great atmosphere. One of the monuments to survive is the effigy of a 14th century armoured knight, and the very fine doorway which once led to the cloisters and now opens on to a modern baptistry.

Three miles to the north-east, at Ullard, west of the river Barrow, are the ruins of a monastery founded by the 7th century hermit, St Fiachra. Little now remains, but the mutilated church has a fine, early Romanesque doorway, and in the corner of the overgrown churchyard is a weathered high cross with carvings on it of King David with a harp, the Sacrifice of Isaac, and a Crucifixion.

There are some enchanting walks in the wooded river valley. The mountain and river scenery, south-westwards to Inistioge, is truly magnificent. Inistioge should not be missed, it is a small, very pretty little town on a bend of the river Nore, which here flows through a deep-cut valley thick with beautiful trees.

[103]

Grannagh Castle S 570146 (Eire ½″ Map 23)

Two miles north-west of Waterford bridge, on the north bank of the river Suir. Also known as Granny Castle. Ruin of a great, 13th century castle belonging to the

Le Poer family. Eustace Fitzgerald Le Poer was executed for treason in 1375, and the fortress handed over to the already powerful Earl of Ormonde. It was finally subdued in the 17th century, by Cromwellian forces. The ruin stands in a fine, prominent position on the bank above the river, which here bends in a great curve to the south, and commands views down to the port of Waterford. Of a once splendid fortress, there remains only the massive tower, now sadly broken, and parts of the curtain walls.

[104]

Jerpoint Abbey S 572403 (Eire ½″ Map 19)

One and a half miles south-west of Thomastown, which is on the river Suir. Magnificent ruin of a great Cistercian foundation, daughter house of Baltinglass and of Mellifont (q.v.). Founded in the 12th century by the grandson of MacGillapatrick, King of Ossory, it stands on the site of an earlier monastery of which there are still traces. The Earl of Ormonde took over the property after the Dissolution, adding to his already extensive properties.

The beautiful 15th century cloisters are remarkably complete and many of the panels on the flat-sided columns bear carvings of figures and animals of startling clarity. Among the ruins of the great church there are some particularly fine grave slabs; and in the chancel lie several huge carved stone tomb chests topped by effigies, one of them of the 12th century Bishop of Ossory, Felix O Dulaney. Some of these great chests are intricately carved around their sides with figures of benign, archaic-looking angels, and 'weepers' with long hair and compassionate faces. (Key from house at 150 yards.)

[105]

Kells Priory S 500433 (Eire ½″ Map 19)

Half a mile east of Kells. Site of one of the largest monastic enclosures in Ireland, covering an area of 5 acres. Founded for Augustinian canons in the 12th century by Geoffrey FitzRobert, who also built a town here and occupied a now vanished castle (the mote can still be seen). There is little else visible from this period except for some tombstones. But ranged over the fields and contained within defensive walls, are the impressive remains of 15–16th century church buildings and strongly fortified towers, as well as some interesting tomb carvings. The ruins are divided into two sections or 'courts' by a tributary of the river Nore, which flows to the east, and by a high wall pierced by an entrance gateway. This is Butler country—the Ormonde overlords—and in common with much of the territory in the region, the abbey settlement came into their hands at the Dissolution.

[106]

Killamery High Cross S 384360 (Eire $\frac{1}{2}''$ Map 18)

Five miles south-south-west of Callan. Fine 8th century high cross which once stood in a monastery founded in the 6th century by St Goban Fionn, and apart from an early tombstone inscribed with a prayer for the soul of Aedan, is the only remaining relic of that time. It stands in an old, overgrown churchyard near an ivy-covered church tower, which can be reached by a signposted farm track. The cross, which is one of the earliest of its kind, is considerably weathered, but its carvings are still impressive. The east face is profusely decorated with geometric designs, and what could be formalized, entwined serpents. The west face bears biblical scenes, huntsmen, and a procession with a chariot.

WEXFORD

[107]

Clonmines S 842128 (Eire $\frac{1}{2}''$ Map 23)

A mile and a half south-west of Wellingtonbridge, at the head of a deep, almost land-locked inlet of Bannow Bay, where the Owenduff and Corock rivers come into the sea. This is the site of an ancient silver and lead mining town once occupied by the Danes, at which time it had its own mint. Prosperous still in the Middle Ages, it fell into decay and was in ruins by the time of the Union in 1684.

All that is left are the shells of four castles and three churches, grouped together on farmland overlooking a lovely, tranquil stretch of reedy estuary country. One of the churches, St Nicholas, is tall and built more in the style of a castle. Another of the ruins is called the Cowboy's Chapel, built by a wealthy landowner who had come up in life from a simple cowherd, and wished to commemorate the death of his mother in a style suitable to his improved station. From its name, he did not seem to have lived down his humble origins. Black Castle, now only a ruinous shell, was once a FitzHenry stronghold.

Three and a half miles to the south, where the road peters out on the eastern side of the bay, is Bannow, another once-flourishing medieval town and rotten borough. Gradually it disappeared beneath encroaching sands, but still sent two members to the Dublin Parliament before the Union. Nothing now remains but a ruined church on grassy land above low, crumbling cliffs. Below stretch miles of sand.

Castle, Co. Laois *(Wonder No. 61)*

Knockeen Dolmen, Co. Waterfo
(Wonder No. 11

Leader's Folly,
Co. Cork
(Wonder No. 147)

Kilcolman Castle,
Co. Cork
(Wonder No. 142)

[108]

Dunbrody Abbey S 705150 (Eire $\frac{1}{2}$" Map 23)

One mile west-south-west of Campile, where a creek runs north-eastwards from the tidal river Barrow. Splendid medieval ruin, one of the finest in the country, built in the 12th century by monks of St Mary's Abbey, Dublin. Because it was a place which had the right of sanctuary, it also became known as the monastery of St Mary of Refuge.

The great, roofless church, cruciform in shape, is 200 feet long and 140 feet broad at the intersection, and has six transept chapels with narrow, one-light windows. A low, though heavily built and turreted tower, rises from the centre. There are traces of some of the monastic buildings. Fine views along the creek and across low-lying meadows to the great river beyond.

[109]

Great Saltee Island Surrounding X 950970 (Eire $\frac{1}{2}$" Map 23)

Five miles south of Kilmore Quay, which is just east of Forlorn Point on the south Wexford coast. The largest of the Saltee Islands, about a mile long and up to $\frac{3}{4}$ mile wide, the haunt and nesting place of several million seabirds. One of the most important of Ireland's wildlife sanctuaries, it is on the direct route of the great lines of bird migration. Well over 30 different species can be observed, including vast colonies of gulls and puffins, and in lesser numbers, razorbills, cormorants and many others.

The whole island is covered with spongy, grass hillocks and riddled with rabbit holes, and in spring and summer, carpeted thickly with wild hyacinths, sea pinks, campion, and tiny, star-faced rock flowers. On the south and south-east the coast is a ragged line of great, indented cliffs and off-shore rock stacks, and the birds fill every ledge and crack, and quantities of them lie like great, anchored flotillas on the face of the sea. The din of their squawking and honking, unheard from the landing side, is deafening at close quarters. The best time to see them in their greatest numbers is at nesting time in late May or early June, though at these periods they can be vicious, if disturbed.

The owner of the island is now only a summer visitor, but when in residence, hoists his personal flag from his house on the hill. Self-crowned Prince Michael the First, his limestone throne stands on the flank of the hill and bears his arms—a shield held by two mermaids, its quarters each containing a different sort of bird. A near-by obelisk and plaque carved with his profile, explains that the throne was erected in memory of his mother, to whom he vowed when only 10 years old, that one day he would own Saltee Island and become its first prince. He cautions his heirs that they can only become his royal successors by being garbed in the robes and crown of the island (regalia which he bought when he had himself crowned), and taking the oath from the throne. Finally, the inscription exhorts all children with ambitions to work hard to achieve them.

The island can be reached by boat from Kilmore Quay, the trip preferably arranged a day before through the Wexford Tourist Office, your hotel, or by personal inquiry at the quay. When the wind is northerly, landing or leaving the island is dangerous, if not downright impossible. There is no proper landing stage, and larger boats anchor off-shore, transferring passengers to motorised dinghies which can negotiate the shallows. After that, visitors only have, themselves, to negotiate a narrow wooden plank to reach the stony foreshore.

[110]

Hook Head

X 735975 (Eire ½″ Map 23)

Long, thin peninsula jutting south-westwards into the sea, and forming the eastern shore of the great Waterford Harbour. At the Head a lighthouse stands above rock ledges and coves. Near-by are the ruins of a tiny church in an overgrown graveyard. Here, in 1649, Cromwell landed his forces and vowed to conquer Waterford 'By Hook or by Crook'. The remark is also claimed as being made by Richard de Clare, Earl of Pembroke (Strongbow), when he took Waterford in 1170. Either way, the phrase has stuck.

There is no Crook headland as such, but on the Waterford shore of the harbour is a small village called Crooke, with a ruined castle and church. From the Head there are magnificent open views across to the rocky, western shore of Waterford Harbour, and eastwards to the Saltee Islands (q.v.).

A mile short of the lighthouse, on the eastern shore of the peninsula, in the fishing village of Slade, is the great, tapered and crenellated tower of ruined Slade Castle, a 15th century fort with a later fortified house beside it. They stand together above the stone mole which encircles the little harbour, now part of the scene. (Key in village.)

[111]

Johnstown Castle

T 020165 (Eire ½″ Map 23)

Three and a half miles south-west of Wexford. Stately 19th century Gothic mansion, its corner towers crowned with ornate, castellated turrets, set in the midst of lawns and splendid trees. The original 13th century castle, part of which is incorporated in the present building, belonged to the Anglo-Norman Esmonde family and was dismantled by Cromwell. It was sold eventually to John Grogan of Yorkshire in the late 17th century, and his descendants, one of whom, ironically, married an Esmonde, owned the castle until 1945, when it was given to the nation. It is now administered by the Agricultural Institute and used for research purposes.

It looks very stately, reflected in the waters of a small lake edged with trees, along which stone nymphs pose statuesquely on their plinths. The lake is one of three in a demesne which covers over 1,000 acres and includes about 600 acres of exceptionally fine woodland. Some 30 acres have been landscaped and shrubs are grouped around the lakes. (Grounds and gardens open to the public.)

[112]

Rathmacknee Castle T 030140 (Eire $\frac{1}{2}''$ Map 23)

Five miles south-south-west of Wexford, to the north-west of the Kilmore road. One of the finest of Wexford's 15th century castles, once the seat of the Rossiters, a Lincolnshire family. Built of warm-coloured stone, the square tower house, some of its crenellations still intact, stands among trees within a walled courtyard, which is entered through a lofty, pointed archway. Over it is a well-preserved machicolation; yet another, shaped like a great crown, projects from a corner of the wall. Through either or preferably both of them, defenders could hurl missiles or pour boiling oil on their attackers. The tower rises through five storeys to a turreted roof with parapet walls and a walk. From here, another machicolation overlooks the ground floor doorway.

[113]

Tintern Abbey S 795100 (Eire $\frac{1}{2}''$ Map 23)

Three and a half miles north of Fethard, near a creek on the west shore of Bannow Bay. Remains of the Cistercian abbey church of Tintern Minor, a daughter house of the more famous Tintern Major, the great abbey in Monmouthshire. Founded by William, the Earl Marshal, about 1200, in thanksgiving for his safe crossing from England in a bad storm. The first monks came from the parent abbey. After the Dissolution, the layman to whom the property was granted, built a house into the church, and it is still inhabited by one of his descendants. The ruins, hidden in a grove of fine trees, include the nave, the south transept, and the presbytery, and some of the architectural details resemble those of the Monmouthshire abbey. The unusually massive square tower is ruinous and thickly overgrown with ivy. The delightful, small, arched bridge which spans the near-by creek, was built from stones of the original church. The ruins are romantically sited and completely obscured from view when the great trees are in leaf, until you are close to them. They can be reached through a signposted gate, by a long, gated drive which runs through grazing and woodland.

[114]

Ardmore Monastic Settlement X 188773 (Eire $\frac{1}{2}''$ Map 22)

Five miles east of Youghal and the Waterford/Cork border, on a southern slope above the village of Ardmore. Site of a monastic foundation of 6th century St Declan. The remains romantically grouped above the sea include a 95-foot round tower with string courses, one of the last and finest to be built in Ireland. The roofless medieval cathedral dates from the 12th century and has a unique west wall, the outer face of which is splendidly decorated across its width with blank arcading in two rows of round-headed niches, most of them containing sculptured figures. Although many of the carvings are badly weathered, some are still identifiable: Adam and Eve with the Tree and the Serpent, the Judgment of Solomon, and the Virgin and Child. It is a moving piece of work.

Inside, there are great tomb niches and three Ogham stones. St Declan's Oratory, standing near, is a very small building with high-pitched gables and projecting walls. A deep, tomb-shaped cavity in one corner is thought to have been the grave of the saint, in whose honour is an annual pilgrimage to the site on July 24. After the Suppression of the Monasteries, Ardmore was leased for a time to Sir Walter Raleigh.

On the shore, somewhat difficult to identify because there are a lot of other stones, is a huge block known as St Declan's Stone. It is alleged to have carried the saint's bell over the sea from Wales, and is credited with curative powers.

[115]

Cheekpoint Hill S 690140 (Eire $\frac{1}{2}''$ Map 23)

Five miles east-north-east of Waterford, at the confluence of the rivers Barrow and Suir. Prominent headland jutting into the broad stream of the two fine rivers, here joining to flow in a great sweep southwards into Waterford Harbour. Mighawn, a wooded hill above the harbour, is an exceptional vantage point. From its summit there are remarkable views of the two rivers, the estuary and the open sea, with the constant movement of shipping; and on a clear day, across seven counties to include the distant Comeragh Mountains and Slievenamon, the Blackstair Mountains, and Mount Leinster.

[116]

Curraghmore S 437155 (Eire $\frac{1}{2}''$ Map 22)

On the western edge of the village of Portlaw, which is 5 miles south-east of

Carrick-on-Suir. The estate of the Marquis of Waterford. The long drive winds its way beside the river Clodagh, through primeval oak forests, suddenly to come upon a vast courtyard, flanked on both sides by stable blocks—possibly designed by Francis Bindon (1742–50). At the end rises the original castle tower dating from the 12th century, with wings on either side and other structural alterations added in the 1780s. Surmounting the tower, outlined against the sky, is St Hubert's stag, the crest of the de la Poers, with a crucifix between his genuine antlers.

Behind the tower is the square block added in the 18th century, its west end being surmounted by the Beresford crest—a dragon with a broken spear through its neck. The house stands amidst elaborate formal gardens, designed by Louisa, 3rd Lady Waterford, supposedly from a plan of Versailles, with a view across an artificial lake to the Comeragh mountains. Trees and shrubs abound—the conifers being of particular note.

Almost hidden away, to the right of the house, is the Shell House, the exotic creation of Catherine, Countess of Tyrone, in the 18th century. Heiress to the de la Poers, she married Sir Marcus Beresford, this being the only occasion that the property has passed through the female line. Inside, it resembles a grotto, completely encrusted with thousands of different shells, some of them rare; many of them mother-of-pearl. In the centre stands the marble statue of its creator—Lady Catherine Power, by John Van Nost, Jr—clad in nymphlike drapery, a shell in her hand.

To the north-east rises the hill of Mother Brown, on top of which stands the de la Poer tower, erected by Catherine's heir, the 1st Lord Waterford, in memory of his eldest son who, aged 12, died from a fall from his pony. Below the tower, overlooking the demesne, is Clonegam Church and graveyard. In the church there is a particularly fine memorial, erected by the 5th Lord Waterford, depicting the reclining figure of his first wife and her child with whom, at his birth, she died—executed by Boehm in 1873. Their grave lies outside the church door.

(Curraghmore House is private. The grounds and Shell House are open to the public on Thursdays and Bank Holiday afternoons. Admission charge.)

[117]

Doneraile Cliffs X 568985 (Eire $\frac{1}{2}$" Map 23)

Two miles south-west of the resort of Tramore, on the western side of Tramore Bay. Precipitous, jagged cliffs, with grassy slopes above them. They line the bay in dramatic sequence from Tramore southwards to Great Newtown Head. Above the sea, on top of the headland close to the cliff edge, three giant white pillars have been erected as navigational aids. Crowning the centre one is 'The Metal Man', a huge, painted iron figure of an 18th century sailor in white breeches and blue jacket, his arm pointing seawards in warning to approaching ships. He has a more romantic function, according to local legend. If a girl hops three times round the base of the pillar without touching the ground with the raised foot, she will marry within the year.

There are magnificent coastal views westwards from the cliff top, and eastwards across Tramore Bay to Brownstone Head, where two more high pillars can be seen. They were erected on both headlands to distinguish Tramore Harbour from Waterford Harbour to the east.

Four miles north-north-east and about a mile inland, is ruined Dunhill Castle, once a stronghold of the de la Poer family, high on a great, craggy rock. The remains are very ruinous but there are splendid sea views from them.

[118]

Geneva Barracks S 696077 (Eire ½″ Map 23)

Two miles south of Passage East, where passenger ferries cross to Ballyhack on the eastern shore of Waterford Harbour; and one mile south of the village of Crooke (see Hook Head). Overgrown ruins of a settlement occupied by gold- and silversmiths from Geneva who, in 1785, came to live here and ply their trade, having managed to get a grant of £50,000 from the Irish Government. The settlement, which became known as New Geneva, failed to prosper and died out. Thirteen years later the site was taken over by the British as military barracks and used to house prisoners from the '98 Rising, who were known as 'croppies', immortalized for the Irish in the ballad, 'The Croppy Boy'. The '98 rebels were greatly influenced by the French Revolution, very much the news of their day, and among other things, they affected the cropped hair-styles of the revolutionaries.

[119]

Knockeen Dolmen S 574063 (Eire ½″ Map 23)

Four miles south-south-west of Waterford; three miles north of Tramore. Enormous portal tomb in the overgrown graveyard of the old church of Kilburrin, which is now disused. The dolmen looms up from a corner of the graveyard where it huddles, almost surrounded by thorny banks and hedges over which you must clamber to get at it. It faces towards an adjoining farm field from which, if you can manage to keep to the edge to avoid crops, the view is much more impressive. The portal stones stand 9 feet high, the space between them closed to within 15 inches of the top by a door—another massive stone slab. A great capstone, over 11 feet long and 7 feet wide, and supported at its back by yet another boulder, closes the tomb chamber. It can be reached from the minor road from Waterford to Tramore, which curves to the west of the main road. A gate in the hedge, opposite some farm buildings, leads across one field to the dolmen.

[120]

Master McGrath Memorial X 223952 (Eire $\frac{1}{2}''$ Map 22)

Two and a half miles north-west of Dungarvan, at the junction of the roads to Cappoquin and Clonmel. Railed-in limestone obelisk on a high, square base, commemorating Master McGrath, the greyhound which won the Waterloo Cup three times—1868, 1869 and 1871—and was only beaten once during the 37 courses which he ran in public. The stone is engraved with a very aristocratic picture of the champion, and cites the various cups which he won.

Section 3

Cork

Kerry

[121]

Ballincollig Castle W 587697 (Eire ½″ Map 25)

Six miles west-south-west of Cork; 1 mile south of Ballincollig, in the lovely valley of the river Lee. Lonely ruin of a great castle dating from the reign of Edward III, standing amid fields in a commanding position on a rock ledge. From the massive square tower an ash tree sprouts, and there are remnants of walls and the outline of the moat. This was the fortress home of the Barret family, subdued and taken over as a garrison first by Cromwell's troops, and later by James II. It can be reached from a minor road running south of Ballincollig village; then over a farm gate and along a cart track. The castle can be seen on the skyline ahead.

[122]

Ballybeg Abbey R 542076 (Eire ½″ Map 21)

One mile south of Buttevant. Ruinous shell of a 13th century fortified abbey founded by Phillip de Barry for Augustinian canons. Close beside it, in a corn field, is a large, circular dovecot. Not much remains of the church except the belfry tower, in which carved heads can be seen by the holes for the bell ropes. A narrow stairway leading to the top is worth climbing for the views. In Buttevant itself, a ruined friary next to the modern Catholic church, contains a heterogeneous collection of decorated stones and parts of pillars. It has a faintly sinister crypt and sub-crypt.

[123]

Ballycatteen Ring Fort W 582459 (Eire ½″ Map 25)

Four miles south-west of Kinsale; ½ mile west-south-west of Ballinspittle at the eastern end of a high ridge. Fine, circular fort covering an area of 3 acres, with an overall diameter of nearly 400 feet, and a flat central area measuring about 200 feet across. The three great ditches are cut to a depth of 6 feet and over, leaving a solid entrance causeway at the south-eastern end. Here, around the year 600, lived workers in iron and bronze, who defended their settlement by a series of strong wooden gates built across the causeway, and a substantial palisade behind the innermost bank, within which were wooden dwelling huts and souterrains. From the top there are fine views to Ballinspittle and over lovely, undulating countryside. From the depths of the grassy ditches, between the hedge-like growth of weeds and wild flowers, hardly a sound can be heard. The atmosphere is mysterious and one feels like an intruder.

[124]

Ballycrovane Ogham Stone V 657529 (Eire $\frac{1}{2}''$ Map 24)

Close to the shore of Ballycrovane Harbour, which is a northern, rocky inlet of Coulagh Bay on the rugged, mountainous Beara Peninsula; 250 yards south-east of the coastguard station. Impressive pillar stone rising like a great, bare tree-trunk, 17½ feet above the rocky ground. It is the tallest ogham stone in Ireland or Britain. (Ogham refers to the Ancient British and Irish alphabet of 20 characters, often found inscribed on stones by means of strokes of varying lengths and groupings.) From the irregular markings near the top, it has been assumed that the inscription was made on the stone *in situ*, and that it had probably been erected centuries earlier. (Ask permission to see it from the bungalow on the small harbour road.)

[125]

Bantry House V 987483 (Eire $\frac{1}{2}''$ Map 24)

South-west of Bantry, beautifully sited on the shores of Bantry Bay. Originally the property of Richard White, first Earl of Bantry, who purchased it in 1765, it is still owned by the same family. Georgian, brick-built mansion considerably enlarged by the second Earl, a great traveller, who brought home many of its heterogeneous treasures: French, Dutch and Flemish tapestries, fireplaces from the Palace of Versailles, floor tiling from Pompeii, a fine old carved chest from Spain, some 18th century French prints, all kinds of period furniture, a letter from Lord Nelson ordering a new foresail, and a great deal else.

There is a splendid air of dilapidation in the somewhat gloomy but resplendent dining room; the Rose Drawing Room, with its pastel carpets and beautiful, delicate glass and china, has lovely views from its tall windows. The grounds, with rough lawns and flower beds gone wild, rise behind the house to a fine vantage point overlooking Bantry Bay. In front, a flagged path flanked by statuary and ornamental urns in the Italian manner, leads down to a balustrade above the water. The views are very beautiful. (Admission charge to house and/or grounds.)

[126]

Bawnatemple Pillar Stone W 119705 (Eire $\frac{1}{2}''$ Map 21)

Two and a half miles north-west of Ballingeary, which is at the western end of Lough Allua. Massive, tapering pillar stone, nearly 20 feet high, one of the tallest in Ireland. Weathered, enormously thick, and leaning, it stands embedded in a field bank almost concealed by trees, a strange monster to find in a farmyard. It is almost invisible until you are within touching distance of it. (Ask at the farm for permission to look at it.)

[127]

Belvelly Castle W 790708 (Eire $\frac{1}{2}$" Map 25)

At the northern tip of Great Island in Cork Harbour, 3 miles north of Cobh. Fifteenth century tower, all that remains of an original Anglo-Norman fortress, owned for a while by Sir Walter Raleigh. In a commanding position close to the water, it overlooks tranquil estuary country where an occasional heron wades. Close to it is the fine arched stone bridge that links Great Island to Foaty Island to the north, and from which beautiful reaches of the channels that lead from Cork Harbour up to the city, stretch out in all directions. Martello towers, one wreathed with ivy, guard the inlet points.

[128]

Blackrock Castle 722720 (Eire $\frac{1}{2}$" Map 25)

Three miles east of Cork City centre, on a promontory which juts into the river Lee estuary at the point where it turns seawards and widens into Lough Mahom. Nineteenth century castellated and turreted tower, already sprouting weeds in its crevices. Originally a 17th century fort built by the Lord Deputy Mountjoy to defend the water approaches to the city; rebuilding was started in 1828. Ageing picturesquely, it stands by the water edge, with splendid views of the constant stream of shipping in and out of the complicated waters and channels of Cork Harbour. Similar views can be seen from the secondary road that runs beside the river to the west and south of the castle which, incidentally, looks more romantic than it really is when seen across the width of the river from the north bank.

[129]

Carrigadrohid Castle W 414723 (Eire $\frac{1}{2}$" Map 25)

Four miles west-south-west of Coachford. On a rocky, near-impregnable site beside a bridge over the river Lee, here very beautiful. Much ruined MacCarthy fortress with a breach in the walls leading abruptly down to the grass-grown, weedy interior. At one side is a boat entrance, very dark and dank. Cromwellian troops overpowered the garrison after hanging the Bishop of Ross within sight of the men, for refusing to persuade them to surrender.

[130]

Carrigaline Church and Drake's Pool W 729622 (Eire $\frac{1}{2}$" Map 25)

On the Cork–Crosshaven road at the head of the estuary of the river Owenboy. A fine, Perpendicular Protestant church, with a forest of small, needle-like spires.

It contains a notable monument with a leaden effigy of Lady Newenham, who died in 1754.

East of the church, the Owenboy estuary widens into Drake's Pool, a lovely wooded creek where, in 1587, Sir Francis Drake and five of his ships took refuge to evade capture by a superior Spanish force. Still further east, on a rocky cliff above the water, are the remains of Carrigaline Castle, built in the late 12th century, and one of the oldest in Ireland. Often besieged, it belonged originally to the Cogan family, was later acquired by a branch of the Desmonds, and was finally taken by troops of Elizabeth I.

[131]

Castlelyons W 838928 (Eire ½″ Map 22)

Four miles south-south-east of Fermoy. The village contains a fantastic collection of ruins associated with the Barrymore family. Set back from the main street is the huge shell of a Carmelite friary founded in the early 14th century by John de Barri. The ruins, chiefly of the 15th and 16th centuries, are of the church, tower and extensive outbuildings.

At the southern end of the village is Barrymore Castle, of the Tudor period. Viewed across fields, looking northwards, it has the illusory appearance of a fine, compact, turreted mansion. Close to, it is two-dimensional—length and breadth only—no depth. Apart from encircling lumps of wall and grass-grown foundations, all that remains are the great, vertical walls, topped by precarious turreted chimneys, all shrouded by a heavy sheath of ivy.

Further south, and west of the village, is a third and even more extraordinary ruin. An 18th century Protestant church, now badly battered, has been added to an even more ruinous medieval nave which, except for its dense overgrowth of ivy, would probably fall apart. The churchyard, packed with decrepit, lop-sided tombs, is approached by a dismal avenue of great, overhanging trees whose foliage casts a sinister green shade in summer. Birds, unaccustomed to disturbance, swoop angrily from the branches. The noise that fills the air like the sound of some hidden dynamo, is the ominous humming of innumerable resident bees. By the side of the church ruin, half-concealed by a near-impenetrable mass of creepers, is the Barrymore mausoleum, hexagonal, and apparently roofed with ivy. This is Gothic gloom at its gloomiest.

[132]

Castletownshend W 184313 (Eire ½″ Map 24)

Exceptionally beautiful village on the west side of Castlehaven, 5 miles south-east of Skibbereen. A single street of old houses shaded by splendid trees, runs steeply down to the water. On 420-foot-high Knockdrum, a hill to the north-west of the village, is a fine ring fort (W 172310), its 10-foot-thick dry-stone walls enclosing a circular area 75 feet in diameter. At its centre is a roofless clochan—a dwelling with a chambered souterrain hewn out of the rock. Near the entrance passage is a small guard-chamber, outside which stands a massive boulder with about 40 cup marks on it. North-north-west of the fort, three slim pillar stones known as the Three Fingers (W 175315), 12–14 feet high and firmly fixed in the exposed rock, stand against the skyline. A fourth, broken stone, is out of alignment a few yards away. There are fine views over the coastline of Castlehaven, and of the ruins of an O Driscoll fortress above the western shore.

[133]

Clear Island Surrounding V 960220 (Eire ½″ Map 24)

Six miles south-west of Baltimore, with Sherkin Island lying between it and the mainland. Rocky island with splendid cliff scenery, about 3 miles long and 1½ miles at its widest point. Almost bisected by the great inlet of South Harbour (Ineer) and the lesser North Harbour (Trawkieran), which is named after St Ciaran (Kieran) who preached Christianity some 30 years earlier than St Patrick, and was born on the island and is its patron saint.

In the north-west corner are the ruins of the 12th century Church of St Ciaran, and an ancient pillar stone—Gallan Chiarain—the site of an annual pilgrimage. Not far from the church ruins are the gaunt remains of Dunamore Castle, perched on a rock. This was once a fortress of the O Driscolls, rulers of the island.

At the southern end is a small lake round which a strange story has grown. If you leave your dirty linen here overnight, it will be cleansed by morning. It is no miraculous phenomenon. Millions of tiny insects appear during the night and literally eat the dirt. It could be worth trying *in extremis.*

Looking to the north and the west, there are tremendous views of a sea full of islands—Carbery's Hundred Isles—Horse, Long, Calf and Hare Islands, and a multitude of smaller islets and rock stacks, at the mouth of Roaring Water Bay and stretching away down the coast. Four miles beyond Cape Clear is Fastnet Rock, its lighthouse the most southerly in Ireland. (Boats from Baltimore take passengers to Clear Island.)

[134]

Clonmel Churchyard W 797680 (Eire ½″ Map 25)

Three quarters of a mile north of Cobh, which is on Cork Harbour. The churchyard contains the plain, communal grave of victims of the wrecked *Lusitania,* commemorated by one small slab set on the neatly clipped grass, and maintained by the Cunard Steamship Company. In the same big churchyard, in part of an old chapel enclosure, is the tomb of the Rev. Charles Wolfe, who wrote 'The Burial of Sir John Moore'. In the ancient, heavily grass-grown section of the graveyard, close to the road, is the tomb of James Verling, surgeon to Napoleon on St Helena for one year (1818–19), and who died at Cobh in 1858. The tomb, weathered and sunken, has a warped grille through which—with enough light and imagination—his remains can be glimpsed.

[135]

Coppinger's Court W 261358 (Eire $\frac{1}{2}''$ Map 24)

One and a half miles west-south-west of Ross Carbery. An imposing Elizabethan mansion built by Sir Walter Coppinger about 1610, and heavily fortified. According to tradition, it had a chimney for every month, a door for every week, and windows for every day of the year. The gables were painted and the windows richly mullioned. It was attacked and burnt down in the 1640s. Now it stands deserted amid fields, weeds sprouting high inside it, its fine, tall chimneys broken and overgrown with creepers. It is still a romantic sight, especially from far off.

[136]

Drombeg Stone Circle W 247352 (Eire $\frac{1}{2}''$ Map 24)

One and a half miles east of Glandore. Prehistoric stone circle 30 feet in diameter, in a lovely position on a grassy terrace, high up in the midst of hills with rocky outcrops and bracken-covered slopes. It is made of 17 great boulders, two of them portal stones over 6 feet high, decorated with oval cup marks. In the centre of the ring is a flat altar stone found to cover a burial cyst containing the bones of a youth, and cremation ashes in an unornamented urn of the early Iron Age.

Fifty yards to the west, partly enclosed by a high bank of boulders and scorched stones, are the remains of a cooking pit and two stone huts. The pit, a rectangular construction, is roughly lined with flat stones. Adjacent to it is a hearth, and a well with partly corbelled roof from which the pit would have been filled. The surface of the well water, looking like a small, dark pool, is covered with tiny water flowers, beneath which newts dart in and out, and from the well a shallow channel, dug to follow the descending curve of the hill, carries away the overflow.

The circular huts, one of them large with 4-foot-thick stone and rubble walls, the other smaller and containing a roasting oven, are linked by a central doorway. This was probably a place of assembly where pagan rites were performed. There are beautiful views westwards to the sea, and over peaceful farming country. In the evening, when the sun is setting, it is full of the mystery of forgotten ceremonies.

[137]

Fort Camden W 810615 (Eire ½″ Map 25)

One and a half miles north-east of Crosshaven, on the south side of Rams Head, guarding the entrance to Cork Harbour. Great, extended fortifications backing on to the cliffs, above a small, sandy foreshore. Hemmed in by castellated walls and arches, and gaping with gun emplacements, from a distance it looks more like the deserted palace and outbuildings of some troglodytic royalty and their attendants.

These were fortifications first built by the British at the end of the 18th century to withstand a feared Napoleonic invasion. Later the site was enlarged and refortified, and used by the Royal Engineers.

A second fort, Templebreedy, was erected during the first world war, close by on a strategic hill overlooking Church Bay. Both these forts, together with a third, Fort Carlisle, which faces across the water from a height on the opposite, eastern side of the harbour, were handed back to the Irish Government in 1938. Magnificent views of a run of beautiful, wooded headlands, the estuary, and Crosshaven Harbour full of small boats, of splendid Cork Harbour and, to the south, the open sea.

[138]

Garinish Island V 936560 (Eire ½″ Map 24)

Small, hilly island off-shore from Glengarriff in beautiful Bantry Bay. Also known as Ilnacullin—the Island of the Hollies. It was transformed by its previous owner, John Annan Bryce, with the assistance of Harold Peto, into an entrancing island-garden, covered with many fine trees and exotic flowering shrubs which flourish in the mild climate. The exquisite Italian Gardens are centred on a rectangular lily pool around whose paved edges are massed a riot of variegated foliage and brilliantly coloured blooms, while at the seaward end steps lead up to a Grecian temple through whose arches can be seen incomparable views of the islet-dotted sea and the dark backdrop of the distant hills and the Great Sugar Loaf Mountain. Shady paths lead through shrubberies, and to miniature Japanese and overhanging rock gardens. The highest point of the island is crowned by an old Martello tower from which there are more spectacular views. Herons nest on some of the wooded islets which surround Garinish. Here Bernard Shaw wrote part of *St Joan.* (Admission charge; boat service—15 minutes' trip—from Glengarriff.)

[139]

Glenbeg Lough Surrounding V 705530 (Eire ½″ Map 24)

One mile south-east of Ardgroom, a village on the northern shore road of the mountainous Beara Peninsula; about 17 miles south-west of Kenmare. Remote and sombre lake just over a mile long, hemmed in by a great circle of rugged mountains, Toureennamna to the east, Maulin to the south. A narrow road from Ardgroom edges the northern shore and peters out altogether at the end of the lake, where there is a small, lonely farm. Great, savage rock faces rise sheer from the road on the southern side, enclosing the water in an impenetrable mass of cliff and crag. It is a wild, desolate place, but very beautiful.

[140]

Gougane Barra W 092663 (Eire ½″ Map 24)

Twelve miles north-north-east of Bantry. A beautiful small lake in the midst of the wild Sheehy Mountains, which drop to the water on three sides in sharp precipices. Best seen after rain, when streams dash in cascades down the rock faces. On a small islet in the lake, joined by an artificial causeway to the shore, is the site of the hermitage of St Finbarr, patron saint of Cork. St Finbarr's Well is at one end of the causeway. On the island is a modern chapel, and beyond it, an 18th century courtyard enclosed by thick walls in which are niches and plaques representing the stations of the cross. A large stone cross on a stepped base and overhung by an ash tree at the centre of the courtyard, marks the site of St Finbarr's cell. There is a Patron (Saint's day festival) on his feast day, September 25. At the courtyard entrance is a stone commemorating J. J. Callanan (born in Cork in 1795), the poet who wrote 'The Beautiful Lines on Gougane Barra'.

South of the lake the main road runs to the coast through the Pass of Keimaneigh (Pass of the Deer), part of it a narrow mountain defile across which, according to legend, a deer sprang to avoid the huntsmen. North of the lake, a new road leads through beautiful National Forest parkland, opened in 1966. In the park, beside the road, a small stream coming from the mountains, is the source of the river Lee which continues through Gougane Barra, and ends in great style in Cork Harbour.

[141]

Kanturk Castle R 386018 (Eire ½″ Map 21)

One mile south of Kanturk. Otherwise known as MacDonagh MacCarthy's Court or Folly. Remains of an immense fortified mansion begun about 1609, but never finished. Work on it was stopped by order of the Privy Council, who thought it too splendid for an Irish subject. They were provoked, no doubt, by jealousy or by fear that MacDonagh was becoming too powerful. Building stopped short of the parapets and the great mansion now stands, almost concealed within a grove of gigantic trees—a great, square, roofless shell, rising through four floorless storeys. Immense flocks of rooks nest there, and weeds grow waist-high within and around it.

[142]

Kilcolman Castle R 581113 (Eire ½″ Map 21)

Two and a half miles north-east of Buttevant, which is on the Mallow–Charleville road. Tall, ivy-covered ruin of a Desmond stronghold granted to the Spenser family in the 16th century. Here Spenser wrote *The Faerie Queen* and other works. Heartily disliked by the Irish, who burnt the castle in 1598, Spenser and his wife escaped, but his son was thought to have perished in the fire. The ruin stands on high ground above a small, beautiful and solitary lough, edged thickly with wild iris and banked with reeds where water birds nest. At the opposite end of the lake from the castle, a walled track leads to the water's edge, and alongside it is a deserted farmhouse where old, rusting farm implements lie idle, as if abandoned because of some sudden calamity. A wonderful, secret place, with a tranquil, melancholy air.

[143]

Kilcrea Friary and Castle W 508685 (Eire ½″ Map 25)

Five miles west-south-west of Ballincollig, on the banks of the small river Bride. Great, solitary ruin of a 15th century Franciscan friary in a graveyard near a lovely old four-arched stone bridge. Opposite it, divided from it by a lane, are the remains of Kilcrea Castle, its huge square tower and broken turrets standing high amid fields and trees. Both the abbey and the castle were built by Cormac Laidir MacCarthy, Lord of Muskerry, who is buried in the abbey. His descendant, Donagh MacCarthy, Lord Clancarty, defended his estates desperately against Cromwellian forces, but was eventually subdued and confined to the Tower of London. The castle and abbey, their treasures stolen, were dreadfully mutilated, and the lands sold. The huge abbey ruin stands in a graveyard packed tight with grave slabs and immense tombs, some with large iron rings set in them and very old.

[144]

Kinsale Museum W 640508 (Eire ½″ Map 25)

At Kinsale, old historic seaport at the mouth of the Bandon river estuary above Kinsale Harbour. Early 18th century Market House, repaired and now used with good effect as a small museum of regional relics. Amongst its collection are three fine beribboned charters granted by Elizabeth I, James I, and James II; tragic pictures and newspaper reports of the sinking of the *Lusitania* off the Old Head of Kinsale in 1915;

records of the feats of Patrick Cotter O Brien, the 8 feet 6 inch Kinsale Giant (1760–1806), who made a fortune on the English stage; ancient weights and measures; a black, hooded, voluminous Kinsale robe—an ancient local dress called the Kinsale cloak, and worn into the 20th century. Near-by in Church Street, is the church of St Multose, dating from the late 12th century, though with many more recent alterations and additions. It has some good sculptured slabs, hatchments hung high on the walls of the nave, and a huge, old square font.

The beautiful coast around Kinsale, with its deeply indented shore line, has always been of strategic importance. On the wooded promontories of the almost land-locked harbour, are the ruins of 17th century fortifications built by the English.

[145]

Labbacallee Grave R 774020 (Eire $\frac{1}{2}$" Map 22)

Three miles north-west of Fermoy, beneath trees at the side of the Glanworth road. Also known as Leaba Cailllighe (the Hag's Bed). Huge, wedge-shaped gallery grave of the Early Bronze Age, the largest in Ireland. Enormous blotched boulders form the walls of the tomb which, externally, measures 20 feet at its widest, western end. The interior, divided into two chambers by a large upright slab, is 5 feet wide and over 25 feet long, and 9 feet at its highest level above the ground. Three immense capstones seal the roof. Excavated in 1934, the smaller chamber was found to contain a headless female skeleton and bones of animals, while in the main chamber were human cremations and pottery sherds, and evidence of burials and food vessels of a later period. Scarcely damaged, except that the covering cairn no longer exists, it is a remarkable memorial to Neolithic endeavour.

One and a half miles to the north-west, at the wool manufacturing village of Glanworth, the charming river Funshion is spanned by a decorative, ancient bridge. Made of stone, it is narrow, with 13 arches. Near it are the crumbling remnants of a Roche castle, and of a 13th century Dominican abbey. But primarily this is a district rich in prehistoric remains: tombs, standing stones, circles, some of them defaced and hard to identify.

[146]

Labbamolaga R 765179 (Eire $\frac{1}{2}$" Map 22)

Five miles north-west of Mitchelstown. Also known as Leaba Molaga (St Molaga's Bed). Ancient monastic site founded by the saint. The humble remains are in a lonely field with trees, and consist of some fragments of an early church, a very small and ruined, roofless oratory and a broken cross slab, all contained within an old, drystone wall, wild flowers sprouting from its crevices. The oratory is entered by a low doorway. On the ground, inside the south wall, is a longish, slabbed stone with a shallow, dank cavity beneath it, scarcely long enough nor even high enough for a man to insinuate himself into it. This was the saint's 'bed'. A night spent in it is said to cure rheumatism. Faith apart, it looks more likely to provoke it. In an adjacent field to the south, stand four bulky monoliths, as if they had sprouted out of the earth.

[147]

Leader's Folly W 466768 (Eire ½″ Map 25)

On the river Dripsey, 1 mile west of Luskin's Bridge, reached by a narrow, little used road. Remains of an aqueduct built around 1860 by a Mr Leader, a wealthy local landowner, to carry water across the valley. It collapsed after the first attempt to use it. Five great, creeper-covered pillars remain, straddling the densely wooded and overgrown narrow river valley, the scrub and weeds so thick and high that the huge, monolithic columns can only be seen from the roadside through breaks in the banks and hedges. A mile or two downstream are the ruins of Dripsey Castle, romantic and lonely on high ground above a dam.

[148]

Lough Hyne W 095285 (Eire ½″ Map 24)

Three and a half miles south-west of Skibbereen. Also known as Lough Ine. Beautiful salt-water lake surrounded on three sides by hills. It has a very deep sea inlet fed by a quarter-mile-long channel, almost like a river, which has a natural sill or weir at the entrance. This gives rise to an unusual tide—a three-hour rise, and a nine-hour fall. Close by is the Marine Biology Station of University College, Cork, appropriately situated in an area where unusual forms of sea life are common: sea urchins, starfish, and jelly fish, sometimes the poisonous sort—summer migrants that come with the Gulf Stream.

On a small islet in the middle of the lough are the shattered remnants of Lough Ine Castle, once a fortress of the O Driscolls. A holy well (Toberbreedy) and an ancient ruined church (Templebreedy) are at the southern end.

[149]

Mizen Head V 737235 (Eire ½″ Map 24)

Most south-westerly point of the Cork mainland, from which the length of Ireland is measured. Wild, windy, grass-grown headland 765 feet above the water, with a Fog Station at its extremity. Awe-inspiring sight of an arc of great, stratified cliffs round which the sea churns ominously, breaking in a cloud of flung spray over half-submerged rock ledges. Magnificent views to the north across Dunlough Bay to Three Castle Head where, beside a tiny lake near the cliffs, are the ruined towers of an old Mahoney fortress, and traces of Dun Locha promontory fort.

On the southern shore of the Mizen Head peninsula, the road runs inland almost encircling Barley Cove, a deep, narrow bay with a beautiful, creamy-white sand beach at its head. Here the sea runs up in long, white-topped rollers, frothing over the Rock of the Devils in the middle of the bay. On a clear day, Fastnet Rock looms up from the sea, 10 miles away to the south-east.

[150]

Old Head of Kinsale W 630393 (Eire ½" Map 25)

Seven miles south of Kinsale, at the southern end of a long, projecting peninsula from which the Head bulges from a thin neck of land like the head of a sea serpent. Grassy promontory with splendid cliff scenery and outlying rock stacks, the home of thousands of gulls and guillemots. On the clifftop are the remains of an old de Courcy castle with battlemented walls, built in the 15th century on the site of a very much older fortress, the stronghold of Cearmna, one of the early Irish kings, and from which he ruled half the country. Beyond the castle ruins, at the tip of the Head, is a lighthouse. Magnificent cliff and sea views.

Ten miles off-shore lies the wreck of the *Lusitania* (see Clonmel Churchyard), where salvage is going on. Records of the sinking in May 1915, are on show at the Kinsale Museum (q.v.).

[151]

Ovens Caves W 554702 (Eire ½" Map 25)

Seven miles west-south-west of Cork; 3 miles west of Ballincollig. Extensive natural caverns and a labyrinth of passages in a limestone ridge above the river Bride, near a quarry. There are estimated to be some 2,000 feet of tunnels, but may be considerably more. Local people claim that they extend anything up to 8 miles. There are several entrances, none of them easy to find. One is about 100 yards east of the bridge at Ovens where, over a low wall, the rough ground drops down to overgrown cliffs. At the lowest level, some 200 yards from the road, is a smallish hole in the cliffside, which can be entered by lying down and wriggling through. Exploration is perfectly possible by caving enthusiasts impervious to the streams and boulders, the mud, and the low dark entrances. Wear clothes that don't matter, and take a strong torch and preferably somebody local who is willing to act as a guide. You could become hopelessly lost in the passages.

[152]

Penal Altar W 220648 (Eire $\frac{1}{2}''$ Map 24)

Three quarters of a mile south of Inchigeela, a village on the north shore of beautiful, indented Lough Allua, an expansion of the river Lee. A road crosses the river valley, bending slightly south-westwards. Just off the roadside, and visible from it, is a rough stone altar, half hidden beneath the low branches of trees. A plaque on it is inscribed: 'Altar of Penal Times. Mass was said here 1640–1800'. Such services were, during that time, forbidden.

[153]

Riverstown House W 734752 (Eire $\frac{1}{2}''$ Map 25)

Three and a half miles north-east of Cork city centre; $1\frac{1}{2}$ miles north of the confluence of the rivers Lee and the Glanmire. Beautiful Georgian home of Dr Jemmett Browne, Bishop of Cork, who rebuilt and beautified it in 1745 with plasterwork by the Francini brothers, stuccodores brought to Ireland in 1738 by the Earl of Kildare. Saved from its fate as a potato store by the Irish Georgian Society, and in part restored at great expense, it was opened to the public in 1965. So far only the beautiful dining room can be seen. The ceiling represents Time rescuing Truth from the assaults of Discord and Envy, from a design painted by Poussin for Cardinal Richelieu and now in the Louvre. Magnificent wall panels depict: Heroic Virtue; Aeneas carrying his father, Anchises, on his shoulders; Grammar, a classical figure inverting a pot over a plant in an urn; Fides Publica, bearing fruits and ears of corn; Fortune, holding a rudder resting on a globe; Achilles drawing on his greaves; and Roma Aeterna, a helmeted lady rather like Britannia holding a statuette of Victory. (Admission charge.)

[154]

The Rock Close W 606750 (Eire $\frac{1}{2}''$ Map 21)

In the grounds of Blarney Castle, which is 5 miles north-west of Cork. A path from the castle leads to an old, stone-built tunnel, which is the entrance to the Rock Close. This is a grove of great, ancient yew and ilex trees, and where massive outcrops of rock have weathered into curious shapes. Some of the boulders, standing in a grassy glade, are formed into a circle; another boulder, on a lower level than the rest, is a great rocking stone. There are two caves and a pool. According to legend, the grove was a centre of Druid worship in pre-Christian days. They used the ancient stones—probably part of an even more ancient cult—in their ceremonies. The yew and the ilex were sacred to them.

It is easy to dismiss the whole fabric of Druidic lore, witchcraft, and fairy magic that has been built up round the place, as mere fancy. Prosaically, it could all have stemmed from James Jefferyes, 18th century owner of Blarney, who planned an ornamental garden here after designs used by Garzoni in Italian villas of the day. Jefferyes could have constructed Rock Close to look as it now does, or merely juggled with an existing, far older construction. But the Druid wood remains a strange, mystical place in spite of its many visitors (try to go early, or late, when they are busy kissing the Blarney Stone up at the castle). Many of the enormous trees—Californian redwood, cypress and incense cedar, as well as yew and ilex, are a thousand years old, perhaps more, and are amongst the oldest in the world. (Admission charge to castle and grounds.)

[155]

Rostellan Dolmen W 882672 (Eire ½″ Map 25)

Five miles east of Cobh; just over ½ mile north-east of the village of Rostellan on the south side of a tidal creek opening into Cork Harbour. Chambered tomb about 10 yards from high-water mark on the shore of the creek, and almost submerged at high tide. Its great stone slabs, topped by a rough capstone, stand 6 to 7 feet high, and it emerges from a bed of mud and waving seaweed like some trapped monster. Something of a headache to archaeologists because of its part-time inaccessibility, nonetheless it has been partly reconstructed and its authenticity proved.

In the village of Rostellan, on a creek to the south, an old stone bridge which spans the reedy, tidal water, has three ancient milestones set into its side, inscribed with the distance from Rostellan to almost anywhere.

[156]

St Colman's Cathedral W 918676 (Eire ½″ Map 25)

At Cloyne, 3½ miles east-north-east of Rostellan, which is on the eastern shore of Cork Harbour. Fine cruciform Protestant cathedral which dates back to the 13th century, but which has been greatly altered at regular intervals since. The most recent restoration was in the 19th century, when the aisles of the vast nave were broadened. Here are several outstanding monuments to Cloyne bishops (including one by the sculptor John Hogan of Tallow) and in the north transept, a very beautiful recumbent statue in alabaster done by Bruce Joy in 1890, of the Illustrious Berkeley, Bishop of Cloyne from 1734 to 1753, the famous philosopher. He is buried in Oxford.

Opposite the cathedral stands a 100-foot-high round tower which, after damage by storm, was repaired by the addition of castellations. The tower, and the remnants

ugane Barra, Co. Cork *(Wonder No. 140)*

Dunbeg, Co. Kerry *(Wonder No. 172)*

Gallarus Oratory, Co. Kerry (*Wonder No. 173*)

Gap of Dunloe, Co. Kerry (*Wonder No.*

of St Brigid's Fire House, are all that remain of an ancient monastery founded in Cloyne in the 7th century by St Colman MacLenin, originally a man of letters and a poet, who was persuaded by St Brendan, whom he met at a ceremony at Cashel, to become a priest. In the Fire House, the nuns of St Brigid kept a fire continually burning for the use of the community, fire being a most precious possession.

[157]

St Gobnat's Shrine W 196768 (Eire ½" Map 21)

One mile south-east of Ballyvourney, which is 9 miles west-north-west of Macroom, on the Macroom–Killarney road. Site of a monastery founded in the 6th century by St Gobnat, who is the patron saint of bees, and much revered for her care of the sick. Here, in a quiet, countrified corner, facing towards the foothills of the Derrynasaggart Mountains, are the ruins of a medieval church (Teampall Ghobnatan) and within the graveyard, St Gobnat's grave, a small mound where discarded crutches and other offerings have been left. Three ogham stones stand by it.

On rising ground outside the graveyard is a modern statue of the saint executed in 1951 by the Cork sculptor, Seamus Murphy. She is represented standing on a beehive from which a bee is emerging, and more bees are carved on its base. Close to the statue is St Gobnat's House, a small, roofless circular hut of drystone walling and, beside it, St Gobnat's Well. Pilgrimages to the shrine are made on the saint's day, February 11th.

[158]

St Mary's Collegiate Church X 096783 (Eire ½" Map 25)

At Youghal. Beautiful, large 13th century church, badly wrecked in the 16th century by the rebellious Earl of Desmond and his troops, who stabled their horses and cattle there. The present church, much restored, still has some remains of the earlier building in it. Particularly fine is the west door, the pulpit carved of bog oak, the revolving lectern, and the 14th century stone font, given a later wood cover. In various parts of the church are any number of recumbent effigies and ancient stone coffin lids. The Boyle Chapel in the south transept contains an elaborately carved monument in the Italian manner, erected by Richard Boyle in the early 17th century as a memorial to himself, his two wives, his mother, and a goodly number of his 16 children. The resplendent painted effigies recline, kneel and stand in various pious attitudes in pillared niches beside and above the tomb chest, on which the effigy of Richard Boyle takes precedence. Adjacent to the church is Myrtle Grove, an Elizabethan house with fine, tall chimneys, all swathed in creepers, where Sir Walter

Raleigh lived from 1588–9 when he was Mayor of Youghal. The house is private but can be seen very well from the church precincts.

[159]

Shippool Castle W 567546 (Eire ½″ Map 25)

Five miles north-west of Kinsale, above the Bandon river which here bends north and then west in a great loop. Shippool, or Poll na Long Castle, was built in 1543 by the Roche family, and stands in a magnificent position above a beautiful, wooded reach of the river, its ground-level gunports commanding the approaches by water. It was one of a great string of fortresses built in the 15th and 16th centuries to defend the valley of the tidal river Bandon, and ruins of more of them can be seen downstream, though mostly in a state of extreme dilapidation. Shippool, too, is very ruinous, but impressive. A short, somewhat perilous clamber over fallen rubble and debris, leads down to the water's edge.

[160]

Templebryan W 386438 (Eire ½″ Map 25)

One and a half miles north of Clonakilty. Ancient monastic site almost obliterated among farm fields, now the home of browsing cattle. Within an overgrown, walled enclosure, about 30 feet across and broken by entrances, are the remnants of a primitive oratory, a lost graveyard, a well, souterrain, and an 11-foot-high pillar stone, tapering almost to a point and greatly weathered. On it can be traced a simple cross and an almost vanished ogham inscription. The whole enclosure, a forlorn deserted place, is contained within a much greater circular one, some 400 yards across, its high, thick bank of earth and stones serving as farm field boundaries, and even more effectively isolating this little, ancient site.

Two fields away, to the south-east, and close to the roadside in yet another field, is a small stone circle. Some of its stones have long since disappeared, but five of them remain—four of them 6 feet high with bevelled tops, and a fifth, which has fallen. In the centre of this diminished circle is a white quartzite pillar, about 2½ feet high. The monastic enclosure and the stone circle are reached by way of the farm and, in fact, are part of it. (Ask permission there to see them.)

[161]

Timoleague Abbey W 475437 (Eire ½″ Map 25)

Three miles west-north-west of Courtmacsherry, on the estuary of the river Argideen, overlooking deeply indented Courtmacsherry Bay. Beautiful remains of a once extensive Franciscan friary—a graceful bell tower, nave, and remnants of the choir, with a high arcade of rounded arches, and an unusual walled courtyard. They stand at the edge of the sea beside an old bridge. It was once one of the more important of the great religious houses of Ireland. The present ruins are those of a 14th century building, constructed by William de Barry on the site of an earlier foundation which, in turn, stood where once was the 6th century monastery of St Molaga, a saint noted for his skill in restoring health.

KERRY

[162]

Ardfert Cathedral Q 780286 (Eire $\frac{1}{2}''$ Map 20)

Five miles north-north-west of Tralee. Site of a monastery founded in the 6th century by St Brendan the Navigator. Here are the ruins of a beautiful 13th century cathedral, to which a chapel at the north-east end, and a south transept were added in the 15th century. It is roofless, but otherwise remarkably complete and very graceful, the walls standing to the eaves, and at the east end there are three very tall, narrow, lancet windows. The west door and remains of arcading date from the 12th century, probably incorporated from an earlier church. The finely carved effigy of a bishop, discovered during work which took place in the 19th century, has been inserted into an arched niche against the wall.

In the same churchyard are the ruins of two more churches, joined together by a wall: Tempall-na-hoe (Church of the Virgin), and Tempall-na-griffin—taking its name from a carving of a dragon on one of its stones. Half a mile east of the cathedral is yet another ruin, that of a Friary in the secluded grounds of Ardfert Abbey, the former Crosby (Earls of Glandore) demesne. Founded in 1253 by Thomas Fitzmaurice for the Franciscan order, the impressive remains include a ruined church dating from the 13th century, with a good later tower which can be ascended to the roof, and parts of the cloisters.

Two miles to the north-west is Banna Strand, where Roger Casement landed from a German submarine in 1916. He was arrested while taking refuge in MacKenna's Fort, an ancient earth hill fort in a field a mile north-west of Ardfert.

[163]

Ballaghbeama Gap Surrounding V 750780 (Eire $\frac{1}{2}''$ Map 20)

Eight miles north-north-west of Sneem, by a northerly fork off the main Sneem–

Killarney road. Precipitous gash in the mountains, a narrow road twisting through the defile where a small, turbulent stream flows. On either side are fierce, boulder-strewn cliffs: Knockaunanattin (1,884 feet) to the east, Mullaghanattin (2,539 feet) to the west; and in the far distance, black against the skyline, fold upon fold of the giant MacGillycuddy's Reeks. A scene of remote and savage grandeur.

[164]

Ballintaggert Ogham Stones V 462997 (Eire ½″ Map 20)

Just over a mile south-east of Dingle, by a signposted lane beyond a small lough, then across two farm fields. Nine ogham stones lying like discarded bolsters within the rough, oval enclosure of an ancient, disused graveyard. Three of them have incised crosses cut into them. About a mile to the north-west, in Emlagh East, is another ogham stone with a cross on it (Cloch an tSagart), and an ancient ring fort.

[165]

The Blasket Islands Surrounding V 255960 (Eire ½″ Map 20)

Off Slea Head at the south-western extremity of the Dingle Peninsula. Group of seven islands and outlying rock stacks, the most westerly of them Europe's nearest point to America. In Blasket Sound, an often stormy and dangerous channel between islands and mainland, two ships of the Spanish Armada struck the rocks and sank in 1588: The *Santa Maria de la Rosa*, and the *San Juan de Ragusa*. The Great Blasket, the largest of the group (4 miles long, just under a mile wide) was inhabited until 1953 when, because of the decline of the fishing and the hard living conditions, the inhabitants were evacuated to the mainland. From this island came some remarkable literature based on the island's life and folklore: *Peig* by Peg Sayers; Thomas O Crohan's *The Islandman*; and *Twenty Years A-Growing* by Maurice O Sullivan, all written in Irish and translated into English.

Great Blasket has dramatic scenery, wild cliffs rising to more than 960 feet and dropping on the west in great precipices known as Fatal Cliff. The ruined settlement of the ex-islanders can be seen from Coomeenoole on the mainland just north of Slea Head. The other islands are: Tearaght (the most westerly), with a lighthouse at its western point; Inishvickillaun (the most southerly), with a ruined church and several clochans; Inishnabro, just north of Inishvickillaun; and Inishtooskert (most northerly), with more ruins and clochans. The two smallest islands, Youngs and Beginish, are at the northern end of Blasket Sound, a scatter of half submerged rocks on their western seaboard. (No regular services; make arrangements on the mainland at Dunquin; or at Dingle, from where excursion boats leave in summer.)

[166]

Caherconree Fort Q 726066 (Eire $\frac{1}{2}$″ Map 20)

Two and a half miles south-east of the village of Camp, which is on the northern coast of the Dingle Peninsula, about 8 miles west-south-west of Tralee. Great prehistoric stone fort, one of the highest in Ireland, on a spur of Caherconree (2,713 feet), a high, craggy peak in the Slieve Mish Mountains. The fort lies 2,050 feet up on a remote, projecting, two-acre rock promontory, shaped like a rough triangle. Impregnable on two sides, which are formed by sheer rock precipices, it is defended on the third side by a massive curving stone wall which, fortified in turn by an outer fosse or ditch, runs for some 350 feet across the 'promontory', forming the third side of the triangle. Best reached from the village of Camp, where a narrow farm lane signposted 'Promontory Fort, 2 miles' follows the course of the little river Finglas. It is possible to drive along this lane, and to start the ascent of the mountain flank from a gate by the side of a ruined burial cyst. The signpost is less than adequate; it is about 2 miles to the *gate* from where the ascent begins; after that, allow a good hour to reach the fort. Magnificent views from the river valley, from where the fort can be seen (when the mountain top is not enveloped in cloud) outlined on a high, dark-grey rock ledge like some giant's eyrie. Magnificent views, too, from the fort, over mountains and the coast.

[167]

Caragh Lake Surrounding V 730920 (Eire $\frac{1}{2}$″ Map 20)

Three miles east of Glenbeigh at the north-eastern end of the Iveragh Peninsula. Beautiful lough, 4 miles long, through which flows the Caragh river. At its southern end, which is ringed by mountains, is Glencar, where there are particularly fine walks along the valley of the Upper Caragh river to Blackstone Bridge, a distance of about 1½ miles. The hills to the east of the lough are strewn with small lakes, easily reached by a minor road which skirts the north-eastern shore. To the south-east is lonely Lough Acoose, from where a mountain track leads to the south of the great MacGillycuddy's Reeks, an awesome belt of high peaks: Beenkeragh (3,314 feet), and Carrauntuohill (3,414 feet), Ireland's highest mountain.

The best ascent of Carrauntuohill is from the north, where a track leads southwards through the starkly beautiful Hag's Glen. A footbridge crosses the river Gaddach, and beyond, the track continues upwards to the small lost lakes of Gouragh and Callee, in high mountain cirques to the east of the summit. Here is mountain grandeur at its most splendid. Superb views take in counties Limerick and Cork, the Dingle Peninsula to the north, and the Shannon beyond.

[168]

Carrigafoyle Castle Q 987476 (Eire ½″ Map 17)

Two miles north-north-west of Ballylongford, on the west side of a creek running in from the Shannon estuary. Great broken castle within a walled courtyard which also encloses a boat dock at the foot of the tower. Seat of the O Connors of Kerry. Defended for the Earl of Desmond against a force led by Sir William Pelham, it was remorselessly battered and taken after a two-day battle, and the survivors hanged. Finally devastated by Cromwell's forces in the 17th century, it fell into utter ruin. Only part of its wall now stands, but it is still powerful, its massive 80-foot tower with a huge, gaping hole in it, rising above the encroaching reeds in the water, and commanding idyllic views of the flat, dreamy, estuary country with its wide empty skies.

[169]

Connor Pass Surrounding Q 500060 (Eire ½″ Map 20)

Magnificent mountain route, one of the finest in the Dingle Peninsula, starting 2 miles south-east of Cloghane on the north shore and ending at Dingle on the southern shore. Beginning at the northern end, the road climbs through the foothills of the great Brandon Mountain (3,127 feet), and Brandon Peak (2,764 feet), winding along the base of immense cliffs on one side, the valley a dizzy drop on the other. As it ascends to the head of the Pass (1,500 feet), the route is through an incredible, boulder-strewn waste, with small lakes caught in the fastness of mountain hollows. Great, awesome peaks rise on all sides: Ballysitteragh, to the west; Slievanea to the east. From the top of the pass there are wonderful views of the sea on both sides of the peninsula, and the massed, craggy slopes of the mountains. The descent towards Dingle is to return to the less spectacular though no less beautiful sight of Dingle Harbour and the rocky, deeply indented shore.

[170]

Corpus Christi Church R 067355 (Eire ½″ Map 17)

At Knockanure, which is 5 miles east-north-east of Listowel. Impressive though simple modern church built by Michael Scott and Associates in 1963–4. It contains three works by Oisin Kelly: the porch screen, depicting the Last Supper; the Virgin and Child, and a fine crucifix. The stations of the cross, designed by Leslie McWeeney, are worked in tapestry, the symbols done in black wool on lime green grounds. They hang round otherwise bare walls. The church bell stands supported by heavy iron girders, on the wide steps outside.

[171]

Derrynane Bay Surrounding V 525580 (Eire $\frac{1}{2}$″ Map 24)

A mile and a half south-west of Caherdaniel, which is on the south-western point of the Iveragh Peninsula, overlooking the wide Kenmare estuary. Wild rock-bound bay, with golden sand beaches and dunes, almost concealed by the surrounding slopes. Reached by a steep, narrow road descending from the Ring of Kerry corniche, from where there are incredibly splendid and romantic views of rugged inlets, off-shore islands and great wooded heights. The southern arm of the bay is a long protecting peninsula ending at Lamb's Head. Half-hidden on the slopes amid thick woods, is Derrynane House, home of Daniel O Connell, the 19th century Irish 'Liberator', somewhat over-restored, and containing a collection of personal relics (Open to the public.) Relics are a feature of the area: the shell of Derrynane Castle; off-shore Abbey Island (reached on foot at low tide) with the remains of an early monastery on it; and above the shore of Derrynane beach, a big ogham stone.

[172]

Dunbeg V 351972 (Eire $\frac{1}{2}$″ Map 20)

Two miles east of Slea Head at the south-western extremity of the Dingle Peninsula; signposted from the coast road across farm fields. Spectacular promontory fort occupying a triangular headland cut off by a great drystone wall 150 feet long, 10 feet high, and up to 25 feet thick with three small enclosures built into it. The outer edges of the fort, where there are only broken pieces of the wall, drop sheer to the sea in 90-foot, savage cliffs, much eroded by the pounding of the sea. The landward fortifications are highly complicated. The entrance is long and tunnel-shaped, with built-in cell-like apertures from which the interior of the tunnel could be watched. A ruinous circular building stands in the inner enclosure, probably a clochan (small stone building, corbelled, often beehive-shaped). On the outside, the whole intricate defence work is further fortified by great, earthen banks and trenches, with a path cut through to the wall; and beneath the path is a souterrain reaching to the second bank, which probably extended a great deal further. It is an astonishing structure on a superlative site. Go now, before further erosion of the cliffs destroys it.

Above the fort, in the Fahan district, on the rough slopes to the north of the road, and also on Slea Head, is a fantastic quantity of ancient monuments; there have been counted no less than 400 clochans (some still in use as domestic outhouses), as well as numbers of standing stones, promontory forts, crosses, and souterrains. Time is all that is needed to find them.

[173]

Gallarus Oratory Q 355049 (Eire $\frac{1}{2}''$ Map 20)

One and a half miles north-east of Ballyferriter, near the mountainous north-western end of the Dingle Peninsula. The most perfect and best preserved of early Christian churches in Ireland, probably dating from the 8th century. Built of un-mortared stone slabs, this marvellous little corbelled oratory is shaped like an upturned boat; it has a high, ridged roof, and has remained completely rain-proof after more than a thousand years. The walls are more than 3 feet thick and enclose an area 10 by 15 feet. A small, round-headed window is inserted at the east end; the doorway at the west end narrows at the top where there are two sockets which probably held door jambs. It stands in fields within an encircling drystone wall, at one side of which there is a 4-foot-high incised pillar stone, with a cross in a circle and other markings on it. (Signposted from the road.)

Two and a half miles east-north-east, at Kilmalkedar, is an early 12th century Romanesque church with The Alphabet Stone (ogham) near the chancel door, and an old sundial. South of the village, is the ruined Chancellor's House, a holy well, and St Brendan's Oratory, a collapsed version of Gallarus.

This is a beautiful district, with fine prospects of high mountains, and distractingly full of prehistoric and other remains—stones, crosses, wells, and the ruins of countless churches.

[174]

Gap of Dunloe V 880897 to 870840 (Eire $\frac{1}{2}''$ Map 20)

Six miles south-west of Killarney, the northern entrance lying to the west of Lough Leane. Great mountain defile through which runs the river Loe, opening into three small, beautiful lakes on its course. Steep, craggy mountains enclose it: on the east the Tomies Mountain, the Shehy Mountain, and the Purple Mountain, while on the west are the awe-inspiring MacGillycuddy's Reeks. The northern entrance to the Gap starts just below Kate Kearney's Cottage (drink and souvenirs), where Kate used to sell illegal liquor to passers-by, in the 19th century. The narrow, rough road that twists through the valley is not for motorists. It can be traversed by pony-trap or on horseback—a popular ride is to the head of the Gap, at 800 feet, and back, a distance of some 3 miles each way. Walkers could make a more leisurely day of it. Touristy in a district already famed for its outstanding beauty, it is nonetheless a spectacle not to be missed for the sheer splendour of its views.

[175]

The Healy Pass Surrounding V 785545 (Eire $\frac{1}{2}''$ Map 24)

Mountain route crossing the centre of the Beara Peninsula over the Kerry/Cork border. Magnificent road reaching its highest point (1,050 feet) at the pass on the summit ridge of the Caha Mountains, Knockowen looming to the east. Dizzy hair-pin bends, and magnificent views in every direction of desolate, empty hills and the rugged coastal mountains. Begun in the 19th century as a military road, it was completed as an incomparable tourist route in the early 1930s. Best followed in a south-north direction, starting at Adrigole Bridge, on Bantry Bay, the road begins at once to climb towards the pass, descending to Lauragh Bridge on Kilmakilloge Harbour on the wide estuary of the beautiful Kenmare river.

[176]

Leacanabuaile Fort V 446811 (Eire $\frac{1}{2}''$ Map 20)

Two miles north-west of Cahirciveen at the southern end of the Iveragh Peninsula; north of the Valentia river, on a hillside, reached by a minor road to Cooncrome Harbour. Leacanabuaile ('Hillside of the Summer Pastorage') is a fine, partly-reconstructed stone fort on a massive, rock foundation, its stone walls enclosing an almost circular area 70 feet in diameter. Protected on three sides by steep grassy slopes, the entrance is on the eastern side. The walls, mostly 10 feet thick and with irregular steps leading up on the inside, contain the remnants of a square dwelling house built on top of earlier circular ones; another clochan on the western side has a cavity leading to a long souterrain. Excavation produced Iron and Bronze Age objects, suggesting the existence of an early Christian farming community. From the top of the ramparts there are fine views down to the coast, where the gaunt ruins of Ballycarbery Castle, a fortress of the MacCarthys, stand black against the skyline. At least two other similar, but lesser forts, and some standing stones, are in the district.

[177]

Lislaughtin Abbey R 003460 (Eire $\frac{1}{2}''$ Map 17)

One mile north-north-east of Ballylongford, at the head of a narrow creek. Roofless ruin of a 15th century friary founded by O Connor Kerry for the Franciscan order. Although very mutilated, it rises majestically almost to its original height above the placid inlet surrounded by farm fields. It stands in the midst of a vast graveyard, and there are many more tombs inside it. The doorway is very fine, and so is the pointed east window, and three graceful, carved sedilia. Peaceful views across the wide Shannon estuary.

[178]

Minard Castle

V 556992 (Eire $\frac{1}{2}''$ Map 20)

Three miles south-west of Anascaul, on the south coast of the Dingle Peninsula. The shell of a large fortress built by the Knight of Kerry, and shattered in due course by Cromwellian forces. One of the most ruinous of ruins, and dangerous too, by the look of the great splits showing in the crumbling walls. It stands on a high grassy eminence, above the shore of a small, stony, sheltered cove where a stream running down from the mountains is spanned by an ancient stone bridge with three squared-off arches. Lovely tranquil views of the rocky, indented Kerry coast and the distant mountains.

One and a half miles to the north-west, just west of the village of Aglish, is a 12-foot pillar stone known as the Aglish Boulder. It stands in the middle of a high, boggy field full of mosses and bog cotton—a huge, bulky stone, with a sunken dolmen beside it. To reach the stone, climb over a grass-covered wall on a lane just west of the village where it will be seen, standing on rising ground, about 50 yards away. Marvellous views of Dingle Bay and the mountains to the north.

[179]

Muckross Abbey

V 976870 (Eire $\frac{1}{2}''$ Map 20)

Two and a half miles south of Killarney, on the shore of Castlelough Bay, an indentation on the eastern shore of the greater Lough Leane, the Lower Lake of Killarney. Beautiful and extensive remains of a Franciscan friary founded in 1448 by Donal MacCarthy Mor; suppressed in the 16th century, when it was attacked by Elizabethan troops, and finally wrecked in the 17th century by General Ludlow's Cromwellian forces. The ruin—remarkably complete, though roofless—stands peacefully amid fine trees in the Muckross demesne. Here are buried the famous Kerry poets, Aodhagan O Rathaille and Eoghan Ruadh O Suilleabhain, and many of the powerful Desmond chiefs. The cloisters, a fine range of 22 pointed arches, enclose an open courtyard with a great ancient yew at its centre, optimistically dated from the abbey's foundation, but undeniably very old and considerably reduced in height by age.

Muckross is one of a dozen or more Wonders in a district very much visited. One of the most spectacular views of the beautiful Killarney Lakes is from the north, looking southwards over the lakes and mountains from Aghadoe Hill, where there are the ruins of a monastery, the stump of a round tower, and the remnants of a small 10–12th century church with an ogham stone in the chancel.

[180]

Rattoo Q 877334 (Eire $\frac{1}{2}''$ Map 17)

One mile south-south-east of Ballyduff. Round tower, 92 feet high and the remains of a monastic settlement founded in the reign of King John for the Knights Hospitallers. The 10th century tower, which has a restored cap, is one of the most perfectly preserved in Ireland. It stands in peaceful farming country within a walled monastic enclosure, where there are the ruins of a medieval church, destroyed in 1600.

[181]

Reenagoppul Stone Circle V 903708 (Eire $\frac{1}{2}''$ Map 21)

Quarter of a mile south-west of Kenmare, which is at the head of Kenmare Bay. Reached by a gated track into what is known as 'The Shrubberies', at the top of a hill. Stone circle consisting of 15 standing stones with a shallow chambered tomb at its centre covered by a massive, rounded capstone. In spite of its somewhat unprepossessing surroundings (one has to pass what is almost a rubbish dump), the circle has a great atmosphere. There are two holy wells in the district; Our Lady's Well and Shrine at Gortamullin, $\frac{1}{4}$ mile from Kenmare, and St Finan's Well, near Kenmare Old Church. Both are still visited; their waters are reputed to have healing properties.

[182]

Robber's Cave W 070825 (Eire $\frac{1}{2}''$ Map 21)

Above and south of Glenflesk, about 8 miles south-east of Killarney, on the northern slopes of Carrigawaddra. Great cave, the hideout of 16th century Owen MacCarthy, a noted robber. (Ask locally the best way to reach it.) Here, in the safety of his mountain lair, MacCarthy trained his apprentices—many of them children of the local peasantry—in the art of cattle thieving and highway robbery. Among the host of legends that surround his name, is the sad one of a widow's son, caught by the O Donoghue overlords who lived at Killaha Castle in Glenflesk near-by, and who was sentenced to be beheaded, though later proved to be innocent. Unfortunately, the chieftains drank too much and forgot to instruct the servants about the pardon. He was beheaded at noon before they sobered up, and the widowed mother put a terrible curse on the family. Curse or no, the castle was duly destroyed, as was customary, by Cromwellian troops. The ruins can be seen on the west side of the Killarney–Macroom road, 6 miles south-east of Killarney itself. A side road turns off below the castle, leading westwards to Lough Guitane, very lonely and beautiful in the midst of the mountains.

[183]

Rossbeigh Strand V 644912–645950 (Eire ½″ Map 20)

One and a half miles west of Glenbeigh, at the north-eastern end of the Iveragh Peninsula. Two-mile-long, curving spit jutting into Dingle Bay across the entrance to Castlemaine Harbour. Composed entirely of yellow-white sand backed by high dunes, where the surf breaks endlessly. At its northern, seaward end is a 19th century stone tower, built as a guide for ships entering the harbour. From Inch, on the opposite shore of Dingle Bay, a similar spit, extending for almost three miles, reaches out towards Rossbeigh Strand, leaving a gap of less than a mile between the two. A third spit cuts into the harbour to the east from the southern shore, Cromane Point at its seaward end. The three great spits, providing incomparable bathing and walks, are often deserted, even in the holiday season. Superb views from all three, especially from their points; and looking back at them from the corniche roads of the Dingle and Iveragh Peninsulas, from where they appear to be an enormous, continuous beach isolating the considerably silted-up harbour behind them. In fact, a deep water channel snakes between the three spits, dividing into narrow waterways at the head of the bay.

[184]

St Brendan's Oratory Q 460118 (Eire ½″ Map 20)

Near the top of Mount Brandon, Ireland's second highest mountain (3,126 feet). Three miles north-east of Ballybrack, near the north-west end of the wild and beautiful Dingle Peninsula. Ruined oratory and well of St Brendan the Navigator, a Kerryman who founded the important monastery at Clonfert (q.v.); also several broken clochans, all contained within drystone walling just below the summit. To this wild and lonely place came St Brendan, by way of The Saint's Road, a mountain track which he is said to have made himself. Pilgrims follow the same route, which is marked by stations of the cross, on the saint's day, June 29. Fantastic views of incredible grandeur over the rugged Brandon Mountain group, the great Kerry peaks to the south, and to the sea and County Clare to the north.

To reach the summit, start from Ballybrack, a village on the road which crosses the western end of the peninsula from Milltown on Dingle Bay. The Saint's Road is a rough trackway, easily discernible, which ascends the western flank of the mountain.

From the summit, a descending ridge running northwards makes a not too difficult hill ramble to Mastiompan (2,509 feet); a great coastal peak, with St Brendan's Monument—a recumbent ogham stone with incised crosses—on its slope. Beyond is Brandon Head, where savage cliffs, in some places 1,000 feet high, drop down to the water, and extend in great arcs south-westwards to Brandon Creek.

[185]

The Skelligs Surrounding V 300608 (Eire $\frac{1}{2}''$ Map 20)

Eight miles west of Bolus Head, the south-westernmost point of the Iveragh Peninsula. A fantastic pair of rock islets composed of grit and shale veined with quartz, rising sheer out of the Atlantic. The home of seals, innumerable nesting gannets, and of puffins, stormy petrels, fulmars, shearwaters, gulls, and many other sea birds.

Little Skellig, rarely possible to land on, is uninhabited. Great Skellig (Skellig Michael—dedicated to St Michael, patron saint of high places), lies to the west, an ominous rock mass covering more than 40 acres, the peak of some long-submerged mountain. Sharply-angled twin peaks tower 715 feet above the water—often turbulent. Permanent inhabitants are lighthouse keepers, and rabbits whose holes riddle the spongy moss—and the birds.

Scored into the precipitous cliffs are narrow roadways with hewn steps, the choice of path being determined by the state of the wind and weather. Perched dizzily on an eastern rock ledge, 600 feet from the summit, are the remains of a monastic settlement traditionally linked with the 7th century St Finan. Here, confined within drystone walls, is a ruinous medieval church, two wells, two corbelled, boat-shaped oratories similar to the one at Gallarus (q.v.), a number of crude crosses and cross slabs, and half a dozen stone beehive dwellings, with thick walls rising in some parts as high as 17 feet. Here, too, are the melancholy remnants of gardens constructed laboriously by the monks—soil had to be collected from the rock crevices and brought there—and a small cemetery with ancient gravestones.

Pilgrimages to Skellig Michael could never have been less than perilous. If ever they could land, pilgrims performed the stations of the cross from the landing place to the monastery, then ascended the final peak, a hazardous climb involving a rock chimney (The Eye of the Needle) and then a ridge terminating in a vertical, 12-foot rock, which had to be climbed by means of hewn holes serving as hand- and footholds. At the top, a narrow spit of rock, projecting outwards for several feet, has a cross carved on its seaward end. Along this the pilgrims crawled to kiss the cross, clinging like limpets 700 feet above the Atlantic.

Access to Skellig Michael is only possible in calm weather. The journey, either from Cahirciveen, or from Knightstown Harbour on Valentia Island, is first down a long, often choppy channel, then into the open Atlantic, taking over two hours. The landing place, Blind Man's Cove on its eastern side, is no more than a giant rock arch, impossible for a boat to enter if seas are breaking into it. Skellig Michael is the experience of a lifetime. The views are stupendous—and indescribable.

[186]

Smerwick Harbour Surrounding Q 360070 (Eire ½″ Map 20)

North-western extremity of Dingle Peninsula. Deep, natural harbour scooped out of the northern coast, protected at its mouth by fine sweeps of high cliff. South of the somewhat gloomy village of Smerwick on the western shore of the bay, are the remains of Dun an Oir (the Fort of Gold), constructed by James Fitzmaurice's invading force of Italian, Spanish and Irish troops in 1580. The fort was besieged and overpowered at once by an English sea and land army under Lord Deputy Grey and Admiral Winter, who spared the officers, but massacred 600 of the men. The handing over of Father Laurence Moore, Oliver Plunket and other hostages, was disastrously futile. Refusing to acknowledge English supremacy, they were tortured and hanged.

Magnificent cliffs edge the shore on either side of the bay, from Sybil Point to the tip of the western arm of the harbour, where the skyline is dramatically broken by the Three Sisters, jutting upwards like the spiny back of a rhinoceros. The eastern arm culminates in Ballydavid Head (830 feet), a rugged promontory with a tower on it.

[187]

Staigue Fort V 591620 (Eire ½″ Map 24)

Two miles north-east of Castlecove, a coastal village at the south-western end of the Ring of Kerry. Fine approach by a narrow road climbing gradually through rocky outcrops, its hedges thick with fuchsia, willow, hawthorn and bog iris. Massive circular fort thought to belong to the Iron Age, standing against a background of formidable, boulder-strewn mountains. It is beautifully constructed of unmortared stone slabs enclosing an area 90 feet in diameter. The walls stand 10 to 18 feet high, 13 feet thick at the base, narrowing to 7 feet thick at the top. The entrance is through a single doorway, nearly 6 feet high, with sloping sides and heavy lintel stones. Inside the walls, 10 flights of steps arranged in a double line of chevrons, and made of jutting, regularly spaced slabs, which enable anyone using them to ascend and descend in various directions, reach from the ground to the top of the walls. Within the walls, at the north and west, are two small chambers entered by transverse passages. This is early defensive construction of an unusually sophisticated standard. The fort, strategically placed with mountains at its back, appears to melt into them, naturally camouflaged. It commands a superb vista down the narrow valley to the sea. (Key to entrance from adjacent farm.)

Section 4

Limerick

Tipperary

Clare

[188]

Adare Manor R 473460 (Eire $\frac{1}{2}''$ Map 17)

At Adare, a pretty village on the river Maigue, its English character contrived by thatched cottages and the familiar appurtenances of inn, church and manor house. Adare Manor, seat of the Earls of Dunraven, stands amid fine trees and gracious parkland, a 19th century edifice of silver-grey stone beset with batches of high chimneys, turrets, gargoyles and balustrading. The result is impressive. It is erected on the site of a smaller Georgian house built by the second Earl who took 30 years over it, largely to his own design. It has some curious, decorative features. The balustrade along the south front is composed of 4-foot-high stone lettering: 'Except the Lord Build the House their labour is but lost that build it'. Other texts and inscriptions are also employed including one which reads: 'Love God onely. Honour and obey the Queen. Eschew evil and do Good'. Augustus Pugin designed the fine dining room, the minstrels' gallery and ceiling, and some of the carved mantelpieces. It was his Lordship's pride that the house was built entirely without debt. Material was transported to the site, often by way of the river Maigue which flows decoratively through the grounds, and paid for on the spot. Broad steps lead to the river, where there is an exceptionally fine cedar of Lebanon. Walks along the banks lead to two ruins, one of a 15th century Franciscan friary, the other an early Desmond castle. In the grounds is a stone commemorating a visit in 1752 of John Wesley. (Admission charge to house and/or grounds.)

[189]

Ardagh Fort R 274385 (Eire $\frac{1}{2}''$ Map 17)

About $\frac{1}{2}$ mile west of the village of Ardagh, which is 3 miles north of Newcastle West. Ancient ring fort with an overall diameter of about 250 feet, grass-grown, and easily visible from the roadside. St Patrick is reputed to have founded a church here. In 1868 the famous Ardagh Chalice was discovered hidden under a thorn bush, an outstanding example of ecclesiastical metal work, now in the National Museum, Dublin. It is a beautiful two-handled cup, 7 inches high, wrought of gold, silver and bronze, and richly decorated with crystal, amber, and enamel. Four brooches were also found.

[190]

Carrigogunnel Castle R 498552 (Eire $\frac{1}{2}''$ Map 17)

Five miles west-south-west of Limerick; 2 miles north-west of Mungret. Haggard wreck of a great 14th century O Brien fortress high on craggy rocks above the river Maigue near where it flows into the Shannon estuary. A prominent landmark for miles around. It was the predecessor of another castle built about 1200 by William de Burgo, son-in-law of Donal Mor O Brien. In 1536 the castle fell to Lord Deputy Grey, who attacked it ferociously for two days and subsequently hanged the garrison. Its final downfall was in 1691 when it was surrendered to the Williamites in the second siege of Limerick, and later demolished by explosion. There remains the massive though shattered keep, a round bastion, and remnants of the great hall, creeper-covered and roamed over by grazing cattle. Lovely views across the tranquil marshy estuary country.

[191]

Castle Oliver Demesne Surrounding R 667190 (Eire ½″ Map 22)

Two miles south-east of Ardpatrick. Nothing now remains of Castle Oliver itself, one-time residence of 'Silver' Oliver who, in the 18th century, brought German Palatinate families (originally settled at Rathkeale) to live in the district. Today Rathkeale is a great centre for tinkers who live in houses crammed with shining brasswork.

Castle Oliver was claimed as being the birthplace of Marie Gilbert—the notorious Lola Montez—who so ensnared the mad King Ludwig of Bavaria, that she was virtually in control of the government. Now, in the vast demesne, approached by two avenues of fine trees, stands Clonodfoy House, a fantastic and somewhat grim 19th century Victorian-Gothic mansion set about with towers, spires and battlements. On the hill above it is a curious double-turreted folly, built to give employment during the famine. (The demesne is private, but ask permission at the farm to go in and look.) Four miles north-east, just east of Kilfinane, is Palatine's Rock, an eminence used by the settled Palatine families as a place of assembly.

[192]

Duntryleague R 779284 (Eire ½″ Map 18)

Eight miles south-west of Tipperary; about a mile to the west of Galbally. Heather-covered hill (922 feet)—Dun Tre Liag (the Fort of the Three Pillar Stones), where Cormas Cas, a 2nd century King of Munster, died from a head wound inflicted in battle and was buried. A well at the summit was enclosed within three stones and the bed of the king placed on them so that his wound might be bathed with the fresh water. To the west of the summit is a partially defaced though clearly marked passage-grave, its long entrance leading to a burial chamber roofed with stones. Near it is a broken stone circle and some ring barrows, and the remnants of a stone fort known as

rigogunnel Castle, Co. Limerick
onder No. 190)

The Rock of Cashel, Co. Tipperar
(Wonder No. 221

Grubb's Grave, Co. Tipperary
(Wonder No. 209)

Stained glass window showing
the Little Ark,
Moneen, Co. Clare
(Wonder No. 248)

Brian Boru's Fort. Superb views from the hilltop across undulating farmland to the Galty Mountains on the southern horizon. Three miles south-west, just to the north of the village of Ballylanders, is a ruined church and holy well, the site of devotions and festivities on August 14th.

[193]

Glenaster Waterfall R 235384 (Eire $\frac{1}{2}''$ Map 17)

Four miles north-west of Newcastle West, reached from the lower, secondary road from Newcastle West to Glin. Wonderfully secret fall of the little river Daar, flowing here in a narrow, heavily wooded gorge, and invisible except from paths that wind steeply down to the river. The water pitches first down 20 feet to a rock ledge, then cascades another 30 feet or so to the bottom of the gorge. To reach it, first cross fields from the road, then descend through thick trees and undergrowth by twisting, very narrow and often muddy paths. A lonely and very beautiful place.

[194]

Hospital R 714362 (Eire $\frac{1}{2}''$ Map 18)

At Hospital, on the Limerick–Mitchelstown road. The village is named for the church of the Knights Hospitaller of St John of Jerusalem, founded in the early 13th century by Geoffrey de Marisco, lord of the manor of Ainy (the village of Knockainy, lies to the west). The ruined church has little of note, but there are several interesting tombs. One, standing within an angle of the walls, bears the effigy in high-relief of a Marisco knight; another later Marisco tomb, more dilapidated, has the effigies of a knight and his lady; the third, a 14th century slab, is carved with the indistinct figure of a knight in armour.

Three miles to the north-west is Cromwell Hill (586 feet), with a motley collection of prehistoric ring forts, mounds and caves noted for their connection with ancient legends. One cave, in the glen below the hill, is called Dermot and Grania's Bed (Diarmaid and Grainne), one of the many places where the ill-fated lovers took refuge in their long flight from the wrath of Fionn Mac Cumhail (Finn Mac Coul). (See also Hill of Allen and the Caves of Keshcorran.)

[195]

Kilfinnane Mote R 682229 (Eire $\frac{1}{2}''$ Map 22)

At the village of Kilfinnane. Enormous flat-topped mound, 200 feet across, encircled by three great earthen banks and fosses, with a total over-all diameter of about

100 yards. Originally an ancient ring fort, it was adapted to accommodate a now vanished medieval fortress. It entirely dominates the village.

Three miles to the north-east, on the south-western slopes of Sleavereagh (1,531 feet), is the site of a prehistoric farming settlement. At about 800 feet are the remains of several ring forts where excavators found souterrains, dwelling houses, and Bronze Age burial chambers. Fine hill scenery, and splendid views from the summit.

Just over a mile north of the Cush crossroad, among quiet fields, is St Molua's Well, with a modern statue of the saint in bishop's dress holding a crook. The holy well is at the back of a large, ancient churchyard and rounds are still made on the Saint's Day, August 4. Two stone slabs mark the path taken by the pilgrims.

[196]

Kilmallock Friary R 610280 (Eire ½" Map 17)

In Kilmallock. Huge ruined friary church, founded in the 13th century by Gilbert, son of Lord Offaly, for the Dominicans. The considerable remains include a very fine five-lancet east window, a south transept with some good carving, and a 90-foot-high broken tower, as well as remnants of the conventual buildings and cloisters. Among the several dilapidated tombs in the choir, is that of Edmund Fitzgibbon (1552–1608), last of the 'White Knights', who betrayed the 'Sugan' Earl of Desmond to the English. ('Sugan' means straw; the Earl being regarded as a man of straw because he was given the title after the death of the last rightful heir. See also Mitchelstown Caves.)

On the north side of the town, between the road and the river Loobagh, is the handsome ruin of the Collegiate Church of SS Peter and Paul, dating from the 13th–15th century. Until recently the walled-off chancel was used for Protestant worship; the arcaded nave and the south transept had long fallen into disrepair. The belfry is a broken round tower incorporated into a corner of the north aisle. There are some fine old 17th century tomb slabs, one carved with a skeleton with a spade, other skeletons below him; another bearing the rather endearing figures of a knight and his lady.

[197]

Lough Gur Surrounding R 640405 (Eire ½" Map 18)

Two miles west of Herbertstown, which is on the Hospital–Caherconlish road. Lovely lake full of water birds and wild swans. It lies in the midst of low, sculpted limestone hills, with sudden outcrops of rock, Knockadoon Hill thrusting into the eastern shore, Knockfennell rising to the west.

Scattered over the slopes and down near the lake is one of Ireland's biggest and most remarkable concentrations of antiquities from neolithic and successive civilizations. Since excavations in 1936, there have been countless finds of pottery, broken sherds, food vessels, arrow heads and fragments of bronze.

To reach one of the most important groups on Knockadoon Hill, take the narrow road to Bouchier's Castle, a ruined tower in the north-eastern corner next to a farm, and from there follow a track round the hill then down towards the lake. Above the water, amid clumpish grass, nettles and crowded undergrowth, are the remains of a neolithic rectangular dwelling, a walled enclosure with a standing stone, and an excavated neolithic cemetery. From here there are fine views over the lake to the hills. On the east side of the lake, close to the narrow road that skirts it, is a wedge-shaped megalithic tomb; on the western shore, at the foot of Knockfennell, is a ring fort and a small broken stone circle.

Near the southern shore, close to the Kilmallock–Limerick road, is an enormous stone circle, the largest in Ireland. The close-packed ring of standing stones, up to 9 feet high, stands within a great earthen bank, 30 feet wide, enclosing a flat inner area 150 feet across. The entrance, which is on the east side, is paved and flanked with massive uprights. It is an amazing monument, all the more wonderful for the giant ash trees that thickly surround it.

There is a great deal more to discover, not all easy to find, and a lot of time and patience is needed. There are hut settlements, cairns, ruins, ring forts, remnants of stone forts, and any number of burial places, broken circles and standing stones. There are two crannogs – man-made islands: Crock Island, small and now connected to the mainland by the overgrown marshy ground in the south-western corner of the lake; and Bolin Island at the top of the northern arm near Bouchier's Castle. Garret Island, picturesquely set in the middle of the lake, is a bird sanctuary where a wide variety of wildfowl breed.

According to an old legend, one of the Earls of Desmond lives at the bottom of the lake condemned by some curse to surface once every seven years and gallop across the water. Legends apart, it is a wild and enchanting place where often the only inhabitants are the cattle that graze there. Frustrating to anyone who expects clear definition and signposts to point the way, it is boundlessly attractive not only to archaeologists, but to anyone with a curiosity about very old things, or just a love of natural beauty. Some of the monuments are under State care; others just exist and have to be looked for.

[198]

Monasteranenagh Abbey R 551408 (Eire ½″ Map 17)

At Monaster, 2½ miles east of Croom. Vast, impressive ruin of a Cistercian abbey – daughter house of Mellifont (q.v.) – founded in the 12th century by Turlogh

O Brien, king of Thomond, as a token of gratitude for his defeat of the Danes at the battle of Rathmore (1148). It overlooks the small river Camoge, here very pretty, with wild iris at its edge. Although the walls are fragmentary, parts of the monastery church still stand to the eaves, with five high moulded arches of shattered transepts and some interesting stone carvings. Good views of the ruin from the road, where it crosses a narrow, ancient bridge.

TIPPERARY

[199]

Athassel Abbey S 011364 (Eire $\frac{1}{2}''$ Map 18)

One and a half miles south of Golden, by the minor road immediately west of the bridge. Vast, rook-haunted ruins of a 12th century Augustinian priory, covering several acres, the largest of their kind in Ireland, in deep meadows on the right bank of the river Suir. From the road a low stone bridge of four arches crosses marshy ground, once a mill stream, to a gateway which had a portcullis and a gatehouse with a porter's lodge. Beyond, to the east, are the principal ruins—a great central tower over the cruciform church and all that is left of the long nave below it. Between nave and chancel there is a magnificent doorway. In the church is a tomb, perhaps that of the Norman William de Burgh who founded Athassel, with figures of knights carved on a panel below it. There are other statues, one erect, and impressive relief carvings. Below the east window the Suir flows. The cloisters, which have some remains of their arcades, lead off into vaulted chambers. The approaches to everything—church, cloisters, chapter house, dormitories, storehouses and other secular buildings—are now overwhelmed by tall grass. One of the most romantic of the great ruins of Ireland. It was destroyed in 1447. Here, Richard de Burgh, the Red Earl of Ulster, having spent his last years in retreat, died, 1326. Here, surrounding the priory, was a town burned in 1319 and again in 1329 or 30 by Brian O Brien, so completely that scarcely a sign of it remains.

[200]

The Baurnadomeeny Tomb R 847603 (Eire $\frac{1}{2}''$ Map 18)

Three quarters of a mile north-east of Rear Cross on the main Newport–Thurles road. Otherwise known as Dermot and Grania's Bed. (Diarmaid and Grainne; see also Hospital and The Caves of Keshcorran.) A magnificent megalithic tomb in a splendid situation on the south-west flank of Mauherslieve (Mother Mountain). It has two chambers, the largest one 14 feet long, separated from the smaller antechamber in which there is a grave. In the tomb and its cairn, which is surrounded by a kerb of stones, a very large number of cremations were found. Some of the stones of the tomb and cairn have enigmatic marks on them. In summer bracken sprouts from the roof.

To reach it take the road north from the main road at Rear Cross, and when it turns sharply to the left continue straight on by a track which leads to a farmhouse. On the way to it there is a great, club-shaped standing stone about 9 feet high. Ask permission to view the tomb at the farmhouse.

On the summit of the mountain above is the Terrot, a pile of stones, said to cover the body of a boy who went hunting instead of going to mass and perished in a snow storm in summer. People used to climb the hill to gather berries on a special day and deposit a stone, brought from below, on the cairn.

[201]

Brittas Castle S 126614 (Eire ½" Map 18)

Two miles north of Thurles. Marvellous 19th century moated folly, in a beautiful, private demesne. A projected replica of Warwick Castle but left unfinished when the owner, a Mr Langley, was hit on the head by a piece of falling masonry which killed him. From the west side the unfinished walls rise in steps to the upper parts of the castle, and this appears to be the only way of reaching those rooms in the tower which were completed. Under the tower a triple arched pointed gateway with limestone stalactites hanging from it, drops straight into the moat. Pine trees sprout from the top of the tower. The cut limestone blocks of which the castle is constructed, are beautifully put together. Partly enclosed by the water-filled moat is the house which the castle may have been intended to supplant. The archway of the tower can best be seen from the demesne to the east of it, in which there are many great trees. (Private, but the owner might give permission to view it.)

[202]

Burncourt House R 951182 (Eire ½" Map 22)

Half a mile east-north-east of the village of Burncourt, which can be reached from the main Cahir–Mitchelstown road at Glengarra Bridge. Glengarra Bridge is half-way between Cahir and Mitchelstown, approximately 8 miles from either place. Otherwise known in Gaelic as An Cuirt Doighte. The remains of a 17th century fortress house, with four square towers, one at each angle of the central block, built about 1640, and now a shell. It is hidden from the road behind a modern farmhouse on the bank of the Burncourt river. The house was burned by its chatelaine, Lady Everard, in 1650, during the Cromwellian wars, to prevent it falling into enemy hands when it was barely 10 years old. Her husband was hanged at Limerick the next year by General Ireton after the town fell. The house has 26 gables and many tall chimneys. There is a walled, fortified enclosure between it and the river. (Ask permission to view at the farm.) Two miles to the south-south-east, in a demesne, is Shanbally Castle, designed by John Nash, burned in 1958.

[203]

The Clare Glens R 731598 (Eire ½″ Map 18)

One and a half miles south-east of Newport. A singularly beautiful wooded gorge on the western flank of the Slievefelim Mountains, through which the little peat-stained river descends in a series of rock pools and falls. It forms the border with County Limerick. Reached by a minor road southwards from the main Newport–Thurles road, ½ mile west of Newport.

[204]

Coolbaun S 217416 (Eire ½″ Map 18)

At Coolbaun crossroads, 4 miles north of Fethard on the road to Killenaule. A large earthwork with 4 ditches completely hidden in a dark spinney of thorn, beech and oak trees on the north-east side of the crossing. The eastern end of this impressive fortification is lost in a very wet bog. There are a number of other prehistoric forts in the vicinity.

[205]

Derrynavlan S 189495 (Eire ½″ Map 18)

Two miles south-east of Horse and Jockey on the Cashel–Urlingford road (marked CH with spot height 459). Roofless ruins of a 13th century church on a grassy mound in the middle of an enormous peat bog, in which the bog cotton flowers. A few hawthorn trees grow here, and there is sometimes a herd of cows grazing. Ruan and Goaban, saints of the 6th century, are associated with it. Ruan founded a monastery at Lorrha in northern Tipperary. He was supposed to have cursed Tara (q.v.) so that it sank into the ground. His bell, which was preserved at Lorrha, is in the British Museum. Less is known about Goaban, but his grave is a mound near the church at Derrynaflan. This is a very remote place, which can be most impressive at sunset. It can be reached by vehicle from Horse and Jockey on the Cashel–Urlingford road. Follow the lane eastwards from the village. Near Heathview House a track used by peat cutters, motorable in good weather, leads through the bog to the place where the cutting is going on. From here the church is about 400 yards to the south.

[206]

The Devil's Bit S 055738 (Eire ½" Map 18)

Four miles west-north-west of Templemore. Here the sandstone mountain which rises to 1,577 feet is cleft by a remarkable windswept gap, Bearnan Eile (the Gap of Eile) the result of glacial action. It is said to have been bitten from the mountain by the Devil who, finding it uneatable, spat it out some 20 miles to the south at Cashel (q.v.), where it now forms the Cathedral Rock. (The Rock, however, is of limestone.) On the western side of the Gap an enormous cross has been erected. Below, to the south, there is a castellated circular tower, Carden's Folly. The view is worth the climb, extending over the green vale of the Suir to the Slieve Ardagh Hills, Slievenamon, the Galty Mountains 30 miles to the south-west, to the north into Offaly, and to the west. The long inclined ramparts of the Devil's Bit Mountains—of which the Gap forms the southern end—are very remarkable when seen from the Templemore–Roscrea road to the east. To reach the Gap follow a long, winding, signposted lane from the road immediately north-east of the Barnane House demesne. This terminates in a locked gate and there is no turning space for vehicles. From here it is about 20 minutes on foot. The valley below the Gap to the north, with its great green slopes, is very beautiful.

[207]

Golden Hills S 004403 (Eire ½" Map 18)

One and a quarter miles north-north-west of Golden. Here are the remains of an eccentric, grey stone, castellated residence with a walled enclosure. It stands next to a modern, cream-coloured bungalow off a minor road just west of a bridge over the Multeen river.

[208]

The Graves of the Leinster Men R 734777 (Eire ½" Map 18)

Four miles north-north-east of Killaloe. A group of stones high on the north-west slope of Tountinna in the Arra Mountains, a few yards from the road that runs along the side of them. Said to be one of the first inhabited places in Ireland. It has legendary associations with the death of a Leinster King who came to visit Brian Boru near-by. Boru himself took his title from Beal Boru, the great ring fort across the Shannon in Co. Clare (q.v.), which is visible from here. The site is disfigured by some sort of scientific pylon which has been erected immediately opposite it. Half a mile north-east along this mountain road, at the Gap between Tountinna and Laghtea Mountain, is Chocan Ri Laighean (Knockaunreelyon), the Hillock of the Kings of Leinster.

It is unmarked on the map and on the ground. Great views from here up Lough Derg and also from the Graves.

[209]

Grubb's Grave S 035106 (Eire ½″ Map 22)

Two and a half miles south-east of Clogheen on the 'Vee' road to the Knockmealdown Gap on the border of Co. Cork. Here, on the north slope of Sugar Loaf Hill, 2,144 feet, in the Knockmealdown Mountains, are buried the earthly remains of Mr Samuel Grubb, Quaker, who died in the 1920s. He was entombed bolt upright in a sugar loaf construction, a cairn of whitened masonry, overlooking his estate, Castlegrace House, in the valley below. Whether the name of the hill inspired the shape of the tomb or vice-versa is not clear. The grave is on the hillside a couple of hundred yards above the road, just west of the hairpin from which the 'Vee' road takes its name. Splendid views over the plain below to the Galty Mountains.

This is not the highest burial in the Knockmealdowns. According to Lewis's *Topographical Dictionary*, 1850, Henry Eeles, who published several papers on electricity, is buried on the actual summit of Knockmealdown Mountain, 2,609 feet above sea level.

Below the Knockmealdown Gap, to the west of the 'Vee' road, is Bay Lough, a mountain tarn about 90 feet deep with a great cliff rising above it. Here the mountainside and the western shore of the lough have beautiful growths of pink rhododendron. This was once an abode of eagles. What must have been the old road to the Gap, now a track, passes close to it. This is a more pleasant route for walking to the Gap than the main road.

[210]

Kilclispeen Stone Crosses S 413291 (Eire ½″ Map 18)

At Ahenny, 5 miles north of Carrick-on-Suir, by a signposted road from Ahenny, a strange, rather forlorn miniature village street of very small white cottages. In St Crispin's churchyard, at the bottom of a field on the edge of the Slievenamon Hills, are two remarkably carved 8th century crosses, among yew trees. Although parts are now very worn, the decorations are still beautiful; both are elaborately incised with interlaced and geometrical patterns, and have pediments depicting horsemen, holy men, chariots and animals in relief. There are also two 18th century tombstones to Denis Finisy and Bridget Comerford, decorated with motifs of the crucifixion: ladder, cross, crown of thorns, hammer, sponge, dice, a cockerel and a purse with thirty pieces of silver.

A mile to the south-south-west, to the east of the main road near Scogh Bridge in

Co. Kilkenny, is an overgrown graveyard with four more great stone crosses in it, beside a ruined medieval chapel (S 423264). They are more primitive looking monuments; two have solid, wheel-like forms; one is decorated; another is tall and whittled away by the elements.

[211]

Kilcooly Abbey S 290577 (Eire $\frac{1}{2}$" Map 18)

Three and a half miles south of Urlingford. A long drive leads to it from the east side of the Urlingford–Killenaule road. Massive ruins of a Cistercian abbey in the demesne of Kilcooly House. It stands alone in a great meadow, hemmed in on three sides by fine trees, close to the border of Co. Kilkenny. The church was built about the end of the 12th century by Donal Mor O Brien, King of Thomond. It was destroyed by marauders about 1445 and partly rebuilt. In the chancel there is the remarkable tomb of James Butler of Clonamicklon, who is buried beneath it, together with his parents and his son. On the tomb chest is the recumbent figure of a knight in armour. One of the panels is ornamented with mandarin-like figures of the Apostles. It is signed by the man who made it, Rory O Tunney. Facing the south door is a screen with carvings of the crucifixion, St Christopher, a panel of a mermaid holding a mirror, and a pair of friendly fishes—also a jester. All were originally coloured. There are many other tombs. In the field in which the abbey stands there is a circular vaulted dovecot. Near-by, in the woods, by the lane which leads to the abbey, there is an austere little grey 19th century church.

[212]

Knockelly Castle S 230388 (Eire $\frac{1}{2}$" Map 18)

Two and a half miles north-north-east of Fethard by a minor road off the Killenaule road. Magnificent edifice with a tall central tower and a huge walled bawn (fortified enclosure attached to a castle) among pines on a high, windy hill overlooking a valley. The tower has three tall chimneys. Below it, to the west, the walls of the bawn meet at a sharp angle, and here there is a turret. The farm is inside the bawn. With the roofs of its buildings rising above the walls, the place has the air of a small fortified town.

[213]

The Knockgraffon Mote S 044290 (Eire $\frac{1}{2}$" Map 18)

Three miles north-west of Cahir and west of the Cahir–Cashel road. Reached by a turning to the west, 1 mile south of Newinn. Follow this road past the ruins of a 16th century castle of the Butlers, and turn left at the next junction. The mote is on the right. It is a huge, grass-covered mound, contoured with sheep runs and over 50 feet high surrounded by a fosse. This is the site of a 12th century Anglo-Norman castle. The entrance is on the west side by a stile. The ditch in front of the bailey is thickly wooded. The whole place is well protected by stinging nettles. In the bailey there are the ruins of a stone building. Splendid views of the Galty Mountains and glimpses of the Suir winding through the meadows below, a crossing of which the mote commanded. Just to the north are the picturesquely overgrown ruins of a medieval church standing in a graveyard. Beyond it the tower of the ruined Butler castle can be seen.

[214]

Loughlohery S 086238 (Eire ½″ Map 22)

Two and a half miles east-south-east of Cahir by a minor road which passes Loughlohery House. Three quarters of a mile east of the house and on the north side of it are the ruins of Loughlohery Castle. Just to the north-west of it, at the end of a field, is a small ruined oratory reached by a stone stile. The building is rendered invisible by ivy and a pair of huge ash trees. The graveyard is also completely overgrown. In it there is a modern plaster crucifixion. There is little to see and it is not worth a long detour as there are hundreds of such places in Ireland, but Loughlohery is a charming and solitary place.

[215]

Loughmoe Court S 118668 (Eire ½″ Map 18)

On the east side of Loughmoe village, 3 miles south of Templemore. Reached by a path through a farmyard which is close to the railway bridge in the village. Magnificent castle of the Purcells with a 15th century tower to which was added a 17th century house, with numerous mullioned windows and with an even larger tower at the western end. All is now ruined. The ragged skyline is very impressive. The ancient, east tower of 5 storeys can be climbed by a spiral staircase. In it are vaulted chambers, one of which has a great fireplace carved with leaves and with initials. Good view from the tower. Nicholas Purcell—Baron Loughmore—was a member of the Jacobite army and one of the signatories of the Treaty of Limerick, on October 3, 1691 after the great defeat at Aughrim in July of the same year.

In the churchyard of the ruined church in the village west of the railway, there is a tombstone 'Given by Patk. Sweeny of Garrenrow, in mem. of sister Bridget, also Aunt Mary'. On it is carved what appears to be an infant crucified, a bodiless angel with the face of a harlequin, and another blowing a trumpet with the words 'Come to Judgm'. At the west end of the village on the bank of the Suir, is a fine, tall mill-house with slatted wooden window shutters.

[216]

The Mitchelstown Caves R 920165 (Eire ½″ Map 22)

Two and a half miles north of Ballyporeen, by the road to Coolgarranroe Bridge. At the T junction by the bridge turn west for ½ mile. There are two sets of caves: The New Caves and the Old Caves, the latter more difficult to enter. The New Caves are behind a farm on the south side of the road at the head of a field. There is a sign at the farmhouse, where a guide can be engaged. At the head of the field there are some old quarry workings, a depression among the limestone rocks. In it a modest, green-painted door, reminiscent of *Alice,* leads to extraordinary underground wonders for those who enjoy caverns. These New Caves were discovered by a quarryman in 1833. The various parts have been given the usual prosaic names—House of Lords, Commons, the Organ, Drum, Pyramid, Table, Cathedral, Gallery of Arches, Chapel, Demon's Cave, Lot's Wife, Victoria Cave and the Closets—to name a few. The best is said to be the Kingston Gallery, 240 feet long and absolutely straight with coloured walls. In all they are nearly 1½ miles long. The services of the guide are more or less obligatory.

The Old Caves (otherwise Uaimh na Caorach Glaise) a couple of hundred yards to the east, are more difficult to visit. In them 'the Sugan' (Strawrope) Earl of Desmond, hid from the British with a price on his head in 1601, and here he was betrayed by Edmund Fitzgibbon, the last White Knight of Kilmallock. (See Kilmallock Friary.) The East Chamber in the Old Cave is large—390 feet long and 40 feet high. In all they are nearly 500 yards long.

[217]

Mona Inchna Priory S 167882 (Eire ½″ Map 15)

Two miles south-east of Roscrea. Remains of a tiny priory in Mona Inchna bog, on what was formerly an island surrounded by the waters of Lough Ore until it was drained in the 18th century. It stands in a walled enclosure high above the rush-filled meadows. Beautiful Romanesque west door and chancel arch. By the door there is a tall stone cross with worn carvings on the base, and a crucifixion with Christ wearing a robe, on the head of it. In a vaulted side chapel there is the massive black tombstone of Mary Hall of London. Mona Inchna is named after Inis na MBeo (the Island of the Living) because the bodies of those who were buried on it were believed to be miraculously preserved. Another belief is that no one could die on it. This little building of Mona Inchna, in its raised enclosure among the ancient beech trees, is one of the most beautiful places in Ireland. To reach it follow the main road towards Borris in Ossory for 1 mile. Then turn right and first left for 1¼ miles. Signpost.

[218]

Moor Abbey R 810280 (Eire ½″ Map 18)

Three quarters of a mile east of Galbally which is in Co. Limerick, at the north-eastern end of the Glen of Aherlow below the Galty Mountains. Impressive remains of a small Franciscan friary, with a tall, square 15th century belfry tower rising above it, on the left bank of the Aherlow river. It was founded in the 13th century by Donough Cairbreach O Brien, King of Thomond. A fortress in the 16th century, it was burned and ravaged many times. In the War of Independence its position was of such strategic importance that the Royal Irish Constabulary tried to blow it up.

[219]

Peakaun S 004285 (Eire ½″ Map 18)

At Toureen, 3½ miles north-west of Cahir, south of the Cahir–Tipperary road. (Marked 'Well' on the map.) Solitary remains of a monastic establishment, named after St Beccan, standing in a field. The old church known locally as Peacan, is very ruined. It is built of pinkish-grey stone. A very narrow doorway at the west end is partially blocked by a large stone. In the churchyard there are the trunks of two high crosses; a third, on a mound near the west door, is approached by stone steps. One of these crosses is said to have been broken by a mason who died suddenly after doing so.

Further along the lane to the south is Tobar Pheacain, a circular holy well lined with stonework, in the shadow of the trees. Beyond rise the Galty Mountains. To reach Peakaun, turn south off the main road by the 'Scenic Road' which is signposted opposite Toureen House, and then south again after ½ mile by a lane opposite a grey, semi-detached bungalow. Then go over the railway by a level crossing. The church is in a field on the right about 75 yards up a track which runs beside a little stream. A Patron day was celebrated here every August 1, until about 1840.

[220]

Rathurles R 907805 (Eire ½″ Map 18)

Three miles east-north-east of Nenagh. A triple-ringed fort on a slight round hill, hidden among trees. In the middle are the ruins of a 15th century church with a line of yews growing within it. The little churchyard has tombs of the Brereton family in it. Everything except the churchyard is overgrown. It is a mysterious place, heavily defended by insect life in the summer. Lying in a field, just outside the ramparts to the north-east, are two massive stone gateposts cut to support a lintel. The fort and church can only be reached by a rough track from a minor road which links the Nenagh–Cloghjordan and the Nenagh–Toomyvara roads. (Rathurles House is occupied and private.)

[221]

The Rock of Cashel S 073407 (Eire ½″ Map 18)

At Cashel. So much has been written about this ancient seat of the Eoghanacht Kings of Munster and later of the Christian prelates to whom it was given, that it seems superfluous to attempt to describe it in any detail here. But although perhaps too much written about, this great congery of ecclesiastical buildings, most of them ruined and roofless, and the tall round tower which seems to point a finger to the sky as if denouncing the despoilers of the place—the last of whom was Archbishop Price who took the roof off the Cathedral and sold the lead in the 18th century—is something which the visitor to Ireland should see at all costs. (It was also burned by Fitzgerald, the Great Earl of Kildare who, when taken to task for having done so by Henry VII of England, justified his conduct by saying 'I thought the Archbishop was in it'.)

Only the magnificent, barrel-vaulted chapel with its steep-pitched roof, built by Cormac, the Eoghanacht King in the 12th century, and the pointed round tower, survive with their fabric undespoiled—although the tower, struck by lightning in 1965, has had to be restored. Those parts of the other buildings which now lie open to the sky have been cleaned up and gravel has been laid on their ancient floors, no doubt with the best of intentions by the Commissioners of Public Works, but to the point of sterility.

It is from the outside that the real grandeur and melancholy of what are perhaps the most melancholy ecclesiastical ruins in all Ireland, strikes the beholder. Whether they are seen from the bend in the road to Urlingford, dark against the evening sky, with long skeins of birds above them flying home; or seen looming out of the mist in the early morning, high above the deep, damp meadows in which stand the pale, lichen-covered ruins of Hore Abbey; or from far off on the road to Golden, dyed deep red or brilliant ochre in a stormy sunset; or seen from close to, with the soft, very wetting Irish rain falling on them, when the stones seem to be exuding the tears of the dead; whatever the time or the place it always has a myriad disguises and appears always to justify the description of it by an Irish writer—'a regal acropolis, as moving as anything in Europe'.

[222]

St Berrahert's Kyle R 947288 (Eire $\frac{1}{2}$" Map 18)

At Ardane, $6\frac{1}{2}$ miles west-north-west of Cahir on the south side of the Glen of Aherlow. (Marked 'Ch' in Gothic type on the $\frac{1}{2}$" map.) Also known as Kilberrihert. All that remains is a small, oval enclosure in a clump of ancient oak trees. Dozens of cross slabs with worn carvings are embedded in the wall, together with the heads of two old crosses. There is a bullaun (stone with an artificial depression, used for grinding). Rags, rosaries and small, broken images are left here under the wall. In summer the Kyle and the surrounding fields are full of flowers. From the enclosure a little gate leads into a very wet water meadow and through it a track leads to another enchanted grove, $\frac{1}{2}$ mile away to the east. Here a spring emerges in a pool. There are rags and offerings attached to the trees at this holy well. Berrahert, otherwise Berechert, Berihert, Beretchert, Berichter, Beiricheart was an Anglo-Saxon saint of the 7th century, whose brother Gerald, also a saint, came with him to Ireland. Berrahert founded a monastery at Tullylease, Limerick. The Kyle is the site of a church which he founded. It is a lonely, beautiful place.

[223]

St Cominad's Well R 720658 (Eire $\frac{1}{2}$" Map 18)

At Kilcommenty, $2\frac{1}{2}$ miles north-north-west of Newport. On a track to the west of a lane which passes close to it. This pretty little well, still an object of veneration, is hidden away in a hollow under the roots of an enormous, ivy-grown ash tree. In the shrine there are a number of small offerings—rosaries, images and even ball point pens. Above it is a rather forlorn and overgrown churchyard. The church is ruined. There is said to be a boulder here, St Cominad's Bed, with bullauns in it and marks—the imprints of the saint's feet—some say they are of his hands—also his ribs; but we were unable to find it and there was no one to ask.

[224]

The 'Swiss Cottage' S 050227 (Eire $\frac{1}{2}$" Map 22)

One and a half miles south of Cahir in Cahir Park, to the east of the Cahir–Ardfinnan road. To reach it, enter the park by the second entrance on the main road after the clubhouse of the golf course. A *cottage orné* designed by John Nash, standing on a hill beside the river Suir in the demesne of ruined Cahir House, one time seat of the Butlers, Earls of Glengall. Seen from the approach drive at a distance, embowered in trees, it is not at all Irish. It in fact resembles the property of some well-hipped settler in Kenya before the war. The interior is elegant, but very decrepit. One room on the west side has beautiful hand-painted wallpaper by Paul Dufour, showing lively scenes on the shores of the Bosphorus. The paper is in a terrible state of repair, and some panels have been replaced by cuttings of coloured Alpine scenes from magazines. The window surrounds are of lacquered wood with mirrors inset. Some windows have glass with landscapes engraved on them; others are painted with warriors. There are rustic fireplaces. A wooden spiral staircase leads to the upper floor, which is not shown. At the back of the building there is a rustic fence of cast iron. A tunnel leads up through the mound to the house. (Admission charge.) In a near-by wood there is a pavilion, now in ruins. The Suir, at this point spanned by a cast iron bridge, is very beautiful, and the park has many noble and exotic trees.

[225]

The Timoney Stones S 190837 (Eire ½″ Map 15)

Five miles south-east of Roscrea. Several hundred standing stones on the hillside south-east of the road which runs south-westward from Knock crossroads. They have a remarkable aptitude for remaining invisible to the eye, but as one continues to gaze over the fields they begin to spring up like mushrooms before one's eyes. Nearly 300 have been counted, but there are probably more lurking in the woods. A good place from which to see them is a track which runs south-eastwards from a farm with silver painted gates, about 1½ miles from Knock crossroads. Another fine collection can be reached by a lane also to the south-east of the same road, 200 yards nearer the crossroads. Here there is a roughly defined circle with some very large stones in it. In the same field there is a strange little copse of trees which appears to be growing from a raised platform of stones. According to a local inhabitant, the 'Agent's Men' used to run races round the stones. A game of counting them would keep some children quiet for hours. Timoney House is a gaunt, sombre ruin on the north side of the road to Knock.

CLARE

[226]

Ballynalackan Castle M 102005 (Eire ½″ Map 14)

Two and a half miles north-west of Lisdoonvarna. Fine, ivy-clad 15th century tower and enclosure (bawn) of the O Briens, on a long, flat-topped steep-sided rock above a valley, with a wood at the foot of it, and another more windswept one on the hill above. Next to the castle is a low-built, 19th century house, once the residence of High Court Judge Peter O Brien, known as 'Peter the Packer' because of his habit of manipulating juries.

[227]

Beal Boru R 696743 (Eire ½″ Map 18)

One mile north-west of Killaloe. East of the Scariff road. Opposite Ballyvally House. Can be reached across the fields. What at a distance appears to be a noble and symmetrical grove of beech and pine trees above the Shannon, conceals within it a large circular earthwork surrounded by a deep ditch. This is Beal Boru (the Pass of the Tributes) and from it Brian Boru took his title. There are other great trees below it near the water. A place of remarkable beauty.

[228]

Birchfield House R 048890 (Eire ½″ Map 14)

One mile west-north-west of Liscannor. Reached by a drive from the gates of a ruined lodge on the main road. In a park dotted with wind-blasted, dead trees. (Ask permission at the farm to view it.) Remains of a fantastic, castellated house, the 19th century residence of Cornelius O Brien MP, now incorporated in a farm. The entrance to the house, of which fragments only remain in the farmyard, is through a grand central archway, flanked by long curtain walls with castellated towers at their extremities. It seems probable that these walls concealed the stables. A tree as ruined as the ruins, supports a colony of rooks. North-west of the house, ½ mile away on the side of the hill which forms the landward side of the cliffs of Moher (q.v.), is O Brien's Monument, an elegant masonry column, with an urn on a capital which has somehow gone askew. It was raised to him during his lifetime at his own suggestion and at his tenants' expense; a fulsome inscription records their appreciation. O Brien also built the bridge over the river Dealagh.

A little way up the road from the monument on the same side is Daigh Bhride (Brigid's Vat). The water of the well emerges from the rock in a little whitewashed building constructed by Cornelius O Brien, and it is reached by a narrow, curving passage filled with images and offerings which include crutches. If an eel is seen while you are taking the water, your wish will be granted. Outside, on a little mound filled with flowers in the spring, and especially beautiful when the fuchsia are in bloom, are images of the saint in glass cases. Near-by, water runs down a series of steps. It is a magical place.

The well is the resort of local people and those of the Aran Islands who used to come by currach (see The Aran Islands) to Doolin (Fisherstreet) by Crab Island to the north (q.v.), on the Saturday preceding the last Sunday in July, Lughnasa, Garland

Sunday. Here they spent the night in singing, prayer and festivity. This, with the gathering of St MacCreiche's Church (q.v.) is one of the authentic surviving observances of the ancient festival of Lughnasa, the last Sunday of Summer.

There is a legend that when St Brigid stayed in the vicinity, an old woman who owned the land where the well was, washed potatoes in the water in order to defile it so that it would not become a place of pilgrimage, and the water miraculously welled up in its present position on the opposite side of the road. The family vault of the omnipresent O Briens is behind a rusty iron door in the near-by cemetery under a Gothic memorial.

[229]

The Bridges of Ross Q 733505 (Eire ½″ Map 17)

On the north side of the Loop Head Peninsula, 3 miles east-north-east of the Head; 1½ miles north of Kilbaha. A pair of extraordinary arches beneath which the sea flows into dark, rather sinister pools, the outermost one very deep; both, although sheltered, often ruffled by the wind. The arches were formed by the action of the sea on the stratas of carbonaceous slates which are here contorted in a wonderfully serpentine manner. They can be reached by a signposted track from the Ross–Moneen–Loop Head road, then across abandoned fields to a place by the water's edge where another signpost points resolutely in the direction of the American continent. Where the track from the road ends there is another embryo arch in process of formation.

[230]

Cahermacnaghten M 199001 (Eire ½″ Map 14)

Four miles north-north-east of Kilfenora, on the west side of the road to Corkscrew Hill. Splendid ring fort with thick, high walls built of massive stones, standing in lonely upland country within the Burren. It abuts on a white farmhouse and there is a grove of windswept trees. The gateway to the fort faces the road. Inhabited until the 17th century, at which time it was a law school of the O Davorens. An Dubhaltach Mac Fhirbhisigh, the compiler of the *Book of Genealogies of Ireland* (now in University College Library, Dublin), who was murdered in 1671 by an English planter, studied here. (See also Doonflin.)

[231]

Cahermore M 222049 (Eire ½″ Map 14)

Two miles south of Ballyvaghan at the entrance to Ballyallaban House. A grass-covered ring fort in a grove of beech trees, in a beautiful situation in a valley of the

Burren. A deep ditch surrounds it. About 3 miles south, a rock beyond the Caherconnell crossroads on the same road, has on it a primitive painting of a foxhunt in full cry. West-south-west on the road to Lisdoonvarna at Corkscrew Hill, there are great views over Galway Bay.

[232]

Carrigaholt Castle Q 850513 (Eire ½″ Map 17)

On the south side of the Loop Head Peninsula, ½ mile south-east of Carrigaholt village. Noble ruins of a 16th century tower house with a fortified enclosure (bawn). It stands above a deserted jetty overlooking the Shannon and is approached through a gateless brick gateway. There is a winding slate staircase to the top of the tower. On one storey is a great fireplace with the initials 'DB' and the date 1604 inscribed on it. From the upper part of the tower a wall bartizan projects with machicolations in the floor through which the defenders could drop missiles and unpleasant liquids. This was the castle of the MacMahons, lords of this peninsula, which was called the Western Corcabascin. It was last besieged in 1649 and taken then. Here, Charles O Brien, fifth Viscount Clare, who eventually became a Marshal of France, raised and trained the Yellow Dragoons, who fought at Ramilles in 1706, in which action he was mortally wounded. Here, too, in 1642, lived Admiral Sir William Penn, father of the founder of Pennsylvania.

One mile south at Kilcredaun Point there is a 19th century gun battery which commands the Shannon estuary, here only 2 miles wide. Near-by there is a little graveyard with a couple of graves in it, and two churches, both ruined—one on the hill above the battery, the other picturesquely covered with ivy down on the shore of Kilcredaun Bay. Splendid views of the estuary. Ships of the Spanish Armada took refuge in Carrigaholt Road, north of the point.

[233]

Clare Abbey R 348759 (Eire ½″ Map 17)

One mile north of Clarecastle. An Augustinian friary founded in 1189 by Donal Mor O Brien, the last King of Munster, who also founded Killone Abbey (q.v.). In isolated meadowland between the Ennis–Limerick railway and the river Fergus. Spectacular ruins, which can be seen from far off but less easily reached, with a square central tower and a tall, leaning chimney-stack, part of the domestic buildings. Fine east window in the nave and many tomb slabs and graves within the enclosure, some of them modern. Reached by a narrow, signposted track from the main Ennis–Clarecastle road.

[234]

The Cliffs of Moher R 043923 (Eire $\frac{1}{2}''$ Map 14)

Three miles north-west of Liscannor by a signposted lane from the coast road to Lisdoonvana. Five miles of great, dark sandstone cliffs, topped by a bed of black shale, a mural precipice which rises sheer out of the Atlantic.

The highest point, 668 feet, is at the northern end. The best view is from O Brien's Tower, 587 feet above the sea, also at the northern end. The tower, built for the convenience of visitors at the cliff edge by Cornelius O Brien, MP (see Birchfield House), is now a ruined shell. Below it, a stupendous ridge known as Goat Island, runs seaward. Off-shore there is a stack, a slender pinnacle, 200 feet high. It was O Brien, too, who had the fence made from huge flagstones of olive grit set up on the cliff edge for the protection of visitors.

The cliffs immediately to the north of the tower, which are as impressive as those to the south, may be missed by visitors who only stop at the car park. The view from them, northwards towards Black Head, south to the Loop Head Peninsula, and north-westwards over the three Aran Islands (q.v.), is remarkable. In a gale, with the wind setting strongly on the cliffs and carrying the spray of both sea and waterfalls up the face and over the edge, there is no more awe-inspiring place in Ireland.

At Hag's Head, at the southern end, which is 407 feet high, there is a disused signal tower. From here the view northwards is very fine but not so impressive as that from O Brien's Tower.

In between the shale bed which extends to a depth of 40 feet in some places and the sandstone, there is a stratified layer about 5 inches thick which contains fossils and a strange and wonderful structure known as 'A Cone within a Cone'.

[235]

Corcomroe Abbey M 297090 (Eire $\frac{1}{2}''$ Map 14)

Four and a half miles east of Ballyvaghan. Beautiful ruins in a lonely valley, of a Cistercian abbey founded by Donal Mor O Brien of Munster about 1180. Roofless, pale grey, they exactly match the mountains of the Burren which rise in steps above them, except for the even paler lichen with which walls and tombs are encrusted. They are lovely from any angle. The tomb, with a recumbent figure lying in an oval niche in the north wall of the chancel, is perhaps that of King Conor O Brien, grandson of the founder. Above it is the figure of a seraphic looking bishop. A huge 19th century tomb in the graveyard containing James Haynes, is entirely hemmed in with yews. South-east of the abbey, high up towards a saddle of Turlough Hill, are the three ruined 12th century churches of Oughtmama. Here there was a monastery of St Colman Mac Duach, who founded churches on Inishmore in the Aran Islands, and then became a hermit in the Burren. (See St Mac Duach's Hermitage, Kilmacduagh and Dungory Castle.) There is a holy well. Oughtmama can be reached by a rough track from Shamvally on the unclassified road to Kinvarra. It is unsuitable for motors, but the walk is worth it. W. B. Yeats used this country as a background for his verse play *The Dreaming of the Bones.*

[236]

Crab Island R 051970 (Eire $\frac{1}{2}''$ Map 14)

West of the village of Fisherstreet. The island is little more than an uninhabited rock. Great seas break on it explosively in heavy weather. Here, in the week before the Irish Rising in 1916, Dowling, the emissary of Sir Roger Casement, was landed clandestinely from a German submarine believing himself to be actually on the mainland. The real landing is on the coast inshore of it at Doolin (Fisherstreet), which is used by fishermen and sometimes by the Aran islanders who come to it in their currachs. (See The Aran Islands and Birchfield House.) The coastal drive from here to Kinvarra is one of the finest in Ireland.

[237]

Cratloe Wood Surrounding R 500613 (Eire $\frac{1}{2}''$ Map 17)

At Cratloe, 5½ miles west-north-west of Limerick, on the north side of the main road to Shannon. A dark and mysterious oak wood, the remains of one of Ireland's ancient, natural forests. Its trees are said to have provided timber for the hammer-beam roof of Westminster Hall in London when it was constructed in 1399, and for Amsterdam City Hall. The wood can be reached by following the road from Cratloe to Kilmurry and then turning right after passing under a railway bridge along a road which passes a large shrine. A part of the wood is to the south of this lesser road on an eminence overlooking the Shannon in a private, walled enclosure; the greater part is to the north of it. It is a dark, mysteriously beautiful place.

[238]

Cuchullainn's Leap Q 685471 (Eire $\frac{1}{2}''$ Map 17)

North side of Loop Head, westwards of the lighthouse. Enormous, sheer-sided rectangular rock formed of similar carbonaceous slates to those at the Bridges of Ross (q.v.), except that here the strata are in parallel layers. (The rock is shown on the $\frac{1}{2}''$ map as 'Dermot and Grania's Rock'). It is separated from the Head by a deep, narrow chasm in which the sea can be heard working even in calm weather. This is Cuchullainn's Leap across which Cuchullainn, one of the Red Branch Knights of

Kilmacduagh, Co. Galway
(Wonder No. 276)

The Cliffs of Moher, Co. Clare
(Wonder No. 234)

Dermot and Grania's Rock,
Loop Head, Co. Clare
(see under Cuchullainn's Leap)
(Wonder No. 238)

Aran Islands curragh,
Co. Galway
(Wonder No. 258)

Irish myth, leapt in order to escape the unwelcome attentions of a hag who, leaping after him, fell into the chasm and perished. His or her footprint can be seen on the landward side.

The off-shore side of the Rock is whitened by the guano of the innumerable sea birds; the eastern end resembles the prow of a ship and the western end is a sheer cliff on which huge seas break in heavy weather—a time when it is extremely dangerous to attempt to observe them. Great views from the exposed Head over the mouth of the Shannon.

[239]

Danganbrack R 420750 (Eire ½″ Map 17)

Half a mile north-north-east of Quin. Reached by a muddy track to the east of a by-road north of Quin. Colossal, skyscraping, lone tower, thickly grown with ivy, a castle of the Macnamaras, possibly 15th century, with machicolations and later additions. Reached by a tree trunk bridge over a deeply sunken stream. The four tall gables crowned with chimneys are fantastic on the skyline. The ground floor is used as a byre and the doorway is whitewashed. The lower courses supporting the edifice are dangerously eroded.

The splendid, 15th century Franciscan friary at Quin, founded by Mac-Con Macnamara on a bank of the River Rine, has incorporated within it parts of an Anglo-Norman fortress built by Sir Thomas de Clare, who built the first stone castle at Bunratty.

[240]

Doonmore Castle Q 960667 (Eire ½″ Map 17)

Seven and a half miles north-north-west of Kilrush on the Loop Head Peninsula, at the southern end of Mal Bay. Cattle graze about this extraordinary lichen-covered tower, the ruin of a MacGorman castle. It stands on the shore guarding the harbour at the mouth of the Doonbeg river, more like a great crumbling rock than a fortress. Here, upturned currachs (see The Aran Islands) lie high up on the beach, and others are moored off-shore in fine weather. A ship of the Spanish Armada went ashore at the mouth of the harbour in 1588 with a loss of 300 lives, and 60 more of its complement were killed by the inhabitants or else executed by the Governor, Sir Turlough O Brien, who occupied Liscannor Castle. A number of Spanish ships were wrecked on this coast.

Doonbeg was a station on the now defunct West Clare Railway opened in 1892, which connected Milltown Malbay with Kilkee. It cost £120,000. The remains of it can be seen.

[241]

The Druids Altar M 268018 (Eire $\frac{1}{2}''$ Map 14)

Seven miles north-east of Kilfenora. A box-like stone tomb, with a massive, rectangular capstone supported on uprights. From it there are great views of the Burren country towards Abbey Hill above Corcomroe (q.v.) and Galway Bay. It can be reached by a steep winding but motorable track south of a house marked 'Deelin Beg' from the road which links the Kinvarra–Ballyvaghan road with the L 51. It stands in a field to the west of this track.

There are other more impressive prehistoric tombs in the area, notably Poulnabrone (M 236003) east of the Ballyvaghan–Kilfenora–Corrofin road, but the Druids Altar has a particularly fine situation.

[242]

Dysert O Dea R 285848 (Eire $\frac{1}{2}''$ Map 14)

Two and a half miles south of Corrofin. Reached by a minor road (signposted) westwards from the Corrofin–Ennis road. Remains of a Romanesque church and a shattered round tower among lonely hills with ruined farms and houses around it. The doorway has 19 grotesque heads in a semi-circle above it. Through the centre of the lancet window of the roofless nave, the tall White Cross of Tola can be seen standing in a field. Cows use the base of it, which is ornamented with serpents, as a rubbing block. On the east side of the cross there is an impressive crucifixion and below it the figure of a bishop—probably St Tola—holding a crozier. It is as if he, too, were suspended in the air. The cross was repaired by Michael O Dea in 1683 and re-erected in 1871. Dysert O Dea was a hermitage of St Tola who died in 724. He founded a church here and became a bishop. St Tola's Well is to the south-east of the church. The crozier of Dysert O Dea is in the Royal Irish Academy, Dublin.

To the north is the ivy-covered tower of O Dea's castle with one huge, gaping window in its south face and with a single tall chimney rising above it. A great battle was fought here in 1318, between Muirchertach O Brien and Richard de Clare, which interrupted the Anglo-Norman subjection of the country. In it De Clare and his son were both slain.

[243]

Gleninagh Castle M 193104 (Eire $\frac{1}{2}''$ Map 14)

Two and a half miles north-west of Ballyvaghan on the shore of Black Head Bay. Reached by a track from the main road at Gleninagh Lodge where there is a letter box. Ruined tower close to the shore in the shadow of the Gleninagh Mountain, one of the highest summits in the Burren. A spiral staircase leads to the upper part. There is a large fireplace on the floorless first storey; overhanging turrets with machicolations. Near-by is a holy well with a cross over it, ruins of ancient houses, and an overgrown, roofless church with gravestones which are simply unworked limestone rocks from the Burren. A peaceful, beautiful place.

[244]

Inishcaltra R 695850 (Eire ½″ Map 15)

In Lough Derg, 1½ miles south-west of Mountshannon. Can be reached by boat from there. Otherwise known as Holy Island. On this beautiful green island are the remains of an anchorite's cell with two standing stones inside it; four churches, one of which is the tiny Church of the Wounded Men (Teampall na bhFear nGonta). The graveyard in which it stands contains large numbers of tomb slabs and a cross base inscribed 'The Grave of the Ten' (Ilad In Dechenboir). In the church of St Caimin, which has a Romanesque doorway, there is a high cross with inscriptions on it, one of which reads: O DO THORNOC DO RINGNI IN CROIS (Pray for Tornog, who made the cross).

The capless 80-foot-high round tower was said to have been the abode of St Cosgraich, 'The Miserable'. Numerous saints are associated with Inishcaltra including St Caimin, half brother of Guaire, King of Connacht, and a descendant of the King of Leinster, who established a monastery here in the 7th century after endeavouring to live as an anchorite on it. He was plagued with visitors. He wrote a commentary on the Psalms and his monastery was sacked by the Danes. He died about 650.

[245]

Intrinsic Bay Surrounding Q 850600 (Eire ½″ Map 17)

West of Kilkee. A weird and melancholy bay named after the ship *Intrinsic,* bound for America and wrecked here in 1856. Another, the *Edmond,* an emigrant ship, was also wrecked near-by in a great storm in November 1850, with the loss of 100 lives. Above the bay a dark cliff rises 200 feet sheer from the sea. The view from Lookout Hill at the summit is remarkable in clear weather. Equally so is that from Knockroe Point above Diamond Rock immediately to the north, from which Grean Rock, an extraordinary, wedge-shaped formation, sheer on its northern face, and the flat-topped Bishop's Island north of Foohagh Point, can be seen to advantage. Bishop's Island is also known as the Island of the Starving Bishop (Ilawn an Uspug Usthig), from the legend that a bishop having callously abandoned his flock in order to take up residence there during a famine, was unable to return to the mainland from it owing to the widening of the gulf, and starved to death.

Apparently inaccessible on its summit is St Senan's Oratory, a small unmortared beehive construction, and the remains of the saint's house. St Senan died 545. (See Scattery Island.)

Between Diamond Rock and Duggerna Rock towards Kilkee there is a huge sea cave 300 feet long and 60 feet high in the cliffs, and a natural amphitheatre of tiered rocks. They can be reached by a footpath from West End of Kilkee. There is also remarkable scenery at Castle Point and at the long, off-shore island, Illaunonearaun (the Island of the Seal) further along the coast to the south-west. Great views also from the 245-foot cliff above Ballard Bay, 4 miles north-east of Kilkee where there is an old telegraph tower.

[246]

Killone Abbey R 323733 (Eire ½″ Map 17)

Three miles south-south-west of Ennis, in the grounds of Newhall House. Ghostly, grey, roofless ruins of an Augustinian nunnery founded by King Donal Mor O Brien, King of Munster in the 12th century, with buildings of the 15th century, tombs, sculptures and mausolea. It stands by a lake hidden among low hills in a rather solitary place. Under the east end of the church is the eerie crypt of the Macdonnells with their family arms over the doorway. Close to the water is a holy well enclosed in a wall, dedicated to St John, as was the abbey.

Newhall House, in the park to the west, is a fine private 18th century brick mansion, built by the Macdonnells. There is a legend that a mermaid from the lake was killed in the house and that when one of the family is about to die the lake turns red. To reach the abbey from the Ennis–Killadysert road, follow a signposted lane to the north-west. From the Ennis–Kilrush road take an unsignposted lane to the south, 3 miles from the town; then left at the first crossroads, which will land you at the same place. Leave your motor car at the first gate on this lane where there is a ruined building, and walk ½ mile along the west shore of the lake to the abbey.

[247]

Leamaneh R 234934 (Eire ½″ Map 14)

Three miles east of Kilfenora at the junction with the Ballyvaghan road. Wonderful ruin of a tall 15th century tower, enlarged in the 17th century by the addition of a house with mullioned and transomed windows. The building is a shell, the windows, pale openings against the sky. The entrance doorway is very small. This was the house of Conor O Brien and his wife, Maire MacMahon, and of their son Sir Donat. Conor O Brien was mortally wounded in the battle against the Cromwellian General Ludlow, at Inchicronan in 1651. His wife is said to have refused to take him into the house, as she wanted no dead men to help in its defence—she later relented and he died within it. Maire O Brien, to save her son's estate from seizure, subsequently married a Cromwellian cornet of horse whom, according to local legend, she killed by kicking him in the stomach. Not even the proximity of a modern farmhouse and the main road spoils the atmosphere of this place.

[248]

The Little Ark Q 733496 (Eire ½" Map 17)

At Moneen, 1 mile north of Kilbaha towards the extremity of the Loop Head Peninsula. A side chapel in the small grey church in this lonely village contains a dark coloured wooden construction rather like a battered bathing machine with windows, and what appears to be a leather covered roof. The doorway is reached by a step ladder. Inside it there is an altar with a crucifix above it. Originally it was fitted with wheels. This strange, impressive little building—The Little Ark—was constructed by the carpenter of Carrigaholt, at a cost of £10, for the local priest, Father Meehan, in 1852 during the period of Souperism (hot meals given free on condition that the local peasantry should send their children to Protestant schools and themselves be present at Protestant services). There was no Catholic church and the only place where mass could be celebrated was on the shore at Kilbaha between high and low watermarks, where the landlord's authority did not prevail, and here it was celebrated in the Ark between 1852 and 1857. The church contains the remains of Father Meehan and at the west end, over the door, there is a stained glass window showing the Ark in use.

[249]

Magh Adhair R 442770 (Eire ½" Map 17)

At Hell Bridge over the river Hell, 2 miles north-east of Quin, and 3½ miles south-west of Tulla. The inauguration place of the Kings of Thomond. A flat-topped grassy mound in lonely countryside, surrounded by a deep ditch and bank. Standing on it, facing what is partly a natural amphitheatre of low hillocks filled with stones, one has the impression of facing a ghostly audience. A few yards to the west of the mound there is a small cairn and, on the far bank of the Hell, a tall, slender standing stone. Five hundred yards south-south-west is Cahercalla, a stone ring fort. It is about three fields east of the Dangan House road, but ask locally as there is no right of way to it. This ring fort which has three ditches, is one of the most difficult to find Wonders in all Ireland. It is completely overgrown with thorns and vegetation, and the only way into it is by the sheep runs. The inner walls are probably 20 feet thick at the base; the stones of which they are composed are like moss-grown cannon balls. An exasperating ruin but one with a truly magic feeling about it.

[250]

Pollnagollum M 160040 (Eire $\frac{1}{2}$" Map 14)

Four miles north-east of Lisdoonvarna, immediately west of the road which runs along the eastern flank of Slieve Elva (1,134 feet). A 100-foot-deep chasm with a tree growing in the mouth of it, which leads into one of the largest cave systems so far discovered in the karstic landscape of the Burren—and in all Ireland. Some 7 miles of caverns have so far been explored. In them there is a waterfall 25 feet high. Casual visitors are not encouraged. A few hundred yards to the south on the same side of the road, is another cave entrance, Poll Elva, which is externally even more impressive.

[251]

St Fachtnan's Cathedral R 180938 (Eire $\frac{1}{2}$" Map 14)

At Kilfenora. Ruin of a very small cathedral, 12th or 13th century, with a square tower, part of which is now inside the Church of Ireland parish church. The roofless chancel contains strange effigies carved in relief: one of a standing figure with a pear-shaped head, whose neck appears to have been added as an afterthought, and who wears a pleated skirt, has a primitive, almost African feeling about it; another is of a bishop in the act of blessing; another, inscribed, is also of a bishop. Equally strange carvings of human heads support the capitals of the magnificent east window.

There are famous 12th century crosses at Kilfenora (one has been removed to Killaloe), three in the graveyard which also has interesting 18th century tombs, and a fourth, of the 11th century, in a field 50 yards to the west, with a remarkably powerful crucifixion carved on it.

[252]

St Joseph's Well R 049770 (Eire $\frac{1}{2}$" Map 17)

At Stackpoole's Bridge, 1$\frac{1}{2}$ miles south-south-west of Milltown Malbay. Known locally as Tobar Laictin (Lachtnan). This holy well is on the steep, wooded bank of a little river. The water emerges from the rock in a small cavity in the bank, which is adorned with holy images and offerings. A tended, beautiful spot. The well is a place of pilgrimage on March 19, the feast day of the saint.

[253]

St Mac Duach's Hermitage M 327042 (Eire $\frac{1}{2}$" Map 14)

In Keelhilla, at the foot of Slieve Carran, 4$\frac{1}{2}$ miles south-west of Kinvarra in Galway, and a mile inside County Clare. Here St Colman Mac Duach spent 7 years with only one attendant. There is a small limestone cave in the screes of the cliff below the Eagle's Rock (marked on the Ordnance map), which is capable of holding one reclining human. Close to it are the remains of a small church hidden among trees and moss covered boulders. There is also a well and a square stone platform. The curious, water-eroded beds of karstic limestone form Bothar na Mias (the Road of the Dishes) used by King Guaire Aidhneach and his followers on their way from Kinvarra in pursuit of their Easter banquet, which had been miraculously rapt away through the air by angels to Keelhilla where the saint and his companion were dying of starvation. A singularly beautiful place and an exceptionally lonely one even by Irish standards. From the church below the cliff there are splendid views of the strange Burren mountains. A Patron—parish celebration—was always held here on the last Sunday of July.

To reach it: $1\frac{1}{2}$ miles south-west of Cappaghmore crossroads, 3 miles south-west of Kinvarra, follow a lesser road to the west which passes between Slieve Carran and Doomore (831 feet). After about $\frac{1}{2}$ mile a red-roofed farmhouse will be seen to the left (south of the road). On the right (north) a faint track across the limestone karst should be visible. From here the church, close under the screes, is about $\frac{3}{4}$ mile on foot. (See also Dungory, Oughtmama under Corcomroe Abbey, and Kilmacduagh.)

[254]

St Macreiche's Church R 073890 (Eire $\frac{1}{2}''$ Map 14)

Three quarters of a mile east-north-east of Liscannor, south of the road to Lahinch. The low roofless ruins of a small, medieval parish church built above the shore of the bay, on the site of a school founded by the saint, a legendary destroyer of plagues, dragons and a great eel, which came ashore to feast on corpses in the 6th century. His 'bed' or 'grave' consists of two rocks in the sea which are uncovered at low water. People took sand from hereabout and threw it into the sea to calm it. Emigrants are still said to do this. The nave and chancel of the church remain, separated by a pointed arch. The old cemetery is filled with tomb slabs. A new one has been walled in an unseemly fashion with breeze blocks. Through the tall east windows the solitary tower of Dough Castle on a bank of the Dealagh by O Brien's Bridge, can be seen. There is a holy well. As at St Brigid's Well (see Birchfield House) there are gatherings here for Lughnasa—the last Sunday of July. Off-shore a city is reputed to lie submerged beneath the waters of Liscannor Bay.

[255]

Scattery Island Q 970530 (Eire $\frac{1}{2}''$ Map 17)

One mile south-west of Cappagh Quay, Kilrush, from which it can be reached by boat. Treeless, bleak, green, strangely beautiful island in the Shannon estuary with one of the finest and tallest round towers in Ireland, between 115 and 120 feet high. It was once struck by lightning and is unusual in having the entrance at ground level. The island was the abode of St Senan who was born near Kilrush, and it was while walking on the shore as a herdsman that he was inspired to renounce the world, breaking his spear and making a cross of it. The Angel Raphael assisted him to rid the island of a monster and also showed him where to find water using a holly branch which then became a holly tree. He was followed there by St Cannera who wanted to set up a tent on the island but she was rebuffed.

> But legends hint that had the maid
> Till morning's light delayed
> And given the saint one rosy smile
> She ne'er had left his holy isle
>
> Moore

There are also remains in the cemetery of 'The Church of the Dead', as well as five or six churches, all ruined, and Senan's Bed—his burial place—within a walled enclosure. There is also a lighthouse and a 19th century battery. There are many legends about Scattery. The pebbles on the shore protect the bearer against shipwreck and soil from the Bed is used locally as an insecticide in gardens. (See also Intrinsic Bay.)

[256]

Spectacle Bridge R 122978 (Eire ½" Map 14)

One mile west-south-west of Lisdoonvarna. The bridge, a single span over the deep valley of the river Aille, has a round hole, the same width as the arch, in the masonry above it. It can only be seen with difficulty from the roadway above. It is best viewed from the boggy field above the river on the east upstream side. On the other side there is a sewage farm.

[257]

The Toomens R 470810 (Eire ½" Map 17)

One and a half miles north-west of Tulla in the grounds of Kiltanon House. A fantastic, deep gorge and limestone caverns through which a river flows. Just downstream of an ornamental bridge which carries the drive across the river to the remains of Kiltanon House, the water disappears beneath a limestone cliff. It reappears in daylight at intervals where the roofs of the caves through which it flows have collapsed. At one point the side of a cave has also broken, and here cattle go down to the water. Above ground one can stand in the wood which marks the course of the river and hear the sound of water running invisibly below. The whole place is riddled with holes. Petrified shells are found here. The river emerges finally into the open air close to the tall tower of a ruined castle. It is an enchanting place.

Section 5

Galway

Mayo

Roscommon

[258]

The Aran Islands L 940050 (Eire $\frac{1}{2}''$ Map 14)

In the mouth of Galway Bay. (The map reference is of Inishmaan, the middle island.)

The stone forts of the Aran Islands (see Dun Aengus) are only a small part of the wonders of antiquity which include churches, holy wells, saints' beds, pillar stones, cross slabs and other remnants of early Christianity; but even more interesting are the inhabitants who preserve a way of life which must very soon become extinct. Of the three islands, Inishmore, Inishmaan and Inisheer, the first is the largest and the most sophisticated as it has had much more contact with day visitors than the other two. Nevertheless, life is still hard for those who cultivate the soil.

All three islands are little more than bare sheets of limestone from which the labour of succeeding generations of the inhabitants has removed millions of stones, which they have piled up to form a labyrinth of walls which also act as windbreaks. In the thousands of small enclosures so formed the soil has been man-made, too, by the laying down of alternate levels of sand and seaweed. The principal crop is potatoes (a boiled Aran potato is one of the most delicious culinary treats in the world) and cabbages and carrots are also grown. The grass is excellent, cattle flourish (from Inishmaan and Inisheer they are swum out to the ship which takes them to the market at Galway); and in October the fields are filled with giant daisies. There are few trees; a few osiers grow in sheltered places and these are used to make baskets and panniers for the donkeys.

On the two smaller islands everything is carried down the little lanes or boreens on human backs or on donkeys or horses. The islanders also collect seaweed and long, sjambok-like sea roots called 'rods' which they sell to extraction factories at £10 a ton. In summer they do well out of lobsters and tourism.

The men of Inishmaan and Inisheer, but to a lesser extent on Inishmore, still wear the costume of the islands; thick trousers of homespun tweed, split up the sides of the leg so that they can be rolled up when they launch their boats through the surf, kept up by braided, multi-coloured belts with tassels on the ends, called criosanna. They wear thick flannel shirts with stand-up collars and leg-of-mutton sleeves, dyed indigo, and waistcoats made from a hairy, grey-blue tweed in which the ribbed pattern becomes more pronounced when the nap wears off. Some still wear heelless sandals of raw cowhide (called pampooties) with the hair on the outside, which they keep damp so that they will be pliable.

The older women and a very few of the younger ones wear deep, full, red flannel petticoats which they dye a shade of madder. Almost all wear shawls, some of them heirlooms beyond price—the brown Galway shawl is very rare. Until recently all the wool for the flannel and tweed was woven at a mill in Galway, but it has been burned down and now the costume must die out when the present stocks of material on the island are exhausted. A Gaelic mass on the islands is a wonderful sight with the people wearing their dress.

For fishing and transporting passengers and goods to and from the visiting steamer (except on Inishmore where the ship can tie up alongside), the islanders use currachs, rowing boats about 19 feet long with square counters and very turned-up prows to help them in the surf. They consist of a light framework of laths covered with tarred canvas. The oars are tapered laths, almost bladeless, which fit over a single thole pin, which enables them to be left unshipped in the water while the crew is fishing. They are very handy. They can carry phenomenal quantities of people and goods—up to 12 persons (the usual crew is three)—and over a ton of potatoes in good weather, and sometimes tombstones. The currachs are usually left upside down on the shore above high water, where they look like shiny black monsters. Going to sea, the crews carry them down to the water upside down on their heads and the impression is of some strange, multi-legged creature in a painting by Hieronymous Bosch.

[259]

Aughinish M 287132 (Eire ½″ Map 14)

Six miles west-north-west of Kinvarra, by a minor road to the north of the Ballyvaghan road. A narrow causeway, about 2 miles west of Kinvarra, joins this little-known isthmus to the mainland. On the north side of it there is a well-preserved Martello tower on the shingle shore of Galway Bay, built as a defence against French invasion at the time of the Napoleonic Wars. Fine views of the Burren mountains to the south and west. Another similar tower is at Finavarra Point, to the south-west on the north side of Ballyvaghan Bay. It can be reached from Burren, 6 miles west of Kinvarra on the Ballyvaghan road.

[260]

Ballylee Castle M 486060 (Eire ½″ Map 14)

Three miles north-east of Gort. To the west of the Gort–Loughrea road, by a signposted road. Sixteenth-century tower, now restored, on the edge of a pretty little, heron-haunted river. W. B. Yeats lived here in the summer months after the first war, and during that time he restored the adjoining cottages. He left it in 1929. Here he wrote *The Tower*. A plaque on a wall records:

I, the poet William Yeats,
With old mill board and sea-green slates
  And smithy work from the Gort forge,
Restored this tower for my wife George;
  And may these characters remain
  When all is ruin once again.

There is a museum; but the castle is perhaps best seen out of season when everything is closed, and the place reverts to its original solitude.

[261]

The Belview Gateway M 849197 (Eire ½″ Map 15)

Two miles west-south-west of Laurencetown. A very fine gateway on the west side of the demesne of Belview House, formerly Liscregaghan, of which only the foundations remain. The gateway was built by Walter Lawrence—the village is properly Lawrencetown—to commemorate the Corps of Henry Grattan's Ulster Volunteers. The central archway, which has a classical pediment below it, is flanked by two small doorways for foot passengers, and by twin lodges. On either side of the pediment are couchant sphinxes. The one on the left has recently been decapitated. Originally there was an urn on top of the pediment, but it is gone.

To reach the gateway from Laurencetown, follow the main Portumna road for ¾ mile; traversing it one is faced by a remarkable folly, a triple-turreted Gothic façade with finials, central archway and slit windows, supported by a pair of flying buttresses. Follow the drive past it through the demesne. Further on to the left are the scanty remains of Belview House with a few splendid cedars, evergreen oaks and monkey puzzle trees. The drive then passes a small house in the Gothic manner, also with flying buttresses. The gateway is at the west end of the drive where it joins the road from Eyrecourt to Kiltormer.

[262]

Clonfert Cathedral M 960211 (Eire ½″ Map 15)

Four and a half miles north-west of Banagher (Offaly), which is on the Shannon. From a distance the cathedral seems just another Church of Ireland foundation. Reaching it, one is ill-prepared for the sight of a great Romanesque doorway under a 15th century tower with a modern parapet. Six orders of arches are supported on shafts and piers. The jambs of the actual doorway are turned inwards. The carving is profuse. What gives the doorway its strangeness is the great triangular pediment above it, supported by an arcade of columns. From between their arches five disembodied, sculptured heads look down dispassionately on the beholder. Above them 10 others, each in a triangular niche, each separated from its neighbour by a triangle which exactly echoes the form of the pediment, do the same. There is nothing like it in Ireland, or anywhere else for that matter.

Here, at Cluain-Fearth (the Meadow of the Grave, or according to Lewis's *Topographical Dictionary of Ireland*, 1837, 'A Retired Spot') St Brendan the Navigator founded a monastery in 558. Its history is one of unmitigated disaster, exceptional even in Ireland. Accounts vary as to the number of times it was destroyed, but it seems to have been burned and plundered a minimum of six times between the 8th and 12th centuries, twice by Vikings, who also reduced the town to ashes, and also by various native kings and chieftains. It was further damaged in the 16th century, and became Protestant at the Reformation. Inside, the 13th century east window of the chancel is very fine. The interior has been awfully restored, but there is a lovely carving of a black mermaid and some strange 17th century figures carved in wood, from the bishop's palace. Clonfert itself is nothing but a pretty hamlet; nothing remains of the town or the bishop's palace. From the village a road to the north-east crosses the Grand Canal before reaching the Shannon where it ends abruptly. At the time when the canal was cut through the bog, an ancient wooden causeway was discovered; but on being exposed to the air it immediately crumbled into dust. On the right bank of the Shannon, opposite Banagher, there is an ivy-grown Martello tower and a battery of the Napoleonic period; also a picturesque canal house by the silted-up canal.

[263]

Coole Park

M 440050 (Eire ½" Map 14)

Two miles north-west of Gort, to the west of the Galway road. Reached by a long, signposted drive. Extremely melancholy remains of the great house, demolished 1941, the home of Augusta Pearse, Lady Gregory. The drive to it runs through a beautiful tunnel of yew and other trees. Coole was resorted to by numbers of the most important poets, dramatists and writers of the 19th and 20th centuries. Lady Gregory turned Yeats towards popular drama and was herself no mean playwright—*Spreading the News, The Workhouse Ward, The Gaol Gate,* etc. in dialect, and many other works. She died in 1932.

Nothing but a few low walls remain of the house. The demesne is very overgrown and the walled garden is planted with conifers which will shortly engulf it. There are still, however, some splendid trees. The bark of the great copper beech in the walled garden still bears, though faintly, the initials of some of the distinguished guests who stayed at Coole—Shaw, O Casey, W. B. and J. B. Yeats, A. E. (George Russell), and Katharine Tynan. Although protected by a railing high enough to deter anything but an ape, they have been added to and sometimes obscured by the cuttings of lesser human beings. South-west of the house is Coole Lough.

[264]

The Derrygimlagh Bog Surrounding L 660460 (Eire $\frac{1}{2}$" Map 10)

Reached by a very rough, signposted track southwards from the Clifden–Ballycionneely road. There is no turning point for vehicles after a warning notice by a solitary house. About 1½ miles from the road in the heart of this lonely peat bog there is a white, beehive-shaped cairn. It lies about 500 yards north of the place where Captain John Alcock and Lt. Arthur Whitten-Brown, on the first non-stop Atlantic flight ever made, crash-landed their Vickers Vimy twin-engined bomber at 8.40 a.m. on June 15, 1919. They left Trepassy Harbour, St John's, Newfoundland at 4.13 p.m. on June 14 and flew 1,960 miles. Both men were subsequently knighted. On the north side of the Clifden–Ballyconneely road there is another, more modern monument.

Close to the cairn, on the shores of a small lough, of which there are enormous numbers in this desolate region, are the remnants of Marconi's first transatlantic wireless station. Some foundations and lengths of chain anchored to concrete blocks are all that remain of the buildings and the masts. The wireless link was with Newfoundland. The station was destroyed during fighting in the Civil War.

[265]

Doonlaur Fort M 283505 (Eire $\frac{1}{2}$" Map 11)

Two and a half miles north-north-east of Headford on the Shrule road. Grass-grown ring fort by the roadside, illuminated with gorse bushes and a single thorn tree. Fine views across Lough Corrib to the west. There is another fort called simply Doon on the way to it, east of the same road.

[266]

Dun Aengus L 817098 (Eire $\frac{1}{2}$" Map 14)

On Inishmore, the westernmost of the Aran Islands. South of Kilmurvy which is 1½ miles west of Kilronan. A horsedrawn vehicle can be hired at the harbourside at Kilronan.

Dun Aengus (otherwise Dun Aonghusa, the Fort of Aonghus, who was a chief of the legendary Firbolgs; see Eochy's Cairn), is the greatest of the Irish stone forts, and is not only one of the greatest Wonders of Ireland, but of the entire western world.

George Petrie (1789–1866), the Irish landscape painter, sketcher and antiquary, thought it 'the most magnificent barbaric monument now extant in Europe' and although this may seem a piece of Irish hyperbole to those who have not seen it, there is really some justice in his claim, especially if its remarkable situation is taken into account.

The fortress, which must have been that of a very considerable person, stands on the edge of a 300-foot-high cliff which overhangs the sea, on a sheet of the bare limestone of which the islands are composed. The walls are drystone, built of unworked blocks laid in courses—some of the stones are between 4 and 7 feet long. Approaching it by the road which traverses Inishmore, which is the largest and in some ways the most sophisticated of the Islands, having become world famous as a result of the filming of Liam O Flaherty's masterpiece *Man of Aran* in the 1930s, Dun Aengus looms on the skyline, a sombre, cyclopean mass, with a single cyclopean eye, an entrance gateway through which the daylight shines in clear weather.

Inside the now ruined outer walls is an enormous enclosure, or outer ward, the first of three, roughly concentric enclosures, the innermost of which is the citadel. Entering it, the visitor is faced by a fantastic, dense forest of stones up to 3 feet high which seem to grow from the living rock in which they are planted, or else sprout from the wall behind it. This abattis, or *chevaux de frise* (although the use of cavalry can scarcely have been envisaged in such a place) extends outwards from the wall for a distance of 80 feet in some places. At the north-western end of this perimeter wall, and outside it, there are the remains of other walls which are outworks. The middle wall has defensive terraces along the upper part of it.

The abattis is pierced by a sloping path which enters the second, middle enclosure wall through a gateway with a huge lintel stone over it. From it, a passage leads into the wall. Beyond this middle ward is the citadel, a stupendous construction with walls in three parts, 18 feet high in places and nearly 13 feet thick. They, too, have terraces, reached by steep flights of steps.

A low gateway leads to the innermost part, a semi-circular enclosure, the walls of which, as do all the others, terminate at the cliff edge. It is a dramatic denouement to reach the heart of Dun Aengus which, in a gale, is filled with spray and spume, and to hear within it the waves booming on the foot of the cliff and the melancholy cries of the sea birds. Here, one feels very near to Hy Brasil, the enchanted island of the west which is supposed to be visible from the cliffs of the Aran Islands at certain times.

Dun Aengus is only one of a number of similar forts on the Aran Islands. Their origins have been attributed to various periods from the Bronze to the Dark Age; confronted with them, a few thousand years can only be of importance to the pedant; it is the situation which counts. Among others on Inishmore is Dubh Cathair

(Doocaher—The Black Fort; L 872075), on the south-west coast. It stands in a fearful situation on a 400-foot-high headland, protected by water on three sides. A single wall, 20 feet high, built of smaller, less well-laid stones than those of Dun Aengus, separates it from the mainland. There are cells, remains of huts and a *chevaux de frise.*

Dun Oghil (The Fort of the Oak Grove) near Oghil village, 1 mile north-west of Kilronan (L 863098), is on the highest point of a ridge. It is an oval fort and its walls are built of stones, some of them very large, laid horizontally and with great skill. A third, Dun Onact (L 810114) ½ mile north-west of Kilmurvy, is almost circular. It stands on a knoll.

On Inishmaan, the middle of the three islands, and perhaps the least known because of the difficulty of landing on it, is Dun Conor (Dun Conchuirn or Conchobhair). This is very fine. It stands on a rocky platform on the highest point of the island and can be seen for many miles out in the Atlantic. The walls are 20 feet high and the thickest of any of the Aran stone forts—18½ feet.

[267]

Dungory Castle M 380107 (Eire ½″ Map 14)

On the shore of Kinvarra Bay, ½ mile east-north-east of the town of Kinvarra. Sixteenth century building on a rock connected with the mainland, with an enclosing bawn, constructed in the 17th century. This rock was probably the site of the castle of King Guaire Aidhneach of Connacht, whose Easter banquet was spirited away by angels to supply provision for St Colman Mac Duach. (See St Mac Duach's Hermitage, Kilmacduagh, and Oughtmama under Corcomroe.) It is said that on November 18, 1775, the day of the great earthquake at Lisbon, a castle on the western outskirts of Kinvarra was destroyed and part of it swallowed up, and on the same day chimneys and battlements of another (Cahirglissane) rocked and fell into a chasm several fathoms deep.

[268]

Dunmore Castle M 500640 (Eire ½″ Map 11)

Half a mile west-north-west of Dunmore on the Ballindine road. Magnificent and mysterious hulk, a castle of the Berminghams, half-hidden in a clump of sycamore trees above a crossing of the Sinking river where there is a bridge. Huge pieces of masonry lie on the riverward slopes. The keep is a hollow shell. Beautiful view downriver over water meadows in which sheep graze. At the roadside are some ancient ruined cottages.

[269]

Fiddaun Castle R 410958 (Eire $\frac{1}{2}''$ Map 14)

Four and a half miles south-west of Gort, and about $\frac{1}{2}$ mile west of the Gort–Tubber–Crusheen road (west of the Gort–Crusheen railway line), by a lane. Wonderful ruin of a 16th century castle of the O Shaughnessys. It stands on the edge of the fields of the karstic limestone Burren country between two small loughs—Lough Aslaun and Lough Do, $\frac{1}{2}$ mile from the borders of Clare. The tower is smooth, slender and immensely tall with a long plume-shaped growth of ivy on its western face. The east side is shattered. The tower is enclosed by a six-sided bawn. There are the remains of a gatehouse.

[270]

Finbhearra's Castle M 362485 (Eire $\frac{1}{2}''$ Map 11)

On Knockmaa Hill, 6 miles west-south-west of Tuam and south of the Tuam–Headford road. In the demesne of Castle Hacket, an 18th century mansion. From the main road, opposite the castle, a beautiful wooded ride leads to a deserted lodge at the foot of Knockmaa Hill. To the east of this ride are the ruins of an ancient castle of the Hackets, with trees growing inside it. A spiral stair leads as far as the first floor; the supports for the joists have designs cut in them. A path to the left from the lodge leads up through the dense woods and rhododendron groves to the summit of Knockmaa (522 feet). Tremendous views to the south, east and west. Those to the north are obscured by the woods. The ridge itself, and the south flank of the hill, is a wilderness of eroded limestone. Finbhearra's Castle is a walled cairn said to be partly a Georgian folly, partly ancient, but no less impressive for that. There is a modern memorial stone close to it. Near-by is a genuine, prehistoric cairn. There is a souterrain on the south-east flank of the hill for those who have the energy to descend in search of it. Knockmaa is the legendary seat of Finbhearra, ruler of the fairies of Connacht, who here fought a battle against those of Munster.

[271]

Glinsk Castle M 714672 (Eire $\frac{1}{2}''$ Map 12)

Three miles south-east of Ballymoe. Fine, empty shell of a three-storeyed, 17th century fortress house, by a bridge over a tributary of the river Suck, close to the border of Roscommon. The house is on a hill among trees. It has two sets of fine chimneys and small overhanging machicolations at the corners. The first turning to the left, west of the stream, leads to the small, ruined and roofless church of Ballynakill. Inside it there is a splendid effigy of a knight, a member of the Burke family, dressed in a short skirt of mail and wearing a pointed helmet on his head. He stands erect, holding his sword with his left and right hand, one above the other.

[272]

Hen's Castle L 998502 (Eire $\frac{1}{2}$" Map 11)

At the north-west extremity of Lough Corrib, $2\frac{1}{2}$ miles south-east of Maum. Caislan na Circe, otherwise known as Castlekirke and marked 'Castlekirk' on the $\frac{1}{2}$" map. Magnificent remains of a 13th century keep with curtain walls on an island at the end of a long green promontory, originally constructed in the 12th century by the last High King of Ireland, Rory O Conor, with the help of Richard de Burgo. It had four square corner towers and once almost covered the island. A few pine trees grow there. It was supposed to have been built by a witch and her hen in one night, and given by her, together with the fowl, to an O Flaherty lord. She told him that if the castle was besieged the hen would lay sufficient eggs to prevent him from starving. The castle was besieged, but O Flaherty killed the bird, forgetting what she had said, and was starved to submission. Best seen from the Maum–Cong lakeside road near Claggen with the mass of Leckavrea Mountain rising up behind it.

[273]

Inchagoill Island M 130491 (Eire $\frac{1}{2}$" Map 11)

In Lough Corrib, 4 miles south-south-west of Cong and about the same distance north of Oughterard from which places it can be reached by boat. Beautiful, lonely island, Inis an Ghoill Craibhthigh (the Island of the Devout Foreigner). Very fine at sunset. On it are the remains of St Patrick's Church, a simple, small oratory and, with a path of flagstones leading to it, Teampall na Naomh, a later Romanesque building with the chancel arch still standing. The doorway is ornamented with sculptures of human heads; those on the capitals have plaited hair. Close by is a stone inscribed with the name of the man who carved it, Lugaedon—this is the oldest remaining Irish inscription in Latin characters.

[274]

Inishbofin L 540650 (Eire $\frac{1}{2}$" Map 10)

Six miles west-north-west of Cleggan. 'The Island of the White Cow', with a present population of 255. In 1912 it numbered 800. Some of them engage in lobster fishing. The island is about $3\frac{1}{2}$ miles long. At the harbour entrance there is 'The Barrack', the remains of a Cromwellian star-shaped fort with bastions, in an enclosure. The island was the scene of much violence when it was captured by the

English – the garrison being thrown down on to the rocks and a bishop chained there and drowned.

East of the harbour is the site of St Colman's monastery. Here there is a cemetery by the medieval church with a considerable ossuary of bones and skulls. St Colman, who came from Lindisfarne, died about 674. The graves of the fishermen of Inishbofin have broken oars planted at either end of them. The boats of those lost at sea were never used again, but were left above the shore upside down. There are sand dunes, unusual cliff scenery, and a colony of seals.

Inishbofin is separated from the neighbouring island of Inishark to the west by Ship Sound, ½ mile wide. The island is 1½ miles long and very precipitous, especially on the western side, which has strange, deep fissures in it called 'ooghys'. An extraordinary rock called Boughil rises 227 feet from the sea off the cliffs on the north-west side. Inishbofin can be reached from Cleggan by the mailboat (times from Clifden Post Office). At Cleggan there are two original Galway hookers, gaff-rigged sailing boats, *The True Light* and the *Ave Maria,* which are still used for transporting visitors.

[275]

Kilconnell Friary M 733315 (Eire ½" Map 15)

In the village of Kilconnell, 7½ miles west of Ballinasloe. Wonderful, pale ruins of a Franciscan friary built by William O Kelly in the middle of the 14th century, on the site of an earlier church of St Connall, Bishop of Kilconnell and Aughrim. They stand in a field on the north side of the village street and are beautiful from almost any angle. A tall, slender central tower rises above the nave, choir and transept. Fine, decorated windows and canopy tombs, one with figures of saints. Magnificent cloisters built with stones with masons' marks on them, including fleur-de-lys. In a small chamber off the choir is a tablet to Baron Trimleston, 'whoe, being transplanted into Conaght with others by order of the vsvrper Cromwell, dyed at Moinivae, 1627'. A notice on the gate leading to the friary gives instructions for obtaining the key.

[276]

Kilmacduagh M 405000 (Eire ½" Map 14)

Three miles west-south-west of Gort, north-west of the main Gort–Corrofin road. A collection of monastic ruins in an extremely impressive situation above a reedy lough and bogs, with great views of the mountains of the Burren to the west. They are dominated by a leaning round tower – 2 feet out of the perpendicular – (Lewis's *Topographical Dictionary of Ireland,* 1837, says 17 feet!) one of the highest in Ireland,

112 feet. The monastery was founded by King Guaire Aidhneach, King of Connacht, for his kinsman St Colman Mac Duach, in the 6th century. (See St Mac Duach's Hermitage, Oughtmama under Corcomroe, and Dungory Castle.)

The site was determined when the saint's girdle fell to the ground in what was then a wood. The girdle was preserved as a relic into the 17th century. In the chancel is a burial place of the O Shaughnessys who were the last custodians of the girdle. St Mac Duach is supposed to be buried here, south-west of the cathedral (Tempall Mor Mac Duagh) on a site now occupied by the tomb of Bishop French who died in 1852. There is a 17th century carving of him in the cathedral, together with one of a crucifixion. Besides the cathedral there are the ruins of John the Baptist's Church, St Mary's Church and O Hyne's Monastery, the last being north-west of the Abbot's House. Near the road a simple wooden cross in the churchyard over a grave records 'Patrick Donoghue (1894–1941) Connaught Rangers. Mutineer, 1920. R.I.P.'

[277]

Lough Nafooey Surrounding L 970598 (Eire ½″ Map 11)

West of Lough Mask. Lonely, beautiful lough. On the north side a roadless glen, which here forms the border of Mayo with Galway, leads deep into the mountains under the rocky cliffs of Leynabricka, an outlier of Maumtrasna (2,207 feet). (See also Lough Nadirkmore.) On the south side are the heights of Bencorragh, Benbeg and Bunnacunneen (2,131 feet). There is a remarkable view of the Maumturk Mountains from the pass, to which the road climbs at the western end of the lough before descending to join the Maum–Leenaun road on the banks of Joyce's river.

[278]

Menlough Castle M 285278 (Eire ½″ Map 14)

Two miles north-north-west of Galway city on the left bank of the Corrib. The first or second minor road to the left, north of the Headford road leads to the village of Menlough. The castle is immediately to the south of it. It is reached by a lane, then by a track past remains of a miniature fortified gatehouse with a tower. Ruins of a castellated 17th century fortified house, with fine chimneys standing in the fields on the bank of the river Corrib above a small jetty. The great windows have been torn down almost to ground level. Once the seat of the Earls of Clanricarde, latterly of Sir Valentine Blake. A fire, started by a candle, destroyed the house and its elderly occupant in 1910. To the north, on the south-eastern shore of Lough Corrib, are the marble quarries of Angliham. Single blocks of pitch black marble, up to 20 feet long, of 4 tons weight, have been cut from them.

[279]

Omey Island and High Island

L 565560 and L 505575 (Eire $\frac{1}{2}''$ Map 10)

Omey Island

South-west and west of Claddaghduff. Green, treeless but beautiful island with rocky outcrops, reached at low water from the mainland at Claddaghduff across an expanse of sands. The way to it is marked by poles. Pony races are held on the beach here in August. There are a few small groups of houses. Remains of Templefeheen on the site of a monastery of St Feichin of Cong. He died of bubonic plague, 664. His holy well is on the west side of the island. The inhabitants of Omey were saved from starvation by King Guaire of Connacht, who sent them food when they were *in extremis*. Beautiful views over innumerable rocks and small islands.

High Island (Ardoilean)

Two miles west of Aughrus Point, from which it may be reached by boat in good weather. Largest and most westerly of a number of islands. 195 feet high and steep-sided. The landing is difficult. Uninhabited. On it are the ruins of a monastery of St Feichin—a church, cells and carved slabs. There are big, stack-like rocks on the west. An extremely lonely place. Fine views of the coast of Connemara.

[280]

Pallas Castle

M 760080 (Eire $\frac{1}{2}''$ Map 15)

Six and a half miles north-west of Portumna by the minor road via Tynagh to Loughrea. A marvellous, remote castle, originally of the Burkes, but confiscated by Cromwell and given to the Nugent family. There is a farm attached to it and the farmer is the custodian. A gatehouse with a low entrance leads into a fortified enclosure—the bawn—in which there is a fine tower house. The wall walks on the bawn and the parapets are still intact, and there is an 18th century malt house. It is worth walking round the outside of the castle to have a look at it. On the east side there are two brick columns, one of which is so overgrown with ivy that it resembles a tree.

To get to the castle turn south by a lane opposite a slate-roofed lodge, 2 miles south-south-east of the village of Tynagh. The lane passes through the remains of a demesne in which there are some splendid evergreen oaks, cedars and yews. Only the foundations of the house remain.

[281]

Portumna Castle M 851037 (Eire ½″ Map 15)

In the demesne immediately south-west of the town of Portumna on the shore of Lough Derg, reached by a signposted drive. Ask permission to view from occupants of near-by cottage. Magnificent ruins of an early 17th century fortress house in a meadow among trees, the one-time seat of the Marquess of Clanricarde, destroyed by fire in 1826 (a later house was burned 1922). A tall, pale grey ivy-clad shell with gaping windows, finials and a strange double staircase to the entrance on the south side. Between the staircases a tablet in the wall bears the epitaph of a favourite dog which reads:

> This stone is erected to the Memory of a much lamented Animal
> Who with a beauteous Form possessed those Qualities which are esteemed most valuable in the Human Species:
> Fidelity and Gratitude.
> And dying about April 20, 1797 aged 11 year
> Was Interred near this Place.
> Alas! poor Fury. She was a dog.
> Take her for All in All Eye shall not look upon her like again!

On the north side of the house a pair of cannon are embedded in the ground, muzzles upwards, on either side of a flight of moss-grown steps. Close by, near the shore of the lough, are the ruins of a Dominican priory with tomb inscriptions. The window tracery in a transept is unique in Ireland.

[282]

The Punchbowl M 455001 (Eire ½″ Map 14)

One mile south of Gort by a signposted lane, east of the road, then by a gated track. Series of beautiful, green, cup-shaped depressions in a wood of chestnut and beech trees. Here the river Beagh runs in a gorge 80 feet deep from Lough Cutra and disappears underground. An enchanting place. Downstream its course is interesting to follow. Besides the Punchbowl there are other holes such as The Beggarman's Hole and The Church. On the west side of Lough Cutra is an early 19th century castle built after designs by John Nash for the first Viscount Gort.

[283]

Rathcronan Fort and Souterrains M 441434 (Eire ½″ Map 11)

Five miles south of Tuam. A grass-grown ring fort, with trees on its perimeter on private land (ask permission from the farm to view) in high country above the surrounding plain. Near the middle of it is the entrance to an extensive system of souterrains, blocked with branches to prevent the sheep from falling into it. There is another a little to the east within the circle. To reach it, take the minor road west-south-west towards the small village of Corrofin, from the crossroads on the Tuam–Athenry road, 4½ miles south of Tuam. These crossroads are indicated by 'Fort' on the ½″ map. Then take the second lane to the north which leads to the farm.

[284]

Roscam M 344242 (Eire ½″ Map 14)

Three miles east-south-east of Galway city, by a lane south from the main Oranmore road which leads past Ross House to the shore. Then by a track skirting the beach. Site of a monastery, with the lower 30 feet of a ruined round tower. The entrance has a huge lintel stone. There is also a roofless, 14th century parish church, and a graveyard. Splendid situation above the rocky shore of Oranmore Bay. Fine views. The walls of the fields have been powerfully reinforced with stones from these edifices. One of the two bullaun stones has imprints of St Patrick's knees on it. A pleasing, solitary place.

[285]

Ross Errilly M 250480 (Eire ½″ Map 11)

One and a half miles north-west of Headford, and west of the Headford–Ballinrobe road. Site of a Franciscan monastery founded in the 14th century—the best preserved in Ireland (also known as Ross Abbey). Sacked by Cromwell, 1656, but remained occupied until 1753. The roof fell in in 1812. Beautiful, small cloister; fish pond, interesting kitchen, mill, etc. This is the burial place of the Burke, Browne, Kirwan and Lynch families. It stands in a very lonely place in a bog close to the Mayo border which runs along the Black river. Approached by a causeway. Fine skyline. Very dramatic at sunset with the mountains silhouetted beyond Lough Corrib.

[286]

St Brendan's Monument and Holy Well L 733423 (Eire ½″ Map 10)

One and a half miles north-east of Roundstone. At the northern end of the curiously shaped island of Inishnee, at the mouth of Bertraghboy Bay. It is reached from the main road by a singularly narrow road bridge. The well is in an enclosure by a solitary farmhouse to the east of the bridge. The monument is a heap of stones. The

Moista Sound, Co. Mayo
(Wonder No. 312)

Croagh Patrick, Co. Mayo *(Wonder No. 298)*
(see under Croaghaun)

Frenchpark, Co. Roscommon *(Wonder No.*

local people visit the well for cures. The situation is very beautiful. To the south-west is Errisbeg (987 feet), above Roundstone, which is worth climbing for a magnificent panorama; to the north-east are the Twelve Bens of Connemara. Several unusual varieties of heather grow on the slopes of Errisbeg.

[287]

St Macdara's Island L 720300 (Eire ½″ Map 10)

One and a half miles by boat from Mace, on the mainland, and 5 miles from Carna. On it there are remains of a partially roofed, minute oratory with windows of the much-revered St Sionnach MacDara, whose help is invoked against the perils of the sea. Sailing vessels dip their sails three times when passing the island. There is a pilgrimage on July 16 followed by a regatta. The roof of the oratory is of an extraordinary kind. There are pilgrimage stations, carved stones and crosses of a sort of blue limestone, and a well.

[288]

St Patrick's Head and Holy Well L 903503 (Eire ½″ Map 11)

Four miles west-south-west of Maum Bridge and 3½ miles east-north-east of Recess; also known as Leaba Phadraig and Tobar Phadraig. A rock with a cavity in it, and a holy well on an exposed and lonely saddle of the Maumturk Mountains between a pair of 2,000-foot summits. Until very recently, at least, a place of pilgrimage on the last Sunday in July. A rough, motorable track from Cur, 1½ miles west-north-west of Teernakill Bridge which itself spans the Failmore river, leads south-westwards into the heart of the Maumturk Mountains. Then an easy hour on foot. On either side there are steep cliffs in the glen above the Failmore river and on the north side of Leckavrea (2,012 feet). Great views from the top of the pass, of Knocknagussy (1,494 feet), of Lugnabrick (1,628 feet) to the north-east, and of the Connemara Loughs and the Twelve Bens to the west. Can also be reached, equally well, from that side.

[289]

Salrock L 780640 (Eire ½″ Map 10)

Six and a half miles west of Leenaun by the road to Renvyle. The small road to Salrock is on the north side of Lough Muck which is joined to Lough Fee by a stream. Salrock is a lonely, beautiful hamlet at the head of Little Killary Bay with fine plantations of trees. Above the bay is a little 19th century church which has a square tower and red-painted window shutters. A very steep path with handholds in the wall leads up to it from the road. A little to the east of the church, in a green valley, is an old cemetery, now very overgrown. Trees have fallen on some of the monuments, destroying them; statues of the Madonna stand half-hidden in the undergrowth. Some of the graves are outlined with stones from the shore, others have hand-painted inscriptions. Here, it was the custom for the coffin to be borne three times round a part of the cemetery before burial, but the place where this was done is now overgrown. Clay pipes were also placed on the grave. There is a holy well near the entrance and another at the far end of the cemetery, but both are now dry. This is the supposed burial place of St Roc, a particularly zealous missionary after which the place is named.

The Pass of Salrock is to the south-east, on the mountain overlooking Killary Harbour. The way through the rocks was made by the saint in his efforts to free himself from the chains with which the Devil had loaded him while he was asleep. There are cairns here. Many rare plants and heathers in this region.

At the seaward end of Little Killary Bay there is a harbour with one or two currachs. Great views of the off-shore islands and the huge precipice of Mweelrea (q.v.), the Giant of the West (2,688 feet), and the dunes on the shore below it to the west. The lonely Lough Fee has an island with a house on it partially hidden in a dense grove of rhododendrons.

[290]

The Seven Monuments M 658147 (Eire ½″ Map 15)

In Moanmore East, 1½ miles south-east of Loughrea, on the south side of the Tynagh–Portumna road. Otherwise known as The Ring. A circle of seven stones set in an earth ring. Near-by there is a sort of small box made of stone slabs. It has been suggested that the stones and 'the construction' were re-erected here in the 18th or 19th century to form a sophisticated folly. Whatever the truth they are well situated in this high and windy place and not even the bungalow next door, nor a network of electric wires, can dispel their real or phony magic.

One mile further eastwards at the beginning of the first turning to the right from the Tynagh road in Rathsonny, is a very fine ring fort 300 feet in diameter with three ditches, hidden in a wood. In the middle there is a souterrain. This was the dwelling place of a considerable chief, or a king. Another near-by ring fort is called Rahannagroagh; it has a single bank and ditch and is less impressive.

Three and three quarter miles north-north-east of Loughrea (M 630223) on the lawn in front of Turoe House, is the famous Turoe Stone, a phallic object covered with decorative Celtic carving. Its setting, surrounded by a modern grating, is not very wonder-making.

[291]

The Aasleagh Waterfall L 892643 (Eire $\frac{1}{2}$" Map 11)

Two and a half miles north-east of Leenaun, on the Galway border. A beautiful, small peat-stained fall of the Erriff river, just above the point where it passes under a metal bridge and enters Killary Harbour. This is a notable salmon river. On the left bank there is a wood of pine and other trees and magnificent rhododendron groves. To the south-east is the peak known as the Devil's Mother, to the west, Ben Gorm. Fine views, too, of the head of the harbour, deep between the mountains and as narrow as a Norwegian fjord. Before and during the first world war this was an anchorage for the British fleet. It extends 9$\frac{1}{2}$ miles westwards to the Atlantic. There is a depth of 40 feet of water within 2 miles of the head of it. (See also Salrock.)

[292]

Aghagower M 035805 (Eire $\frac{1}{2}$" Map 11)

Three miles south-east of Westport, at a crossroads. Remains of a 12th and 13th century church with a slightly leaning round tower 60 feet high. This place was on the old pilgrim road to Croagh Patrick (q.v.) called Tochar Phadraig. There are a couple of holy wells, but they are dry. St Patrick is said to have founded a church here.

[293]

Ashford Castle M 148546 (Eire $\frac{1}{2}$" Map 11)

Half a mile south-west of Cong in Mayo (the castle is actually just over the border in Galway). A fantastic mock fortress on the shore of Lough Corrib, built by Sir Benjamin Lee Guinness, the brewer, in the late 19th century. It is now an hotel. The demesne is very beautiful. Immediately eastwards of Cong village, on the roadside, there are large numbers of crusheens—small wooden crosses. At Cregaree East and Cregaree West there are heaps of stones, also beside the road. It is the custom for any funeral procession entering Cong, to halt at one of these places while the relatives and friends of the deceased add either a cross or some stones to those already in position.

The beautiful remains of Cong Abbey are well known. The last so-called 'Lord Abbot' and the last of the 'monks' of Cong, the Reverend Patrick Prendergast, who died in 1828 aged 88, is buried under the floor of the abbey church which, in its most magnificent period, attracted to it more than 3,000 scholars and students. The splendid Cross of Cong from the monastery is in the National Museum at Dublin.

[294]

The Benaderreen Cliffs G 054409 (Eire ½" Map 6)

On the coast 4 miles west-north-west of Ballycastle. A line of tremendous, sheer cliffs in a bay close to the Ballycastle–Belmullet road. From here there is a distant view of the strange rock called Doonbristy (q.v.), off Downpatrick Head, 5 miles to the east. Two miles east-south-east by a minor road, the second to the right on the main road to Ballycastle, in one of two very old adjacent churchyards, is the tall, impressive Stone of Doonfeeny with a double cross carved on it.

[295]

Benwee Head F 815449 (Eire ½" Map 6)

One and a half miles west-north-west of the village of Portacloy. A tremendous run of sheer cliffs, 829 feet high at their greatest elevation, some of the finest cliff scenery in Ireland. Immediately to the west of them there is an immense bay also very sheer, with a natural arch. Off-shore, to the north-east, are the Stags of Broadhaven, a group of huge stacks, the tallest of which is over 300 feet high. Great views from the Head over Sligo and the coast of Donegal to the north, and southwards over Blacksod Bay to Achill Island. The cliffs can best be reached from the hill above Portacloy to the west, where there are extensive peat diggings, in about ½ hour.

[296]

Castlecarra M 172755 (Eire ½" Map 11)

Seven miles north-north-west of Ballinrobe, on the east shore of Lough Carra. The castle can be reached by a long lane from the road west of the village of Carrownacon. It passes close to the 13th century ruins of Burriscarra Abbey and a church, both roofless. A ruined archway spans the lane. To the north, across an arm of the lough, can be seen the impressive ruins of Castle Burk, now a farm. A long, green ride, flanked by a pair of stone columns, leads to Castlecarra, a castle of the MacEvillys, on a promontory above the shore. In the woods round about are the ruins of houses and outbuildings all moss-grown under the trees. It is an enchanting place. On Castle Island, in the lake, to the west, the remains of George Moore, the novelist, are interred. (See Moore Hall.)

[297]

Croaghaun F 557060 (Eire ½" Map 6)

On Achill Island, 3 miles west-north-west of Dooagh. The highest sea cliffs in the British Isles, 1,950 feet to the sea, at an angle of about 60 degrees. They are not the sheerest. Conachair on St Kilda (see *Wonders of Britain*), the highest cliffs in the United Kingdom, fall a stupendous 1,392 feet sheer into the Atlantic; but nevertheless Croaghaun is awe-inspiring.

From Corrymore House, west of Dooagh—a one-time residence of Captain Boycott—(see Lough Mask Castle), by way of Lough Acorrymore, the summit is an easy 2 hours' climb; more energetic persons will take much less. The end is dramatic. The mountain, 2,192 feet at its highest point, suddenly ceases to be and falls to the sea in a series of vast, rocky, partly grass-grown slopes. The view is immense: to the north over Blacksod Bay, the Mullet Peninsula and the islands to the west of it; eastwards over Achill to the Nephin Beg Mountains; to the south and east over Clare Island, Inishturk and Inishbofin Islands, and Clew Bay and Croagh Patrick, the holy mountain. Beyond Clare Island are the Twelve Bens in Galway. Immediately below Croaghaun, to the west-south-west, is the long, knife-edged ridge, in places only a few yards wide, with a tremendous fall to the sea on either side, which leads down to Achill Head. The descent can be made first towards Achill Head, but then turning away from it down the valley to Keem Bay and from there to Dooagh by the coast road. An alternative—more rewarding—is downhill by the cliffs northwards to Saddle Head (512 feet), 4 miles of huge precipices, in places over 900 feet high; then 2 miles eastwards, leaving a hill marked '881' on the $\frac{1}{2}''$ map on the left, to a ruined signal tower. Then to the ruined village of Slievemore (q.v.) and south to Keel by the road—a full day's walk. Neither Achill Head, the approach to which can be dangerous at any time, nor Croaghaun should be approached in high winds or thick weather, and this is true of any of the other great Irish cliffs. In spite of what most guide books say, the view of Croaghaun from the sea is less spectacular, unless one can contrive to be a considerable way off-shore. When hiring a boat from the islanders at Dooagh vigorous bargaining is necessary.

[**298**]

Croagh Patrick L 926807 (Eire $\frac{1}{2}''$ Map 11)

The great holy mountain of Ireland which rises straight from the southern shores of Clew Bay. Originally Cruach Aigil (the Hill of Holy History), it is a quartzite cone 2,510 feet high, popularly known as 'The Reek'. There is a great dark combe, Log na n Deamhan, under a precipice on its north face, into which St Patrick drove evil spirits. The mountain is very fine seen from Louisburgh to the west and from the east, from which side it appears to be perfectly symmetrical.

It was on the summit, having ascended it from Aghagower (q.v.) on the Saturday preceding Ash Wednesday, in the year 441, that St Patrick passed 40 days and nights in prayer and fasting, tormented by demons, some in the form of great, black birds which swooped about him. Finally he rang his bell, the host of demons fled and were engulfed in the sea beyond Achill Island. He descended from the mountain on Holy Saturday.

The ascent, from Murrisk, is traditionally made at night to reach the top for mass at dawn. The old way is barefoot. This impressive pilgrimage takes place on the last Sunday in July, Crom Dubh's Sunday, but begins on Saturday night. Sixty thousand people took part in 1968.

The climb to the first ridge is slippery because of the small stones. The last part of it is lined with little shelters which are occupied by sellers of refreshment on nights of pilgrimage. In daylight an active person can reach the ridge in 30 minutes. By day the route glitters with the broken glass of innumerable, discarded bottles but this is in no way squalid. At the base of the cone is the first of three penitential stations, Leacht Mionnain (the Memorial of St Benignus). Here the pilgrims recite seven paters, seven aves and the creed and make seven circuits of the station. On the final part, Casan Phadraig (Patrick's Path), the torrents of stones which form the screes are extremely steep and arduous by any standards. At the summit, which can be reached as an athletic exercise in 1 hour from Murrisk, but takes far longer as a pilgrimage, there is a modern chapel. The view is truly wonderful. Here, at Leabha Phadraig (the Bed of Patrick) the pilgrim recites seven paters, 15 aves and the creed, kneeling. Then 15 paters, 15 aves and the creed at the remnants of the altar of the ruined chapel of Teampall Phadraig. This is followed by a circumambulation of the summit 15 times, the pilgrims praying. At Leabha Phadraig, he recites seven paters, seven aves and the creed, on his knees, and makes seven more circuits of this station. At Roiligh Muire (the Resting Place of Mary) sometimes called An Garrai Mor, on the west-south-west side, where there are three heaps of stones, seven paters, seven aves and the creed, are recited and seven rounds made of each of the circles of the station. Lastly, the pilgrim walks round An Garrai Mor (also known as the Great Enclosure) seven times.

[299]

Cross 'Abbey' F 642310 (Eire $\frac{1}{2}''$ Map 6)

Four miles west-south-west of Belmullet. A small roofless church, in the 14th century a priory dedicated to the Virgin. It stands alone in the sand dunes on the exposed western side of the Mullet Peninsula. There are some cross pillars in it. The cemetery which surrounds it is filled with large, ancient tomb slabs; other less sophisticated tomb monuments are nothing more than heaps of stones.

[300]

The Dolmen of The Four Maols G 238178 (Eire $\frac{1}{2}''$ Map 6)

At Cloghogle on the south-west outskirts of Ballina, reached by a road over a level crossing at the railway station. Fine dolmen with a large capstone, hidden behind a hedge in a field on the south side of the road. It is said to be the grave of the Four Maols, foster brothers—Maol Croin, Maol Seanaidh, Maol Dalua, Maol Deoraidh. They murdered Ceallach, a bishop, who was also their tutor, some time in the 6th or 7th century. They were hanged by his brother on Ardnaree (The Hill of Execution) which is on the east side of the river Moy. The whole thing may never have happened at all.

[301]

Doonamo F 644376 (Eire ½″ Map 6)

Four and a half miles north-west of Belmullet. A prehistoric promontory fort on the cliff edge at Doonamo Point, a high and lonely headland on the Mullet Peninsula. The coast is wild and grey with deep inlets and, in one place on the way to the Point, there is a large puffing hole. The fort is very ruined. The wall on the landward side is defended by a ditch and there are the remains of a four-row *chevaux de frise*. The situation is remarkable. Great views of Eagle Island, off-shore to the north-west which has a lighthouse on it at an elevation of 200 feet, with massive, fortress-like walls. There are two light towers but only one is in use. The island is very steep-to. Great seas break on this coast in heavy weather and the cliff top is eroded and bare of vegetation for a considerable distance from the edge.

[302]

Doonbristy G 125429 (Eire ½″ Map 6)

Three and a half miles north-east of Ballycastle. Dun Briste (the Broken Fortress), a sheer-sided, yellow sandstone rock with pale, horizontal bands across it is separated from Downpatrick Head by a chasm 80 yards wide which is said to have opened in a great storm in 1393. It is the same height as the Head, 150 feet. From the west, the headland sloping gradually upwards from south to north with this box-shaped monolith lying off it, has a most extraordinary appearance. There is a legend that St Patrick encountered a pagan god called Crom Dubh on it while it was still part of the mainland and that Crom Dubh was either converted by the saint or else a miraculous rift appeared leaving the god isolated on the rock where he either perished or dwells still. On it there are the remains of a prehistoric promontory fort.

A cavern runs in under the Head and forms shafts open to the sky, the largest being Poll na Seantuinne (the Hole of the Old Wave), or perhaps Seantuine (of the Old Person). The effects in these puffing holes with the sea working in them can be impressive in rough weather.

On the cliffs on the north side of the Head are the scanty ruins of St Patrick's

Church, with a drystone construction called 'The Steeple' close to it. Half a mile south of it, where the headland begins to rise, there is a holy well of the saint. (If you see a fish or a bubble in it you will be cured of your afflictions.) The Head is a very old place of Patron pilgrimage and stations were and are still performed here about the well and near the church on Garland Sunday, the last in July, though now it is a much reduced ceremony.

[303]

Eochy's Cairn M 170600 (Eire $\frac{1}{2}$" Map 11)

In a lonely situation $3\frac{1}{2}$ miles north-east of Cong, 3 miles south-west of Ballinrobe. A huge ruined cairn of pale shining stones, a passage-grave, the entrance to which is invisible, one of the greatest in the west of Ireland. Fine views from it over Lough Mask to the Partry Mountains. Can be reached from the Ballinrobe–Neale road by a lane $\frac{3}{4}$ mile north of The Neale, to the west of it. After about $\frac{1}{2}$ mile, at the first substantial farm, take a track to the north-west then, where this lane bends eastwards, the cairn can be seen straight ahead.

The rough triangle of country comprehended by the Cong–Neale, Neale–Cross, Cross–Cong roads to the south of it, is known as the Plain of Southern Moytura. It is the site of one of the great battles of Irish myth between the Tuatha De Danann, a tall race with magical propensities and the Firbolgs, a small dark people (the Men of the Bag), known as such because they were forced to carry bags of earth while in bondage in Greece. The battle lasted four days and the Firbolgs were defeated. On the fourth day Eochai, King of the Firbolgs, was killed and interred beneath the cairn which bears his name. In the course of the battle Nuada, the King of the Tuatha De Danann, lost his hand and therefore became imperfect and ineligible to rule. He abdicated and there followed a period of misery for his people during which they were subjects of the Fomorians, African sea robbers who had already conquered them, but eventually Nuada's hand was replaced with a silver one and he re-ascended the throne.

The second battle of Moytura (Northern Moytura) was fought seven years later. In it the Fomorians were utterly defeated by the Tuatha De Danann. (See Carrowmore.) The story is told in the *Leabhar Gabhala, The Book of the Invasions of Ireland.* The limestone 'Plain' is a very overgrown, strange, haunted place. It contains within its boundaries a remarkable collection of cairns, stone circles, forts and standing stones—some of them difficult to find.

At Ballymacgibbon North, $2\frac{1}{2}$ miles east of Cong, just north of the Headford road (signpost), there is a wonderful cairn of gleaming stones 60 feet high and 390 feet in circumference, with a kerb of boulders round it. According to Sir William Wilde (see below) it was raised by the Firbolgs who each threw down a stone for the number of Tuatha De Danann they had slain on the first day of the battle when the action was in their favour. Near it, south of the road, is Caher Faeter (the Pewter Fort) with a souterrain in it. Cill Duin, on the west side of the Cross–Neale road, 1 mile south of Neale, is a souterrain in a rather mysterious wood filled with moss-grown stones (M 180570). Sir William Wilde, Surgeon and Irish antiquary (1815–76), the father of Oscar Wilde, rather romantically attempted to link the cairns with the battle, but has been no doubt correctly, but drearily, discredited by modern savants. See his very interesting book *Lough Corrib, its shores and Islands* (1867). In the demesne of his residence, Moytura House, south of the Cong–Cross road on the shore of Lough Corrib is Caher Gerrode, a ring fort. From it rises a tower which he built. On the Cong–Neale road, 1½ miles north-east of Cong opposite an old rectory at Glebe there is a circle of large, upright slabs on a mound among trees. There are others near-by.

[304]

Giant Rocking Stone G 214047 (Eire ½″ Map 6)

At Pontoon Bridge, immediately west of Pontoon Bridge Hotel. A large, delicately poised but unrockable block of granite, hidden in the heather on a hill overlooking Lough Conn and Lough Cullin. It was deposited there by glacial action and there are many similar in the area. The normal flow of the waters of the loughs is from Conn to Cullin, which is the smaller of the two. From it the Moy flows northwards to the sea, but after heavy rainfall Lough Cullin rises more quickly and the water rushes back under the Pontoon Bridge into Lough Conn.

[305]

The Gulf of Aille M 070810 (Eire ½″ Map 11)

Five miles south-east of Westport, ½ mile west of Aille. Reached by a signposted lane from the main Westport–Partry road. The Gulf is near a beautiful, small lough. There is a farmhouse. Great view of Croagh Patrick (q.v.) cone-shaped, to the west. Here, in a tree-clad depression in the fields, the little river Aille disappears underground beneath a limestone cliff. A large sink hole, near-by, opened up in one night 20 years ago. The caves have been partly explored. In Penal Times mass was said in a hidden place close under the cliff. The Aille reappears at Bellaburk, 2½ miles to the east. To see the Gulf of Aille ask permission of the farmer.

[306]

Inishglora and Inishkeera Surrounding F 610300 (Eire ½″ Map 6)

Two low-lying islands about 1½ miles west of the Belmullet peninsula, lonely, windswept, and now uninhabited. Reefs join them together. They can be reached by currach, of which there are a number on the shore near Cross Point. On Inishglora are the ruins of a monastery founded in the 6th century by St Brendan the Navigator, the saint who made such tremendous sea voyages and who is thought by some people to have reached America. Here a ruined cashel (circular drystone wall) encloses three oratories, one of them beehive-shaped, three cells and inscribed cross and tomb slabs. On Inishglora the nails and hair of the dead were said to grow as vigorously as they had done in life:

> 'On Inis Gluair in Irrus Downan, the bodies thither brought do not Rot, but their nails and hair grow and every one there recognizes his father and grand-father for a long time after death; and no meat will putrefy on it even without being salted.'
>
> (*Book of Ballymote, c.* 1400)

Here the children of Lir, who had been changed into swans by their stepmother, swam in the Atlantic for the last 300 years of their enchantment. (See Lough Derravaragh and Fair Head.)

Five miles to the south are the islands of Inishkea North and South, separated by a narrow channel. On Inishkea North, on the south side of the island near the now deserted village by the landing place, is Bailey Mor, a really huge mound, 500 feet wide and 60 feet high. South of it there is a shell mound. Near-by, a prehistoric dye workshop was found, where purple dye was made from shellfish. In the 1900s a whale fishery was established here by the Norwegians. At that time the population of the North and South islands was 212. Each had its own king. They were finally evacuated in 1931. On Inishkea South, 5 miles south-west, there is a ruined small church, also said to have been founded by St Brendan.

[307]

Kilgeever Church L 838808 (Eire ½″ Map 11)

Two miles east of Louisburgh. Roofless remains on the southern slopes of an isolated hill to the west of Croagh Patrick (q.v.). There is a cemetery and a holy well. Wonderful views across a green plain southwards to the Sheeffry Hills. Some pilgrims come here after their penitential exercises on Croagh Patrick.

[308]

Lough Mask Castle M 144604 (Eire ½″ Map 11)

On the east shore of Lough Mask. Splendid, lowering ruin of a great tower of the 15th century castle of the MacWilliams, altered in 1618. It has similar architectural features to those of Danganbrack in Clare (q.v.). The castle is a window-pierced shell with tall chimneys. It stands in the grounds of Lough Mask House, in which lived Captain Charles Cunningham Boycott (1832–97) late of the 39th Foot. He was land agent to Lord Erne in Mayo and as such evicted a large number of tenants. In 1880 his neighbours, inspired by Michael Davitt, the founder of the Land League and a lieutenant of Parnell, stopped the tenantry, and almost every other local person, from having anything to do with Boycott and his family, and in doing so added another word to the English language.

House, castle and demesne are private property (stud farm), but a fine view of the castle can be had from the lough or more distantly from the strange, stone-littered peninsula of Inishmaine, once an island in the lough, immediately to the north, on which there are the remains of an Augustinian monastery. To the west of the monastery there is a square building with two cells in it, floored with stone sleepers, perhaps a sweat-house—a sort of Irish version of a hammam, heated by a turf fire and shared communally among a number of persons. Some such sweat-houses survived in use into the present century. (See Leckemy.)

[309]

Lough Mask–Corrib Canal M 148554 (Eire ½″ Map 11)

Between Lough Mask and Lough Corrib. A wonderful but tragically useless piece of engineering, constructed with vast expenditure of labour during the great famine, to link the two loughs and give work to the starving inhabitants. The work of cutting the channel through the limestone, and the construction of the five locks, took hundreds of labourers over four years, but when the water was finally admitted to the canal it percolated away into the limestone. Only a small section at the northern, Lough Mask end has any water in it at all; but it is worth exploring. A part of it can be seen from a small bridge which crosses it just outside the town of Cong to the right of the Clonbur road, to which point the map reference refers.

[310]

Lough Nadirkmore M 002640 (Eire ½″ Map 11)

Three miles north of the east end of Lough Nafooey (Galway), east of Lough Mask. An extremely solitary, small lough not more than ½ mile long, 890 feet up under a huge semi-circle of cliffs. The situation is extremely dramatic. On the north side of the semi-circle is Buckaun (2,046 feet), to the south-east is a peak unnamed on the ½″ map (1,705 feet). Both are outriders of Maumtrasna (2,207 feet) to the west. There is a smaller lough near-by to the east. Ascent from Cappanacreha on the Owenbrin river. Ask directions locally. Can be very wet; not for the easy-going.

[311]

The Menawn Cliffs North and south of F 650015 (Eire ½″ Map 6)

On Achill Island two and a half miles south-east of Keel. Can be reached from the south-eastern end of Trawmore Sands. There is no point in climbing to the summit of the Menawn Mountain which is 1,350 feet and far back from the cliff edge. An alternative route is by the coast from the village of Dooega, at the foot of the beautiful glen of the Dooega river. The cliffs, which are between 800 and 900 feet sheer to the sea in places, are amongst the most impressive in the British Isles.

Cathedral Rocks are fantastic rock formations south of Trawmore Sands, but the cliffs are at their sheerest further south towards Glennanaff Point. They are far more imposing from seawards than Croaghaun (q.v.), which is not as impressive as one might hope from close to, and ought to be seen from a distance of a mile or so. Great views from the Menawn Cliffs over the landward side of Croaghaun, especially at sunset, and over Slievemore to the north (both of which see), and Clare Island to the south.

[312]

Moista Sound F 940426 (Eire ½″ Map 6)

Four miles west of Belderg Harbour, on the north coast of Mayo. An awe-inspiring sea chasm in a very remote and hidden situation, so narrow that a rowing boat can only enter it with its oars shipped. It is at a place where the trap rock of which the coast is composed has fallen to form what is known as a trap-dyke, a tremendous rift, a couple of hundred yards long, rising 350 feet sheer from the sea on the north side and 450 feet on the south, although the cliff itself rises even higher, though less steeply, above it on the south.

To the west is Illanmaster Island, below a great cliff on the mainland and separated from it by a narrow gut. The Sound is difficult to find, but worth the effort. From the main Belmullet–Ballycastle road, which traverses one of the loneliest and most desolate regions in Ireland, take the road at Belderg towards Belderg Harbour, and after ¾ mile take a rough, narrow road to the west which leads through very lonely country over a saddle on the south flank of Glinsk Hill. The road is only shown on the ½″ map as far as a place called Ballinapark, but it in fact continues much further. After reaching the west side of Glinsk, leave your vehicle and, with a farm to your left, follow the flank of the hill northwards along the 600-foot contour line, until you reach a deep bay with a high cliff on its west side, south-east of Illanmaster Island. Moista Sound is just to the east below the circular eminence marked '800' on the map. It is invisible until you are directly over it.

Three miles westward at Porturlin is another trap-dyke phenomenon—a 30-foot high arch in a 600-foot cliff, which can be rowed through at half tide. The coast westward from Porturlin as far as Benwee Head (q.v.) is among the most magnificent in Ireland. Below the promontory on the west side of Portacloy there is a huge sea cave with an entrance 30 feet high. Inside, it has a high-domed roof. This can only be entered by boat.

[313]

Moore Hall M 194745 (Eire ½″ Map 11)

Four and a half miles south-east of Ballintober, and 1½ miles south of Carrownacon. Large, square, grey 18th century house, on a slight eminence overlooking a bay on the east side of Lough Carra. Best reached by a track along the lake shore from the Carrownacon–Ballygarries road, then by a stile. The house, which is now hidden in a dense conifer plantation, is a shell burnt out in 1923, but the Doric columned portico still stands. Over the entrance is an inscription *Fortis Cadere Cedere Non Potest*, with the date 1795, and there is a tablet in the wall put there by the Ballyglass IRA.

No upper floors are intact, but there are large cellars, and at the back of the house a tunnel hung with stalactites. To the east is a huge, walled garden now overgrown and planted with conifers. This house was the home of the Moore family. John Moore was, for a very short time, '1st President of The Connaught Republic', a post to which he was optimistically elected at a celebration of the early victories of the United Irishmen, aided by a French force in 1798. A tablet placed at the locked, east gate on the road by a Californian Moore records 'John Moore, 1st President of Ireland and the men who gave their lives in 1798'; George Henry Moore, prominent in the Tenant Right movement and George Moore, the novelist, lived here. The area and the lough are described in the latter's books *The Lake* and *Ave, Salve, Vale.* The writer's cremated remains—he died in 1933—are in an urn beneath a cairn on Castle Island to the north-west. (See Castlecarra.)

[314]

Moyne Friary G 228288 (Eire ½″ Map 6)

Two miles east-south-east of Killala by the minor road from Ballina to Killala, eastwards of the main road. From it a signposted path by a farm leads to the friary across the fields. This complex of ruins clustered about a great tower, stands above a little bay on the west side of the Moy estuary only a short way north of another Franciscan foundation, Rosserk Abbey (q.v.). The cloisters are very beautiful with their pairs of plain round pillars. A small stream runs through the friary; it supplied the occupants with water. In the nave there are lively representations of 16th century ships scratched on the wall plaster. The view from the tower, which is over 90 feet high, across the estuary to Bartragh Island, and over the sandhills at the river mouth, alone makes the journey to Moyne worthwhile. The friary was burned and ruined, together with those of Rathfran and Rosserk by Sir Richard Bingham, English Governor of Connacht, in 1590. High up in the little town of Killala itself there is a fine round tower, 84 feet high and, near-by, a very considerable system of souterrains.

[315]

Murrisk L 920824 (Eire ½″ Map 11)

Five miles west of Westport on the coast road. Ruined friary of the 15th century, in a singularly beautiful situation on the shore of Clew Bay, and in the lee of Croagh Patrick (q.v.). In it are the tombs of the O Malleys who founded it.

[316]

The Musical Bridge F 969200 (Eire ½″ Map 6)

At Bellacorick on the main road to Belmullet, 10½ miles west-north-west of Crossmolina. A very singular bridge, built of limestone, which spans the Abhann Mhor in the village. It was built in the 18th century but as early as the middle of the 17th century the Erris 'prophet', Brian Rua O Carrabine, foretold that when it was built it would never be completed. It never was. Musical sounds can be produced by running stones along the northern parapet, which is very worn as a result. Those with some musical ability can actually play tunes on it. The southern parapet is non-musical—possibly because the limestone was set in cement when the bridge was repaired after the Troubles. It is said that anyone who actually completes the bridge will come to a sudden end. Some years ago an official of Mayo County Council did put the last coping stone in place at the north-east end and died almost immediately—he was, however, a sufferer from chronic asthma. An Assistant County Engineer in Mayo had it placed in position in 1920 but the next morning it was no longer there.

[317]

Mweelrea L 790670 (Eire ½″ Map 10)

Six miles west-north-west of Leenaun. Nine miles south-south-west of Louisburgh. The highest peak of the Mweelrea Mountains, the Giant of the West (2,688 feet). There are three principal peaks. On their eastern flank is Lough Doo, to the south Killary Harbour, and to the west the Atlantic. The views from the tops are amongst the most wonderful in Ireland. They extend far along the coast over Clew Bay,

Clare Island and Achill to the north, and south-westwards to Slyne Head; inland over the mountains of Connemara. The northernmost summit is Benbury (2,610 feet). The walk from Mweelrea to it and then south along the ridge to Benlughmore is really impressive, with great combes and screes falling away below. The ascent of any of these mountains should not be attempted alone in bad visibility or high winds.

Lough Doo is a beautiful, lonely lough on a pass between the Mweelrea Mountains and the Sheeffry Hills, which have an enormous scooped-out combe on their southern flanks. The road along its shores from Killary Harbour was built by the Congested Districts Board in 1898 – a tablet records the fact. It passes Delphi, a house in woodland, so named by a member of the Sligo family who made the Grand Tour. A mile to the north of it a very lonely road follows the course of the Glenummera river eastwards between the mountains.

Below Mweelrea, to the north-west, is the immense, remote beach of Kinnadoohy, with dunes at the southern end on the shores of Killary Harbour. When the wind blows, dunes and beach are hidden in a haze of flying sand. On the shore beyond the meadows in which the sheep graze, is a stony mound which could be a cemetery or a midden. Off-shore is Inishturk and, to the north, Clare Island.

[318]

Neale Park M 190593 (Eire ½″ Map 11)

At The Neale, 3½ miles north-east of Cong on the east side of the Ballinrobe road. In a field close to the main road and visible from it is an extraordinary cairn of stones in the form of a nine-tiered pyramid with a block on top of it. It has a faintly oriental air; perhaps it was an inspiration of Lord Kilmaine's, whose estate this was, to give work to his tenants. On the opposite side of the road there is the melancholy ruin of a 19th century Protestant church, with a tower. In the grounds of the ruined house to the south-west, is a curious monument to find in an 18th century demesne, with a stone in it on which are carved figures of a unicorn, a man and a lion. According to an inscription they were found in a near-by cave and the figures, Dine Feale (Gods of Felicity) were worshipped by Edda and Con after whom Connacht was named. East of the house there is an eye-catcher – a classical temple, which stands on an arched sub-structure.

[319]

The Pigeon Hole M 145552 (Eire ½″ Map 11)

Half a mile west of Cong on the Galway border. Can be reached on foot from a lodge on the east side of the first minor road to the south of the Clonbur road, west of Cong. Otherwise known as Poll na gColm. A deep, fern hung, mossy limestone chasm which marks the course of an underground river linking Lough Mask with Lough Corrib (the second largest lough in Ireland). A flight of extremely slippery steps leads to the bottom of it. There are pools in which white trout are supposed to live, and deep caverns which were originally shown to visitors by a woman who carried a burning bundle of straw above her head, which must have added to the grandeur of the scene. The chasm stands on the edge of a conifer plantation in which there are more embryo swallow holes. Other caverns near the village are Horse's Discovery, The Lady's Buttery and Kelly's Cave which is partly a rock-cut tomb. To find them, ask locally.

[320]

Rosserk Friary G 251251 (Eire ½″ Map 6)

Four miles north of Ballina. It can be reached by a signposted lane from the minor road which links Ballina to Killala and which runs parallel to the main road and to the east of it. Magnificent, extensive ruins of a 15th century Franciscan establishment, in a romantic and solitary situation on the west bank of the estuary of the Moy. Rosserk (Ros-Serce, the Wood of Seac) was burned in 1590 by Sir Richard Bingham, English Governor of Connacht. He also destroyed the Rathfran and Moyne Friaries. The roofless buildings with their triangular gable ends and square tower soaring up among them, dark against the waters of the estuary, make a most powerful impression. Close by, to the south-south-west towards the shore, is a little holy well which is visited on the Feast of the Assumption (August 15). It can be reached by a track leading to a farmhouse from the lane to the friary.

[321]

St Dairbhile's Church F 618184 (Eire ½″ Map 6)

Ten miles south-west of Belmullet. At Fallmore, at the south-south-western end of the Mullet Peninsula, in a beautiful situation above the shore. A very ruined little building of the 7th century of which little more than the gable ends remain, and a narrow, immensely solid doorway with some interlaced ornamental designs, at the west end. There are old graves in the rocky cemetery, and a few windswept bushes. St Dairbhile's (or St Derivla's) Bed is the grave of the saint on its north-east side, and to the north of it is the 'Vat', a holy well. Great views of Croaghaun, and Slievemore on Achill (both of which see) and of Black Rock with its lighthouse, 6 miles beyond the island of Duvillaun More to the west-south-west, on which there are the remains of an anchorite's establishment.

[322]

Slievemore Village F 640073 (Eire ½″ Map 6)

Achill Island, 1½ miles north of Keel by a lane. Extensive ruins of a village on the south flanks of Slievemore (2,204 feet), a great quartzite cone shot with mica, the northern slopes of which descend to the sea. The village was abandoned in the late 19th century but continued to be a buaile (milking or pasturing place) to which the islanders resorted in the summer months, living in the 'booley houses', a form of transhumance which is becoming increasingly rare in the parts of Western Europe in which it was formerly practised. To stand in the single street, nearly a mile long, with its roofless stone houses and huts on either side, the walls of which are often well-preserved, is a moving experience.

In the cemetery at Slievemore there is a walled holy well of St Colman and in one part of it, south of the lane, there is a curious construction, perhaps part of his original church. It consists of two stone slabs one above the other with a cross on the topmost one. These slabs are supported by drystone walling, and there is sufficient height under the lintel which they form, for a body to pass. Many of the graves here are outlined in stones from the shore. There are great views of the Menawn Cliffs and Croaghaun to the south and west. From here the ascent of Slievemore can be made easily in an hour by way of a conspicuous white rock called The Star. The view is splendid but the one from Croaghaun is finer. The descent can be made by the ridge to the west side of Dugort village (marked by 'Hotel' and 'Settlement' on the ½″ map).

Just east of Slievemore church, where the lane ends by a couple of inhabited cottages, there is a prehistoric grave with a cairn which has a gallery 20 feet long and a circular forecourt with two upright stones. Another, very much alone in the bog, about 400 yards north-east of it, is marked 'Cromlech' on the map. It has a gallery with a big capstone. There are other remains in the area. The road through the deserted village is so boggy that any conventional vehicle will certainly get stuck in any but the driest weather. In the sea cliffs under the north face of Slievemore, are the weird and marvellous Seal Caves. They can only be visited by boat from Dugort, but the entrance can be seen from the cliff path which runs along the side of the mountain westward from Dugort.

[323]

Termoncarragh Cemetery F 649353 (Eire ½″ Map 6)

Four miles west-north-west of Belmullet by way of the village of Corclogh, then the first turning to the left after ¾ mile, then the next left turning that presents itself. A very old, walled graveyard on a little hill with cropped green grass all around, and distant views of the sand dunes near the shore. To the east is the little lake of Termoncarragh. In the cemetery there is a macabre vault in which a pair of skeletons is visible. There are many old tomb enclosures and graves of British merchant seamen whose bodies were washed ashore on the coast during the last war—and one of a member of the Lovat Scouts. The visit to Termoncarragh can be conveniently combined with that to Doonamo (q.v.).

[324]

Turlough M 208940 (Eire ½″ Map 11)

Four miles east-north-east of Castlebar. Ruins of a 17th century church and a fine pointed round tower, to the north of the Foxford road and visible from it. There is a cemetery. On the west wall of the church there is a carving of a crucifixion. Another, on a slab inside, shows Christ with elongated arms and with his hair standing on end (or is it the crown of thorns?), and splayed, elongated fingers.

[325]

Westport House L 987851 (Eire ½″ Map 10)

West of the town of Westport in a demesne. Pale grey, limestone house built by Richard Cassels in 1730, and subsequently worked on by James Wyatt in 1780. Cassels built the Palladian front in 1730. There is a splendid barrel-vaulted entrance hall. A white Sicilian marble staircase, built by the third Marquess in the 1850s, leads up from it. A statue, the Angel of Welcome, of the same material, stands in a niche at the head of the first flight. Fine chandelier of Waterford glass. Splendid, austere dining room by Wyatt, with beautiful stucco work. There are some impressive romantic landscapes in the house by James Arthur O Connor, painted in the early 19th century. (Admission charge.)

Westport itself is a civilized little town. It was designed by James Wyatt at the same time as the house. He also had plans for a theatre which might have been delightful if it had ever been built. The heart of Westport is the six-sided market place in which stands a truncated-looking column on which stood, or was intended to stand, the statue of George Glendenning, banker and son of the Rector of Westport. A little river enclosed by low walls, and shaded by sycamore trees, runs through the Mall and down to Clew Bay. The place has a very continental air. At Westport Quay, a mile from the town at the head of Clew Bay—the long-defunct port of the town which was established in 1780—there are some fine old warehouses.

[326]

The Castlestrange Stone M 824599 (Eire ½″ Map 12)

One and three quarter miles north-west of Athleague. In the demesne of a castle on the bank of the river Suck, there is an oval granite stone embellished with enigmatic spiral decoration of the Iron Age. Like many such rarities it is protected by a railing which reduces its primitive effect. Reached by a bridge from the Athleague–Glennamaddy road. The castle is now part of a farm. There are some old stables.

[327]

The Doon of Drumsna East and west of M 992963 (Eire ½″ Map 12)

One mile south of the town of Drumsna in Leitrim, on the Roscommon side of the Shannon. Huge earthworks, in place 100 feet wide at the base, with a ditch. They extend across a great bend of the Shannon, north of the canal known as the Jamestown Cut which virtually makes an island of this bend. The builders of the Doon may have had a similar intention. The works appear to face south. Two other lesser earthworks run parallel to it on the north and south sides. At the western end the Doon becomes narrower and when it comes to the river it follows the right bank upstream. There are only two breaks in the entire system, each about 150 feet wide with curious inturned defences. The earthworks are not easy to find as they run through rather close country, but good sections can be seen to the east and west of the road which goes southwards from the Drumsna–Carrick-on-Shannon road, nearly opposite a farm at Drumcleavry, ½ mile before the canal is reached. If in difficulty ask the farmer. A similar but much longer earthwork, which faces north instead of south, runs along the Ulster border in Co. Leitrim from Lough Melvin to Lough Macneen and is called the Black Pig's Dyke (q.v.; also see Mote of Granard). Such dykes are known as travelling earthworks.

[328]

The Drumanone Dolmen G 767023 (Eire ½″ Map 7)

Two miles west of Boyle. An extremely impressive portal grave, one of the largest in Ireland, with a huge capstone, 14 feet by 10 feet, which has partially collapsed on its supports. A door-stone obstructs the entrance. It stands in a field to the north of the Boyle–Sligo railway line. There are some slight remains of the cairn which originally covered it. When it was excavated some cremations were discovered. It can be reached by a little track beside a house on the north side of the Boyle–Tobercurry road, immediately to the west of the place where the railway crosses it by a bridge. The dolmen is just beyond a level crossing on the railway, about 200 yards from the road.

[329]

Frenchpark M 728920 (Eire ½″ Map 12)

Half a mile north-west of the village of Frenchpark. The shell of an 18th century mansion, a central block with wings, once the fine seat of Lord de Freyne. North of the house there is a circular building with a central chimney—probably a brewhouse—all overgrown with ivy, and somewhere there is said to be a large souterrain, but you must ask directions locally, if you can find anyone to ask, which is by no means certain in this lonely, ruined demesne. The entrance to it is by a gate on the north side of the main road to Ballaghaderreen. A little further on, on the south side of this road, is an old ivy-covered church. Here, in the graveyard, is buried Douglas Hyde, who became first President of Ireland in 1937, one of the founders of the Gaelic League.

[330]

Kilronan G 899123 (Eire ½″ Map 7)

Three quarters of a mile north-north-west of Keadew on the shore of Lough Meelagh. In the vault of the Mac Dermot Roes of Camagh in the churchyard of the ruined church, is buried Turlough O Carolan, the last and one of the greatest of the Irish bards. He died in 1738 at the age of 68. Ten harpers were at his wake which lasted four days. Here, for some years, his skull was exhibited in a niche in the church, decorated with a black ribbon. Goldsmith records in an essay the occasion when Carolan, having heard a continental musician, probably Geminiani, play the Fifth Concerto of Vivaldi on his violin, took up his harp and played the whole piece without missing a note. Having done so he immediately composed 'and with such spirit and elegance that it may compare (for we have it still) with the finest compositions of Italy'. It is known as 'Carolan's Concerto'. The melody of the 'Star Spangled Banner' is also his. A plaque records Mulloy MacDermot as being 'The Poor Man's Magistrate the Poor Man's Protector'.

Down by the waterside there is a holy well of St Lasere (Lasair) who is supposed to have founded a church here with her father St Ronan, and a great stone—perhaps the capstone of a cromlech—on which offerings are placed by pilgrims to this spot.

Along the road to the north-west is the gate of Kilronan Castle demesne (private), with a remarkable lodge in the form of a grotto, with pointed windows formed of what appears to be artificial stone. There are two castles, one Gothic with

Strawberry Hill decoration in a terribly dangerous state of dilapidation. It has fan-vaulted plaster ceilings, a minstrels' gallery, and beautiful cast iron work on the upper well of the staircase. The fireplace in the great hall was supported by a pair of wooden blackamoors, but they have been wrenched away.

[331]

Rathcrogan M 800837 (Eire ½″ Map 12)

Three miles north-west of Tulsk on the south side of the Frenchpark road; ½ mile south-south-east of Rathcrogan crossroads. A small hill with steep sides, partly a man-made earthwork, in a bare, windy situation 500 feet up above the plain which extends to the Shannon. Inside it there is a mound, perhaps a barrow. On the edge of the hill there is a standing stone. This was Cruachan, the royal seat of the ancient kings of Connacht; and Maeve the goddess, the much-married wife of King Aillil of Connacht who gained the title by his mystical union with her, had a palace here. The inauguration place of the Connacht kings was on Carnfree, 2 miles south of Tulsk.

Half a mile south-south-west of Rathcrogan there is a limestone cave called Owney-grat—the Cave of the Cats. The entrance to it is roofed and walled with stone for some distance, and there are early Christian ogham inscriptions on the lintels (M 798834). This was the Cave of Cruachu, the entrance to the Other World.

The area around the Rathcrogan crossroads has a variety of tumuli, ring forts, earthworks and stones secreted in it. One hundred and twenty yards north-north-east of Rathcrogan is Miosgan Meabha (Maeve's Lump; q.v.), a recumbent pillar stone, and in the next field to the west, is Maeve's Mill. A quarter of a mile to the south of Rathcrogan is the Burial Place of the Kings (Reillig na Riogh), a round enclosure with some mounds inside it. Here are supposed to be buried Conn of the Hundred Battles and Eire (after whom the island was named), Fodhla and Banba, Queen of the Tuatha De Denann. Nothing of them has been found by excavation. With such associations the area about Rathcrogan can scarcely lack atmosphere.

[332]

The Rinndown Peninsula Surrounding N 050541 (Eire ½″ Map 12)

Two miles east of Lecarrow, on Lough Ree. The peninsula can be reached by a gated track which passes a farm at the end of the road from Lecarrow. Ask permission to go to it. Near-by there is the little ruined church, all that remains of the Hospital of St John the Baptist, a medieval foundation of Augustinians. A path leads through fields in which there are overgrown masses of masonry, to the remains of an immense wall with fragmentary remains of towers and a gateway. This wall, which is over

500 feet long, extends from one shore of the peninsula to the other. South of it again, there is a moated ditch which also spans it. On the eastern side, above the shore, there is a moated castle, completely overgrown with trees and vegetation, and almost impenetrable. The earliest parts are 13th century, with additions as late as the 17th century. At the western end there is a ruined church overgrown with ivy. Beyond it is a deep, mysterious wood, in which there is a circular building with a tower above it which can occasionally be seen above the trees as one advances towards it. These are the only remains of a castle and a town founded in the 13th century. One of the most haunting and haunted places in Ireland.

[333]

Rockingham House G 847038 (Eire ½″ Map 7)

Two and a half miles west of Boyle, by a minor road which leads to an impressive gatehouse. The very melancholy ruin of a great mansion, reconstructed for Lord Lorton, the owner of the town of Boyle, by John Nash in 1810; burned again in April 1863, and a third time in 1957. It was the seat of Lord French, the British General of the first world war. It stands on the shore of Lough Key in a once splendid but now despoiled demesne in which there are still some very noble trees, lakes and interesting buildings. Close to the house there is an equally melancholy 19th century church, also ruined; on the south side of the main avenue are the remains of a medieval church. Two dark tunnels extend outwards from the cellars of the house. One emerges in the park on the east side, the other on the lake shore to the north. This tunnel has a room on one side of it filled with curious machinery, perhaps some form of pumping engine.

Trees are being cut down and roads driven through the demesne, which is now being developed as a public park by the Forestry Department. The house, also, may be restored. On Castle Island, one of the many wooded islands in the lough, are the picturesque remains of a 17th century castle which was also burned down accidentally in 1922. Four miles east of Boyle, on the north side of the main Boyle–Carrick-on-Shannon road, at Ardcarn, there is a large, grass-grown stone cairn in parkland.

[334]

Roscommon Castle M 873650 (Eire ½″ Map 12)

Immediately north of the town on the left side of the road to Tulsk. The shell of a 13th century Anglo-Norman fortress altered about 1580, with a great, twin-towered gate building on the north side, and angle towers connected by curtain walls, of which only the north and south walls remain. With its many windows added in the 16th century, the ruin produces a most powerful effect. It is somehow reminiscent of a French château. It was dismantled by the Cromwellian General Reynolds, in 1652. Reached by a signposted lane from the main road.

[335]

Strokestown M 931808 (Eire ½″ Map 12)

The village was designed for Maurice Mahon, 1st Baron Hartland. Its extraordinarily wide, tree-lined avenue running east and west, intersecting the main road, gives it an outlandish, continental air. At the lower, eastern end is a splendid archway, the entrance to Strokestown Park House and the demesne of the Mahons, a present from Charles I; at the far western end is a 19th century church. The façade of the house is 18th century and very fine. There are two old churches and an ancient, wooded deer park. Both house and demesne are private.

[336]

Tulsk Friary M 832810 (Eire ½″ Map 12)

In the village west of the main road. The very fragmentary remains of a 15th century Dominican friary, a foundation of the Mac Dowells. There is little of historical or architectural interest, but they are romantically ivy-clad to the point of obliteration.

Section 6

Sligo

Leitrim

Donegal

[337]

Abbey Court G 560184 (Eire $\frac{1}{2}''$ Map 7)

Four and a half miles north-east of Tobercurry, near Lavagh, north of the Collooney road. Ruins of a Franciscan friary thick with ivy, in a bleak, overgrown graveyard. The square tower over a crumbling nave is shakily supported by four pointed arches. The ruin is full of tombstones. In it a wall vault has burst open, and a wooden coffin with rusty nails protrudes. Abbey Court is the perfect setting for a Gothic horror novel.

[338]

Ardtermon Castle G 590434 (Eire $\frac{1}{2}''$ Map 7)

Five and a half miles south-west of Grange, on the south side of the Raghly road. Bold ruins of a 17th century fortress with round angle towers, standing in a windswept field overlooking Drumcliff and Sligo Bays. It was built by Sir Nathaniel Gore, ancestor of the Gore–Booths of Lissadell (q.v.). A mile to the north, reached by a lane from the road to Raghly and $\frac{1}{2}$ mile south-west of the Castle, is the over-overgrown enclosure of Teampall Beolain, an ancient church which was partially engulfed in the sands which drifted over this land from the shore in the 18th and 19th centuries ruining the soil, destroying houses and causing misery and desolation. It was halted by the planting of bent grass. The churchyard, hidden romantically deep in vegetation, is a hell of insect life in the summer.

[339]

The Bricklieve Mountains Surrounding G 755115 (Eire $\frac{1}{2}''$ Map 7)

Six miles east-south-east of Ballymote. Among the most extraordinary of the natural Wonders of Ireland are five parallel limestone ridges in the Bricklieve Mountains, separated by deep canyons. Above them, on the ridges, are large numbers of prehistoric cairns, known collectively as the Carrowkeel Cemetery. Some of these cairns are more than 20 feet high and are surrounded by kerbs of stones. Many have passage-graves within them.

The most fantastic of these ridges is the easternmost one above Lough Arrow. It ascends from north to south in a series of terraces, separated one from the other by steep cliffs. On the second of these platforms is the 'Village', some 50 rings of stones, many of them with uprights outside them. This was possibly some kind of human habitation. On the two highest terraces there are impressive cairns visible at a great distance. A whole day can be spent exploring the Bricklieve Mountains. The effects at sunrise and sunset are sometimes very remarkable.

The ridges can be reached by a signposted road at Traveller's Rest, which is on the Ballymote–Boyle road. A road—not shown on the $\frac{1}{2}''$ map—runs between the second and third ridges on the western side of the mountain. About three quarters of a mile up this valley a track with solid foundations leads first north and then eastwards round the head of the third ridge. Above the track at this point there is a long cairn, over 100 feet long and 8 feet high. In the forecourt is an immense stone slab. Just beyond the fourth ridge the track begins to descend towards Lough Arrow. Here a short walk through the heather brings one to the edge of the canyon beyond which the fifth ridge rises majestically.

[340]

Cairns Hill G 705340 (Eire $\frac{1}{2}''$ Map 7)

One and a half miles south-east of Sligo, marked on the map as Belvoir Hill. The summit of this hill once gave a splendid view of Lough Gill to the east. It is now largely obscured by a plantation of conifers. The view in every other direction, including an unusual one of Sligo town below, is magnificent. On the top is a grass-grown ring fort. There are other remains near-by. A much better view of the lough is from the road on the south side of the hill. To reach it, follow the main road south for 1 mile from the centre of the town; take the left fork and the first turning to the left after $\frac{3}{4}$ mile, and carry on along it until the lough comes into view. The hill top can also be reached with some difficulty from this gravel road.

[341]

The Carrowmore Megaliths Surrounding G 663335 (Eire $\frac{1}{2}''$ Map 7)

Two miles south-west of Sligo. An astonishing concentration of Bronze Age chambered tombs, the greatest prehistoric cemetery in Ireland, extending over $1\frac{1}{2}$ miles of undulating country at the foot of Knocknarea. (See Maeve's Lump.) This is the legendary burial place of the warriors who fell at the battle of North Moytura. (See The Labby.) It is difficult for the layman not to feel sensations of awe in the presence of these structures, some of them mushroom-shaped capstones, others sunk deep in the ground with dark, gaping entrances, others surrounded by kerbs of enormous boulders. Originally there are said to have been more than 100 tombs, of which at least 60 can still be identified. Almost all were originally covered with cairns. They are not immediately obvious to the eye, especially when the grass is growing tall in the fields, but the casual visitor will find various kinds within a hundred yards or so on either side of the road, on the south side of which a megalithic cemetery is marked in Gothic type on the $\frac{1}{2}''$ map.

A mile to the north is the remarkable Tobernaveen Holed Stone (G 665350) – otherwise the Speckled Stone – a thin limestone flag 9 feet high and 10 feet long with a large hole near the bottom of it. The Stone is inconveniently situated in a deep, watery ditch at the junction with another similar ditch in boggy ground. At one time children were passed through the hole to cure them of various ills. To reach it from the megaliths, follow the road northwards towards Sligo, and turn first left on the minor road from Sligo to Knocknarea. Continue past a road to the right which leads to Woodville House until a small bridge is reached. The Stone is 100 yards to the south of this bridge in a field.

[342]

The Cave of the King G 720129 (Eire $\frac{1}{2}''$ Map 7)

On the north-east flank of Keshcorran Mountain, approximately 4 miles east-south-east of Ballymote. This lonely, prehistoric monument, a partially collapsed, twin-chambered tomb, stands on a little hill below the mountain. Some of the stones have circular holes in them. Near it, in a hollow, is the overgrown entrance to a cave. Below the hill is a ring fort and beyond it Lough Labe. On the east flank of Keshcorran there is a beautiful little empty valley. Splendid panorama to the north and west. This is a wild, windy, magical place.

It can be reached from the minor road which runs along the north-west side of Keshcorran, and then by a gravel road to the east along the north side of the mountain. This road begins near the place marked 'Carrownacreevy' on the $\frac{1}{2}''$ map. After 1 mile turn right from it and follow a lane to the highest farmhouse on the slope of the mountain. The Cave of the King is reached by walking towards the lesser of two pronounced gaps in the hillocks below the mountain to the south. It is on the left of this gap; but ask at the farm.

[343]

The Caves of Keshcorran G 704123 (Eire $\frac{1}{2}''$ Map 7)

Three and a half miles south-east of Ballymote. A series of caves in the limestone 600 feet up in the cliffs, on the west escarpment of Keshcorran Mountain. About 16 dark entrances and rifts can be seen from the road below and further off. The largest is at the north end of the cliff. Moss and fern grow in them and they are singularly undisturbed except by cattle. The bones of reindeer, elk, bear and Arctic lemming have been found in them as well as traces of human occupation. In one of these caves, now named after him, Cormac Mac Airt, King of Ireland, was born and suckled by a she-wolf. In another lived Corran the Harper who was given the plain below by the Tuatha de Danann, as a reward of his skill. Here, too, Fionn (q.v. Hill of Allen) was prisoner of three hags. Near-by, at Rath Grainne at the foot of the north end of the hill, Diarmaid and Grainne, the hero and heroine of 'Toraigheacht Diarmada agus Grainne' (The Pursuit of Diarmaid and Grainne) lived for 16 years, and it was from this place that Diarmaid set off on the fatal hunt for the Magic Boar which had been his foster brother before he was turned into a pig.

There was also a great battle at Keshcorran between the Vikings and the men of Connacht in 971 in which the Irish were defeated. Their dead are in the old graveyard at Toomour, 1 mile south-east of Kesh on the north side of the main road from Ballymote to Boyle (marked on the $\frac{1}{2}''$ map as 'Ch' in Gothic type). A great well-attended festivity used to take place here, on Garland Sunday (the last Sunday in July, the last of summer and the first day on which new potatoes were eaten). A gathering is still held here.

Fine views from the caves over Lough Fenagh, and much more extensive ones from the summit of Keshcorran on which there is a round cairn. Caves and summit are reached by a steep path from a grey farmhouse on the small road to Kesh, where it runs parallel to the main Ballymote–Boyle road. Ask directions at the farm.

[344]

Classiebawn Castle G 697563 (Eire $\frac{1}{2}''$ Map 7)

One and three quarter miles north-west of the crossroads at Creevykeel (q.v.), which is on the Sligo–Bundoran road. Massive, very private, early 19th century turreted house, high on the cliffs above the Atlantic, erected by Lord Palmerston and never burned, and now the property of Earl Mountbatten. It exactly expresses the attitude of the age in which it was built. Lord Palmerston also built the solid little harbour at Mullaghmore near-by at a cost of £20,000. There is a good view of the castle, looming against the skyline across the reedy waters of Bunduft Lough, from the Creevykeel–Mullaghmore road.

[345]

The Creevykeel Cairn G 721546 (Eire $\frac{1}{2}''$ Map 7)

Immediately north-east of the Creevykeel crossroads, on the Bundoran–Sligo road. Remains of a large court cairn (a cairn enclosing an oval courtyard) near the main road, with the usual network of overhead cables on every hand, and with a burial chamber—this one in two compartments—meticulously excavated. This prehistoric monument is an impressive sight and the great limestone mountains behind it to the south and east make it easier to forget the 20th century intrusions.

[346]

Cruckancornia G 272277 (Eire $\frac{1}{2}''$ Map 6)

West side of the estuary road from Inishcrone to Ballina, 1½ miles south-south-west of Inishcrone. Otherwise 'The Children of the Mermaid'. The Children, seven pillar stones, of which only five appear to be readily visible, are half hidden in thick grass at the foot of a conspicuous tumulus. The Mermaid was turned into a woman by an O Dowd who obtained her magic mermaid's cloak for the purpose. He married her and had seven children. Subsequently, the Mermaid got her cloak back and became a mermaid again. Before going back to sea she changed her children into seven stones. Fine view from the tumulus of the estuary of the Moy and the great sand dunes at the mouth of it.

[347]

The Doonflin Monument G 570324 (Eire $\frac{1}{2}''$ Map 7)

At Doonflin Lower, 1 mile west of Skreen Church on the south side of the main road. Strange, throne-like monument of cement which looks old but isn't, with an inscription in Gaelic on it which can only be deciphered with difficulty. Translated it reads: 'On this spot in the year 1670 was murdered Dubhaltach Mac Fhirbhisigh, the great historian of Ireland. Erected 1931'. This An Dubhaltach Mac Fhirbhisigh was one of a line of distinguished, hereditary historiographers and poets who served the O Dowds of Tieragh from the 14th to the 17th centuries, and conducted their inauguration ceremonies. He compiled the *Book of Genealogies of Ireland*, now in University College Library, Dublin. His murderer was an English planter named Thomas Crofton (See also Cahermacnaghton.)

[348]

Drumcliff G 688420 (Eire $\frac{1}{2}''$ Map 7)

East of the main road, 3½ miles north of Sligo. Most famous because the church-yard is the burial place of William Butler Yeats (1865–1939) whose epitaph, made by himself, is amongst the most definitive ever written. He died at Roquebrune in France, and his remains were brought to Ireland in 1948 to be buried in the place where his grandfather was once vicar. The plain little Church of Ireland of 1809, with its square tower, topped with finials, rising darkly among the trees, is impressive when seen across the green meadows from the lane which runs eastwards from the bridge over the Drumcliff river. Behind Drumcliff loom the extraordinary precipices of Kings Mountain and Benbulben. In the old Roman Catholic churchyard there is a magnificent 11th century cross, 13 feet high, of sandstone, with sculptures of Adam and Eve, the crucifixion, human figures, animals and interlacing scroll work. On the west side of the main road there is the stump of a round tower, part of a 6th century monastery of St Columcille.

[349]

The Fairy Mound of Laughter G 665172 (Eire $\frac{1}{2}''$ Map 7)

Three quarters of a mile north-north-east of Ballymote, by a small road signposted 'Golf Course'—ask in the town for the road to the golf course. It is useless to ask for the Fairy Mound of Laughter. Sidhean an Ghaire (The Fairy Mound of Laughter) is a round, windy tumulus covered in daisies in summer. It is of little archaeological interest, but the view from it is as lovely as its name. It stands on the west side of the road opposite an iron gate which leads to the golf course. There is another smaller, nobbly tumulus in a field by a farm a short distance nearer to Ballymote on the same side of the road.

[350]

Fionn Mac Cumhail's Fingerstone G 395367 (Eire $\frac{1}{2}''$ Map 7)

One and a half miles south-east of the bridge at Easky to the south of the main Sligo road, opposite a school, next to a modern bungalow. Enormous, elephantine, grey granite rock, cleft neatly from top to bottom. Fionn (see The Giant's Causeway, and Hill of Allen), who as well as a warrior was a great poet, as was his son Ossian, tried to hurl it into the sea and failed. He then broke it in two, using another boulder of which there is no sign. If you try to pass through the cleft three times the rock will close on you.

[351]

The Giant's Griddle G 397282 (Eire $\frac{1}{2}''$ Map 7)

Four miles south-south-west of Dromore West. Magnificent, awe-inspiring portal dolmen, standing alone in the bog. It has a great wedge-shaped capstone supported by three other stones, one of which is keeling over. The underside of the capstone is slightly concave. The great piles of turf on the hills around are like prehistoric fortresses. Somewhere to the west-south-west, $1\frac{1}{2}$ miles away across the Easky river, are the Great and Small Griddles of the Fiana—gallery graves. This is a terrible region in wet weather. The Giant's Griddle is reached from the main Dromore–Sligo road east of Dromore village by a road to the south, or by another west of Dromore on the road to Ballina. Both meet to form a crossroads. If travelling by the former go straight on, if by the latter turn right (otherwise you will end up at Lough

The Glen of Knocknarea, Co. Sligo
(Wonder No. 352)

Cast a cold Eye
On Life, on Death.
Horseman, pass by!
W. B. YEATS
June 13th 1865
January 28th 1939

Yeats' grave, Drumcliff, Co. Sligo (*Wonder No. 348*)

Heapstown Cairn, Co. Sligo (*Wonder No. 353*)

Easky), and go straight on until the Buncrowey river is crossed by a bridge (marked 'Ford' on the map). After 1 mile, beyond a big bend in the road, there is a white farmhouse on the right. Some 50 yards short of it a gate to the left of the road leads to the dolmen.

[352]

The Glen of Knocknarea G 624334 (Eire $\frac{1}{2}''$ Map 7)

Four and a half miles west-south-west of Sligo. A truly remarkable chasm in the limestone, $\frac{3}{4}$ mile long and with cliffs on either side 40–50 feet high, festooned with long strands of ivy. It is filled with the trunks of trees and overgrown with vegetation, but a footpath runs through it. The fern Scolapendrium grows here in great quantities. This secret, hidden valley with its unvisited air, is the epitome of Victorian picturesqueness. The entrance to it is by an iron gate on the south side of the road, $\frac{3}{4}$ mile to the west of Grange House from which the ascent of Knocknarea (see Maeve's Lump) is made. The glen is distinguished on the map by a conventional mark which resembles a stretch of mineral tramway.

[353]

The Heapstown Cairn G 773163 (Eire $\frac{1}{2}''$ Map 7)

At the north end of Lough Arrow, 3 miles north of Ballinafad. An enormous cairn of stones over 200 feet in diameter enclosed by a kerb of large boulders in the demesne of Heapstown House, which is on the east side of the road to Riverstown. The cairn is supposed to have been constructed in a single night and to be the grave of Aillil, son of Eochu Muigmedoin. It is partly concealed by chestnut trees and rhododendrons. It has never been excavated and may contain a passage-grave. (Signpost on road.)

[354]

Inishmurray Island G 570540 (Eire $\frac{1}{2}''$ Map 7)

Four miles north-west of Streedagh Point, on the mainland. Low-lying, bleak island, a mile long, with cliffs and rocky shores. The landing is at a pier at the east end. At the beginning of the 20th century Inishmurray had a population of 90. In the census of 1926 it was given as 74. The island was only finally abandoned in October, 1947. In the 19th century it was noted for the illicit distillation of potheen, and in such quantities that a detachment of the Royal Irish Constabulary was established permanently there to stop it. In addition to potheen making, the inhabitants cultivated oats and potatoes and engaged in fishing.

On the island are the remains of St Molaise's Monastery, which was plundered by the Vikings in 807. They are so wonderful that every effort should be made to visit them. The majority of the buildings stand inside an enormous, drystone walled cashel, 12 feet in height and 15 feet thick in places. Steps lead to the upper parts and there are cells within it. This outer wall has four entrances, the southern one being a modern fabrication by official restorers in 1880.

This tapered, oval enclosure is divided into four parts by other walls. In these compartments there is a really remarkable assemblage of buildings, altars and monuments. In the largest is Teach Molaise, an oratory used by the islanders as their church, a minute building, only 9 feet by 8 feet. It has a stone roof and immensely thick walls and early gravestones with inscriptions, one of which reads: OR DO MUREDACH HU CHOMOCAIN HIC DORMIT (Pray for Muredach, grandson of Chomocain who sleeps here.)

In the church was kept an effigy carved in oak, which the islanders believed to be St Molaise. It may have been a ship's figurehead. It is now in the National Museum in Dublin. Also in this enclosure is Teampall na bhFear (the Men's Church), where the men of the island were buried. (The women were buried at Reilig na Mban, outside the walls on the south-east side, and any body buried in the cemetery of the opposite sex was mysteriously removed by night to its proper place.)

Outside the wall, too, on the north side, is a sweat house (an Irish version of a Turkish bath.) Near the Men's Church there is a cross pillar with holes in it by which pregnant women used to raise themselves from their knees after praying there. Here, too, are the 'Speckled Stones' (Clocha Breaca)—strange stones on one of three altars, used for cursing one's enemies.

In the west enclosure is a clochan, which was used as the school before the island was evacuated; and Teach na Teine, the 'Fire House' in which there was a hearth with a perpetual fire, broken up by the 'restorers' employed by the Office of Public Works.

Around the Island, above the shore, there are 11 stations, memorials and wells which are visited by pilgrims. The round begins at Teach Molaise and then continues round the island in a clock-wise direction from St Mary's Station by the harbour. Some of the stations are in remarkably wild situations, with the sea booming and the gulls crying about them. (Reached by boat from Grange, on the mainland; but arrange a price before setting out.)

[355]

The Labby G 796157 (Eire ½″ Map 7)

One and three quarter miles east of Heapstown Cairn (q.v.). Officially known as the Carrickglass Portal Grave. This extraordinary tomb, a travesty of a prehistoric monument, stands improbably at the bottom of a field where it forms part of a wall. It has an immense weathered and eroded capstone 8 feet thick, 15 feet long and 9 feet wide, and is said to weigh 70 tons, with a thick wig of heather on top of it. It is one of the most eccentric looking objects in Ireland.

To reach it from Bellarish Bridge near the Heapstown Cairn, take the minor road to the north-east, then the second turning on the right after about 2 miles. After just over 1 mile some distance beyond a sharp, almost right-angled bend, there is a lane to a farm with a cattlegrid. Ask permission at the farm. The Labby is just beyond it. If the road from Bellarish Bridge is followed without turning, Lough Nasool is reached. This lough (Na-Suil—'Of the Eyes') is reputed to disappear once every hundred years. It last did so in 1933, through a hole in the bottom known as Balor's Eye. Balor of the Baleful Eye was a giant Fomorian chief. He had a fort on Tory Island, and Cloch Cheannfaoladh (both of which see) has bloody associations with him.

A mile to the south-east of the Labby is Moytirra West, a round cairn (G 807151). The name commemorates the great legendary battle of North Moytura in which the Tuatha de Danann triumphed over the Firbolgs. The graveyard of this battle is supposed to be at Carrowmore (q.v.; see also Eochy's Cairn.)

[356]

Lissadell G 622442 (Eire $\frac{1}{2}''$ Map 7)

Three and a half miles west-north-west of Drumcliff by way of Carney. Fine, severe, late Georgian House built 1836, of the Gore–Booth family, designed by the architect Francis Goodwin of London. It stands in a wooded demesne, overlooking Sligo Bay. Here was born Constance Gore-Booth, later Countess Markievicz, who played an important part in the Easter Rising of 1916 (she was condemned to death by the British, but reprieved). Here, too, lived her sister Eva, the poetess. They were the daughters of Sir Henry Gore-Booth, the Arctic explorer. Constance was the first woman to be elected to Parliament. As a Sinn Fein member, she refused to take her seat at Westminster; but she became Minister for Labour in the Dail Eireann, when de Valera formed a government in April, 1919. Yeats stayed here and later wrote the poem, dedicated to the sisters, which begins: 'The light of evening, Lissadell, Great windows open to the south . . .' The house has a noble music room and, in the dining room, extraordinary, elongated murals by Count Markievicz, including likenesses of the family butler, the gamekeeper and one of himself. On a wall of the great staircase are some sensitive portraits in charcoal by Constance Gore-Booth. The demesne is almost always open, with access to the shore. (The house is open afternoons only, May to September; admission charge.)

[357]

Lough Achree G 519296 (Eire ½″ Map 7)

A lonely tarn formed by an earthquake in 1490, and said to be Ireland's newest lake, high up under the north side of Knockachree in the Slieve Gamph (Ox Mountains). A rough road leads up past it through the mountains and down to Coolaney on the south side. Great views from the road over Sligo Bay, and of Knocknarea and Benbulben.

[358]

Maeve's Lump G 637346 (Eire ½″ Map 7)

Four miles west-south-west of Sligo. Otherwise known as Maeve's Mound or Maeve's Heap; Miscaun Meadhbh, Misgaun Medb, Miosgan Meabha, Miosgan Meva are a few of the Gaelic versions. A great, grey cairn of stones—estimates differ widely about its dimensions, but it seems to be about 200 feet in diameter and over 35 feet high—on the summit of Knocknarea, an enormous, truncated cone of limestone, 1,078 feet high. It could conceal within it a Bronze Age passage-grave, but although it is said to have been picked at by gentry, it has never been excavated scientifically—and long may it be left alone! Under it is supposed to be buried Queen Maeve who was killed by a slingshot while bathing in Lough Ree, Co. Roscommon. There are other tombs near-by. What makes the climb worthwhile (it is an easy 30 to 40 minutes from the east-south-east side near Grange House) are the great views from the summit. To the north-east it extends to the cliffs of Slieve League (q.v.) in south Donegal, to Benbulben in the north-east, to the west along the coast to north Mayo, to the Stags of Broadhaven, off-shore stacks; and far to the south, the cones of the Nephin and Croagh Patrick which loom up above the intervening mountains can be seen in clear weather. Knocknarea falls away in tremendous precipices, especially on the north and west. In these steep faces, above the screes, there are caves.

[359]

The Pigeon Holes G 574426 (Eire ½″ Map 7)

North-west of Raghly Point. On this beautiful, green peninsula, joined to the mainland by a storm beach of sand, there is a deep, narrow inlet through which the sea penetrates into a crevasse, and finally into a hole in a field. These holes are said to produce startling effects when the wind is blowing strongly from the west. To the north is Yellow Strand, a deserted sand beach, nearly 1½ miles long. At its northern end is Knocklane Hill, which is haunted by the White Lady (Baintighearna Bhan), the wife of Sir Nathaniel Gore of Ardtermon (q.v.) who rides here in a phantom chariot drawn by horses. To reach the Pigeon Holes: beyond the little village, take the first turning to the right down a narrow lane past a pair of modern cottages, then walk about ¼ mile parallel to the shore.

[360]

St Farannan's Cliff G 415363 (Eire ½″ Map 7)

Two and three quarter miles east-south-east of Easky, and half a mile north of the main Sligo road. Indicated on the ½″ map by 'Well'. Reached by a small road which leads down to the shore from the Sligo road at Ballymeeny. The place is to the east of it, reached through a field gate. St Farannan's Cliff (Alt Fharannain), a beautiful, densely wooded gully through which a little river descends over a series of miniature moss-grown falls, has a modern statue of the saint above it in a little enclosure. It was an ancient place of pilgrimage and still is. The river bed has a railing to support the pilgrims in their passage across it to the Saint's 'Grave' or 'Bed' in the cliff on the far side. Here also is St Farannan's Well. Very muddy.

[361]

Staad Priory G 627495 (Eire ½″ Map 7)

Two miles west of Grange. The only remains of this little building, which is on the site of a monastery founded by St Molaise, is part of the nave and a wall under which cattle shelter from the elements, but its situation is beautiful in the fields above the bleak, stony seashore on the edge of which mounds of seaweed dry in the wind. Inland there is a line of broken-down, thatched cottages and beyond them in the distance rises the fantastic mass of Benbulben. On the lonely Strand of Streedagh, to the north-east, large numbers of bodies from three Armada ships wrecked here were cast ashore and Sir Geoffry Fenton, the Elizabethan translator and statesman, counted 1,100 corpses on the sands. Four miles off Streedagh is Inishmurray Island (q.v.).

[362]

Tober Tullaghan G 620263 (Eire ½″ Map 7)

On Tullaghan Hill at the eastern end of the Slieve Gamph Mountains, 1 mile north-east of Coolaney and ½ mile north of the Collooney road. A track from a white farmhouse on the north side of the road leads up to it through four fields. Tober Tullaghan (St Patrick's Well), a Wonder of early Christian Ireland, because the water in it is said to ebb and flow with the tides of the sea, is a place of pilgrimage. It is near the summit of the conical hill, half-hidden in bracken. To reach it from the foot of Tullaghan Hill go up from the last gate in a stone wall, past a couple of thorn trees. There are some little offerings at the well, left by pilgrims. Fine view from the summit of Tullaghmore Hill on which there are remains of raths (stone forts). The north face is sheer.

LEITRIM

[363]

The Black Pig's Dyke G 954463 (Eire $\frac{1}{2}$" Map 7)

Between Lough Melvin and Upper Lough Macnean. A series of prehistoric earthworks about 6 miles long, said to have formed the frontier with Ulster, otherwise known as the Worm Ditch or The Black Pig's Race; so named because they are supposed to have been thrown up by a rooting pig. There are quite well-preserved stretches of bank in some places, with ditches on either side, in others a single ditch, but persistence is needed in finding them. One easily found section of the dyke crosses the road north of Kiltyclogher about one-third of a mile west-north-west of the height marked 329 feet on the map (reference above), where it is very apparent on the south side of the road, in a field. It is not very exciting. Travelling earthworks of this kind, which may be part of the same defensive scheme, can be seen in Roscommon (see the Doon of Drumsna) and in Longford between Lough Sheelin and Lough Gowna (see Mote of Granard).

[364]

The Corracloona Grave G 997428 (Eire $\frac{1}{2}$" Map 7)

Near the west side of the road north of Corracloona schoolhouse. Otherwise known as Tuomba Mor Liagattach. Remains of a cairn and windswept, chambered tomb among the heather. In the entrance there is an enormous stone with a kennel-hole in the bottom of it which leads into a chamber 11 feet long and 8 feet wide. Another huge slab leans against it. This holed stone is rather like the one at Tobernaveen. (See Carrowmore.)

[365]

The Eagle's Rock G 783489 (Eire $\frac{1}{2}$" Map 7)

Four and three quarter miles south-south-west of Kinlough on the west side of Glenade. Fantastic, limestone monolith, separated from the cliffs of the main mountain by a deep gorge. It can be seen from 5 miles away on the coast road to Bundoran.

Two miles to the south-west of it, detached from the same escarpment, at Peaka-dawn, there is another strange formation with long fingers of rock rising from it. A rough lane, not marked on the $\frac{1}{2}''$ map, leads close under the Eagle's Rock from the minor road through Glenade, west of the main road, and then returns to it. The minor road along the south side of the Glenade Lough passes close to Peakadawn.

[366]

Fenagh H 110074 (Eire $\frac{1}{2}''$ Map 7)

Three miles south-west of Ballinamore. Site of a monastery of St Callin, burned 1360. Two ruined churches, one higher than the other, stand on a slight eminence above a reedy river bed. The one nearer the road has barrel vaulting. The east window is beautiful. To the right of the window is a double monument to the Payton family, with a gryphon and reindeer on it. On the outside of the building the gable-brackets have sculptured heads of men wearing jellybag hats. At the east end of the graveyard there is a strange modern tomb, with a medieval-looking crucifix on it, and in the west wall, the tomb of a bonesetter.

[367]

The Glenaniff Road G 855533 to G 912480 (Eire $\frac{1}{2}''$ Map 7)

A very lonely mountain road which crosses the mountains from the shores of Lough Melvin and descends into Glenaniff. It begins on the Kinlough–Rossinver road about 3 miles from Kinlough. On the right of it, as it ascends, some remarkable pyramidical rock and earth formations can be seen under the cliffs. At the head of the pass there are other prominent but miniature cliffs. From here the road descends the beautiful green vale of the Glenaniff river from which great hills run up on either side.

[368]

O Rourke's Table G 800353 (Eire $\frac{1}{2}''$ Map 7)

Three miles north of Dromahaire. Reached by a footpath west of the junction of the Dromahaire–Manorhamilton road with a minor road to Sligo, by way of Colgagh. It is named after the hereditary chiefs of this district. Great views of Lough Gill from the summit of this flat-topped, grass-covered hill, and of the mountains to the north. Worth the short climb.

[369]

Park's Castle G 784353 (Eire $\frac{1}{2}''$ Map 7)

On the north shore of Lough Gill, 7 miles south-east of Sligo. A splendid, 17th century castle which incorporates a dwelling house. The bawn has a high wall with turrets. Fine gatehouse, with towers on either side. There is a small jetty. (Key at near-by farm.)

[370]

St Mel's Abbey G 842548 (Eire ½″ Map 7)

One and a half miles east-south-east of Kinlough, otherwise known as Rosclogher Church. Ruins of a small religious house on the lonely south shore of Lough Melvin, hidden in a grove of sycamore trees. On a tiny man-made island (a crannog) off-shore among the reeds, are the ivy-grown remains of Rosclogher, otherwise Clancy's Castle. De Cuellar, a captain of the Spanish Armada, shipwrecked on the coast of Sligo, is supposed to have taken refuge here. The ruins are ¾ mile from the Kinlough–Rossinver road by a signposted track.

[371]

Sruth-in-Aghaidh-an-Aird G 762436 (Eire ½″ Map 7)

Eight miles west-north-west of Manorhamilton, on the north side of Lough Glencar, at its eastern end. 'The Stream Against the Height': a series of three falls on the south side of the massif, of which Truskenmore is the highest part (2,126 feet) and Benbulben the most impressive. The lowest, which is accessible by a path from the road, pours over a cliff into a circular pool among trees. The way to this lower fall is signposted. The upper ones can be reached from a forestry road a little to the west; but the gorge to the foot of the final cliff is very difficult and overgrown. The water is said to go up instead of down when the wind is in the south, but it may not do so now as there are many new plantations of trees.

In the lough below there is a small, round island with pines growing on it, that may have been a crannog—an artificial island, made of brushwood, boulders, peat, etc.

DONEGAL

[372]

The Bawan G 702980 (Eire ½″ Map 3)

One mile south of Naran. A really wonderful great fortification, on an island hidden away on an arm of lonely Lough Doon. It consists of a huge drystone rampart about

17 feet high, roughly oval in form, with a walk 8 feet wide at the top. There is a single entrance on the east side. On the left side of the entrance a tunnel and steps lead up through the wall to the rampart; another gallery on the right hand leads into the interior of the wall; other flights of steps lead up the ramparts from the inside of the fort where otherwise there is nothing at all.

At one time, before the level of the lake was lowered, The Bawan appeared to be rising straight from the water. It was partly reconstructed in modern times. It is very impressive at sunset, dark and immutable it seems between the shining waters of the lough and the sky. To reach it from the road from Ardara to Naran and Portnoo, turn left immediately north of Kilclooney and then right again by a signposted road. A boat can be hired (well worth the charge) from the farm, ½ mile further on, or if only a distant view is wanted, it can be seen from a little hill above a ruined cottage along the road a little to the north.

[373]

Burt Castle C 320193 (Eire ½″ Map 1)

One and a half miles north-north-west of Newtown Cunningham. It can be reached from this village, on the Letterkenny–Londonderry road, by a lane. Ruins of a 16th century fortress of the O Dohertys on a hill above Lough Swilly. It has an oblong tower with vaulting and two tall, round turrets at opposite corners, one with a circular staircase in it. Splendid views from it over Lough Swilly, especially at sunset. Down by the shore are the ruins of Burt church.

[374]

The Carndonagh Crosses C 463450 (Eire ½″ Map 1)

Half a mile west of the village of Carndonagh, on the main road. Four early crosses, three of them in the graveyard. The finest is St Patrick's Cross, of khaki coloured sandstone, one of the greatest of the early cross slabs (perhaps 7th century.) It is improbably sited on the roadway, but defies the relative squalor of its situation. The east side facing the road has two broad bands of interlacing ribbons on it which almost entirely fill the arms. Two strange little birds beat their wings on either side. Below them is a crucifixion, the figure with attenuated arms, flanked by two bird-like figures. Beneath, in a separate box, are three owl-like humans which have been identified as ecclesiastics. The west face has ribbons carved on it and the shallow sides are also carved—the south side with three figures, the north with a pattern. The cross is flanked by two small stone tablets with solemn little figures carved on them, from which the American cartoonist, Saul Steinberg, must surely have received inspiration, and other carvings.

[375]

The Cashelmore Bell Tower C 054326 (Eire ½″ Map 1)

One and a half miles north of Creeslough. A strange, castellated, 19th century bell tower, with a huge bell in it but without a church, on a gorse-covered mound above some crossroads. Below it, by the main road, there is a shrine.

[376]

Cloch Cheannfaoladh B 949326 (Eire ½″ Map 1)

Half a mile north-east of the main road at Falcarragh, on the right side of a lane which runs beside a hand-ball court and a sports ground on the south side of the demesne of Ballyconnell House. 'The Stone of the Head of Faoladh': a red-veined, quartzite rock on top of a drum tower hidden away among trees beside the road. The red veins are the crystallized blood of Faoladh, whose head was cut off by the giant, Balor of the Baleful Eye, on one of his disastrous visits to the mainland from Tory Island (q.v.). Balor had stolen a wonderful cow from Faoladh, a champion warrior, and to avoid reprisals he decapitated him using the stone as a chopping block. The stone is also commonly called Cloghaneely. There are many versions of this and the other legends of Balor. The tower was erected by Wybrants Olphert and his wife Sarah in 1774.

[377]

Clonca Church and Cross C 535474 (Eire ½″ Map 2)

On the south side of a minor road from the Moville–Culdaff road, 1 mile south-east of Culdaff. Turn west at a yellow church (signposted). The little church, which is roofless, stands in a field in open country. The west door has a very old lintel stone over it carved with a cross; on the left of it is another stone with vague, primitive shapes carved on it, one of which may be a bird. Inside, on the left by the east window, there is the long, grey, 16th century tombstone of Magnus MacOrristin, with a Gaelic inscription which was read many years ago as 'Fergus MacAllen made this stone—Magnus MacOrristin of the Isles under this Mound', but it can no longer be deciphered to its full extent. On the stones are designs that resemble fleurs-de-lys, a long sword, a hurly stick (it could be a golf club) and a ball.

Outside, to the west of the church, is the shaft of St Bedan's Cross. It is slightly inclined from the vertical and carved with marvellous interlaced designs. On one side is the miracle of the loaves and fishes with Christ sitting in a chair. On the other are two animals above twin, seated figures. In the churchyard is the tombstone of the Rev. McOolgan with a hand, a Bible and a chalice carved on it.

[378]

Cooley Church C 599382 (Eire $\frac{1}{2}''$ Map 2)

Three quarters of a mile west of Moville. Outside the gate is a magnificent monolithic cross, 9 feet 3 inches tall. The shaft has a hole in it and on the slab there is a footprint of St Patrick, who is supposed to have built the first church here. The remains of the present one are very small. In the churchyard is the Skull House, a tiny, drystone building with a moss-grown stone roof of tremendous solidity. It contains bones, but no skulls. In the churchyard is a stone with beautiful lettering modelled on Gaelic forms to Mary Ann Cary. Reached from the main road west of Moville by a signposted lane.

[379]

The Croaghmuckros Coast Road G 654751 to G 615760 (Eire $\frac{1}{2}''$ Map 3)

Runs from Shalwy, $3\frac{1}{2}$ miles west of Killybegs, to Kilcar. The little sandy bays with the green fields above them and, on the side of the steep hills, the white cabins, with their golden thatched roofs guyed to the walls to prevent them being whisked away by the wind make this one of the most beautiful drives, or better walks, in Donegal. Here a more ancient way of life seems miraculously preserved. As one goes westwards along the side of Croaghmuckros, great views open up of the sheer cliffs at Carrigan Head and of the great dark mass of Slieve League beyond (q.v.). From Kilcar another beautiful road follows the north side of Tawny Bay and the estuary of the Glen river up to Carrick.

[380]

Doe Castle C 084318 (Eire $\frac{1}{2}''$ Map 1)

Two miles east-north-east of Creeslough. Reached by a signposted lane from Cashel on the main Creeslough–Carrickart road. Marvellous, tan-coloured town house, a stronghold of the Clan MacSuibhne (MacSweeny), which settled here from Scotland at the invitation of the O Donnells, and became their gallowglasses (mercenaries). It stands on a rocky promontory at the head of Sheephaven, defended on the shoreward side by a rock-cut ditch, formerly spanned by a drawbridge and with a portcullised gatehouse. Eoghan Oge MacSweeny was foster father to Red Hugh O Donnell who lived here as a boy. It fell to the Cromwellians in 1650. Here lived General George Vaughan Hart who fought at Long Island, Brandywine and Seringapatam and died 1832. His initials are over the doorway. At one time, cannon captured at Seringapatam were kept in the courtyard. This labyrinthine castle was occupied until the beginning of the 20th century. It has a great keep with a fine view from the top, and is defended by curtain walls with circular towers. In the adjoining graveyard is a strange MacSweeny tombstone, carved with figures of primitive animals, etc. Another MacSweeny tombstone is at Killybegs (see Killaghtee).

[381]

Donegal Friary G 926781 (Eire ½″ Map 3)

A quarter of a mile south-west of Donegal town, by a signposted track west of the main road. Fragmentary but impressive ruins of a Franciscan friary, above the shore where the river Eske opens into an estuary. It was founded in 1474 by Red Hugh O Donnell, the son of O Donnell of Tir Conaill, and his wife Fingalla, daughter of Conor O Brien of Thomond. They are both buried here as is their son, Hugh, who became a Franciscan monk. The English took the friary twice, and the second time, when it was being besieged by the Great Red Hugh O Donnell, their gunpowder store blew up, destroying the buildings. After the failure of the Spanish landing at Kinsale in 1601, this Red Hugh fled to Spain; but died the next year, possibly by poisoning, and was buried at Valladolid, aged 28. Here, too, the famous history of Ireland, the *Annals of the Four Masters,* was begun in 1632. It covered 1,100 quarto pages and 4,500 years of the history of Ireland up to 1616. There are walls with two noble windows in them still standing, an east window and another in the south transept. The arches of what remains of the cloisters are half buried. Below the rock on which the ruins stand there is a little jetty. Fine views across the estuary to Ballyboyle Island and beyond.

[382]

The Doon Rock and Holy Well C 115197 (Eire ½″ Map 1)

One and three quarter miles west of Kilmacrenan. Signposted by a road to the west from the main road to Creeslough, 1 mile from Kilmacrenan. A great flat-topped rock looming above the moorland, its base half hidden among trees. This is Carraig an Duin where the O Donnells, Lords of Tyrconnell (see St Columcille's Oratory), went through the rituals of inauguration. The stone used during these ceremonies is at the south end of the rock. The medieval Welsh topographer, Giraldus Cambrensis, gives a disagreeable account of the inauguration of an O Donnell in the latter part of the 12th century, during which the chief performed his ablutions in a soup made from a freshly killed white cow which was afterwards drunk by his tribesmen; but nobody believes this.

At the south-eastern foot of the hill there is a holy well. Here, in the green grass, is an extraordinary bed of relics. Dozens of sticks stuck in the ground are wrapped around with rags, pieces of lace, silk and cotton, together with handkerchiefs, scarves and unidentifiable articles of clothing some of them brightly coloured, rosaries, beads and pins; one has the impression of being in the presence of a tribe of midget beggars. It is a strange spectacle. Near-by is the well. It is much visited, especially on Sundays.

[383]

The Druidical Circle C 542475 (Eire ½″ Map 2)

On Mass Hill, 1¼ miles south-south-east of Culdaff. Fine remnants of a stone circle, of which eight pointed stones remain standing, on a windy hill to the west of the main road. Reached by a lane, then on foot. Good view to the west.

[384]

The Eas Dunan Waterfall G 978879 (Eire ½″ Map 3)

Six and a half miles north-east of Donegal. A beautiful cascade on the Coraber river which here falls over a cliff into a deep pool, high up in the hills. A marvellous place for a swim if there are no horse flies about. To reach it follow a lane from the north end of Lough Eske to a farm beyond Edergole Bridge. From this farm walk up what is a well-defined but very boggy track in any but the driest weather, towards a pass to the north-north-east, keeping the gorge of the Coraber on the right. The fall is hidden from view on the right. (Allow about 45 minutes to reach it.) There are splendid views of the lough below.

Two miles northwards is the very lonely Lough Belshade, the source of the Coraber, high up between the Bluestack and Croaghbarnes Mountains. To reach it continue along the right bank of the river by the track above the fall. Allow 1½ hours to Lough Belshade from the farm.

[385]

Errigal Mountain B 928209 (Eire ½″ Map 1)

Six and a half miles south of Gortahork. A huge, white quartzite cone, with loose screes tumbling down its side, the highest mountain in Donegal, 2,466 feet. From some angles it resembles an immense pallid slag heap. The ascent is best made from Dunlewy on the shore of Dunlewy Lough, and takes about 2 hours, first over heather and rough grass, then over loose screes. There are two summits joined by a narrow ridge called 'One Man's Path'. The north-east side, towards Lough Altan, is very steep. The World Domino Championship Congress is held here once every five years, in March. It seems an exposed place for such a gathering. Great views in clear weather as far south as Benbulben, Co. Sligo, and to Knocklayd Mountain above Ballycastle in Antrim, some 75 miles to the east-north-east.

[386]

The Gap of Mamore C 318433 (Eire $\frac{1}{2}''$ Map 1)

Seven miles north-north-west of Buncrana. Impressive pass between Mamore Hill and the Urris Hills. The road climbs to it with steep bends from Lenankee on the west side, a singularly unchanged village in the beautiful green country on the shore of Lough Swilly. The Gap between the mountains is extremely narrow. Fine views over Lough Swilly from the north side. The descent from the Gap to the lonely country to the south-east is by a dead straight road in one unparalleled swoop.

[387]

Glencolumbkille Surrounding G 530850 (Eire $\frac{1}{2}''$ Map 3)

Six miles north-west of Carrick. A place of rare beauty and interest even in the West. Here, among the sand dunes, facing the Atlantic or in the green glen with the stony mountain rising steeply above it on the north side, to the flanks of which St Columcille retired to wrestle with the demons which beset him, it is easy to understand how he and the pilgrims who have followed him here over the centuries became attracted to this place. Here, on St Columcille's Day (July 9) a three-mile-long Turas (pilgrimage) takes place in the course of which 15 stations are visited in the $3\frac{1}{2}$ hours before sunrise. The stations are marked by early Christian and prehistoric remains, sometimes both together in one place.

The first station is a megalithic tomb set in the west wall of the Protestant church, the spire of which is prominent in the glen, and which is on the site of a far older foundation. In the churchyard there is an eerie souterrain which is entered through a trap-door. It extends east and west from the foot of the entrance shaft for a total of 50 feet and the eastern arm has a chamber in it beyond which the passage continues. The fifteenth and last station—a pair of cross-slabs—is also in the churchyard.

The second station is a beautiful, slender stone, probably a cross-pillar, on a hillock west of the church.

The third station is to the north-west of it, $\frac{3}{4}$ mile away across Garveross Bridge, a narrow cement structure. It is called Ait na nGlun (the Place of the Knees) and consists of small heaps of pebbles, 'healing stones' which the pilgrims pass round their bodies. They are in a field to the left of the track which leads to the fourth, fifth, sixth and seventh stations, the first three of which are about $\frac{1}{4}$ mile uphill to the north-west in Beefan where there is a small, beautiful group of old, thatched cabins. Just to the south of them is the fourth station, a circular prehistoric stone enclosure and a cross-slab on Mullach na Croise, a little hill with a beautiful view from it.

The fifth station is another enclosure, the little roofless chapel of the saint with his bed in it, a broken slab, cairns and cross-slabs. To the east of the enclosure is the sixth station, Leac na mBonn (The Stone of the Footsoles), and other stones with curative properties, one of which has a depression in it.

The seventh station is to the north-west on a crest—Columcille's Well—where offerings are left. On the way to it is the Saint's Chair. Above the well, on the rocky side of the mountain, is Screig na nDeamhan, the place where Columcille conquered the demons.

The eighth station is eastwards, at the foot of the mountain, about 400 yards beyond the fourth station, Mullach na Croise. This is Garraidhe an Turas (the Garden of the Pilgrimage) where there are cairns and cross-slabs.

The ninth station is $\frac{3}{4}$ mile away to the east in Farranmacbride, a cairn in a field on the left of the little road which runs northwards towards the mountain east of the church. Here there is also a cross-slab, Clo'n Aoineach, a tall slender stone with a hole bored in it through which the pilgrim can descry heaven.

The tenth station is a cairn with a cross-slab, $\frac{1}{4}$ mile south-east on this side of the road; the eleventh is another cairn a little to the east; the twelfth is a cairn with a magnificent cross-pillar on the other side of the road; and the thirteenth and fourteenth are both cairns with pillars, the first by the police station at Gennew, the second on the other side of the Murlin river which is crossed by stepping stones. The fifteenth is in the churchyard.

Beyond Glencolumbkille, on the south side of the road to Malin More, is a 'Folk Village' built with the help of a grant from the Tourist Board and run by local people. 'Folk Village', with its Teutonic undertones, does little justice to this fascinating collection of old houses, reconstructed from ancient materials assembled here together with their original furnishings and all the necessary gear of life in the glen. The local women who act as guides are refreshingly interesting to listen to. Delicious teas are served with bread baked over the fire in the old way.

[388]

The Greencastle Forts C 657404 (Eire $\frac{1}{2}''$ Map 2)

At Greencastle. Extensive, early 19th century fortifications, built in 1812, at the time of the threat of Napoleonic invasion, to command the entrance to Lough Foyle and the approaches to Londonderry. There are two forts, an upper and a lower. The upper part incorporates a Martello tower and is connected by a winding staircase in a massive tower with the lower part. The upper part is now an hotel. Magnificent views from the ramparts over the strait to the mountains of Derry and the coast of Antrim.

On Magilligan Point in Derry (see Duncrun Graveyard) nearly a mile away, across the strait, there is another Martello tower. This and the Greencastle forts could bring 26 guns to bear. Next to the forts, and in an equally commanding position on a rock, are the huge and impressive ruins of the medieval castle, reduced to its present condition by 16th century artillery bombardment.

[389]

The Grianan of Aileach C 366197 (Eire ½″ Map 1)

Four miles north-east of Newtown Cunningham. An extraordinary great cashel, a circular stone enclosure with drystone walls 17 feet high and 17 feet thick, 803 feet up on the bare turf summit of Greenan Mountain. There is only one narrow entrance, on the east side. Until some time in the 1870s, when it was restored by a Dr Bernard of Derry, the walls were much reduced in height. On the inside there are two, and in some places three walks, one above the other connected by stairways. Long galleries run through the interior of the walls. Surrounding it on the hill there are remains of concentric earthworks. This was a sacred meeting place and the royal summer palace of the rulers of Tir Eoghain (Tyrone). It was destroyed twice—in the 7th century, and at the beginning of the 12th century by Muriertach O Brien of Munster. What one sees now is in part a 19th century reconstruction which is rather sniffed at by archaeologists, but for the layman both the site and the great brooding cashel are memorable. A new motor road to the summit destroys, to some extent, its unique isolation. Tremendous views down Lough Swilly and Lough Foyle towards the sea.

[390]

Horn Head C 012422 (Eire ½″ Map 1)

Three miles north of Dunfanaghy. A road not marked on the ½″ map leads to the great headland, 626 feet high with steep cliffs. Fine views from it of Tory Island (q.v.) to the north-west, and to the westwards of Inishbofin and Inishbeg islands, and eastwards as far as Malin Head. In clear weather the Paps of Jura in the Inner Hebrides can be seen, 100 miles to the north-east. Templebreaga Arch is a magnificent natural coastal phenomenon, 1½ miles to the south-west of the Head.

[391]

Inver G 819780 (Eire ½″ Map 3)

Seven miles west of Donegal. Small fishing village by a sand bar at the mouth of

The Cave of the King, Co. Sligo *(Wonder No. 342)*

ilclooney Dolmens, Co. Donegal *(Wonder No. 392)*

Slieve League, Co. Donegal *(Wonder No.*

the Eany river where it flows into Inver Bay. The little ruined church, in a walled churchyard, stands alone on a promontory by the river, and is surrounded by water on three sides when the tide is high. In the churchyard by the west door is the shattered tombstone of Thomas Nesbit (died 1801), the inventor of the gun-harpoon for whaling. The church is roofless and overgrown. Beyond the wall, a brightly coloured rowing boat lies high and dry in a field. In the distance across the meadows east of Inver Bridge, the tall spire of a Church of Ireland church rises among the trees, in a landscape that might have been painted by Constable.

[392]

The Kilclooney Dolmens G 723967 (Eire $\frac{1}{2}$″ Map 3)

Four miles north-north-west of Ardara on the Naran road, and $\frac{1}{4}$ mile east of a farmhouse at Kilclooney More, between Kilclooney Bridge and the village of Kilclooney. They are visible from the road. There are two tombs, originally covered by the same cairn; the larger one a really remarkable structure with an enormous, roughly triangular capstone, supported by three sloping stones, 6 feet high. From a distance it looks like a flying saucer landed in the bog. The other smaller megalith has a more collapsed appearance. To reach them, ask permission at the farm to go through the farmyard, as this is the shortest way.

[393]

Killaghtee Church G 754755 (Eire $\frac{1}{2}$″ Map 3)

Half a mile south-west of the village of Dunkineely, which is on the Donegal–Killybegs road. The church is reached by a wooded path beyond an iron gate, which is by a disused railway bridge. This lonely, ancient ruin stands in a churchyard overlooking McSwyne's Bay. The roofless church is full of tomb slabs which make an irregular floor. In the graveyard there is an unusual cross slab with a Maltese Cross carved on it in relief. The arms of the cross are not parallel with the sides, and this gives it the look of a catherine wheel in action. Below it there is a knot, symbol of the Trinity. To the south, on the shore of the bay, are the forbidding-looking ruins of a castle of the McSwynes (the MacSweenys of Banagh). A very strange tombstone of Niall Mor MacSweeny stands against a wall of the otherwise rather unattractive churchyard at Killybegs, 4 miles west of Dunkineely. Another, similar stone, also of the MacSweenys, is in the graveyard at Doe Castle (q.v.).

[394]

Killydonnell Friary C 247182 (Eire $\frac{1}{2}$″ Map 1)

Two miles south-east of Rathmelton by a signposted lane (unsuitable for motors), from the minor road from Rathmelton to Letterkenny, which is itself east of the main road. Ivy-covered ruins with great, gaping windows, the west end of which returns powerful echoes, down by the shore of the estuary of the river Swilly. It was founded by the O Donnells for the Franciscans in the 16th century. In a creepy vault under the east end, are the remains of the last of the Stewarts of Fort Stewart. There is a legend that the bell of Killydonnell was carried off by raiders from Tyrone who put to sea with it in a boat. A storm came up and they were drowned. The bell is heard to toll once every seven years at midnight.

At Rathmelton, to the north-west, there are some fine old, multi-storeyed stone warehouses on the quay. The little town was formerly a very busy place with corn mills, a brewery, bleach greens and linen manufacturies, and these buildings must have been connected with one or other of these industries.

[395]

The Leckemy Sweat House C 587437 (Eire $\frac{1}{2}$″ Map 1)

Three and a half miles north-north-west of Moville. Behind a farmhouse to the east of the minor road to Culdaff, $\frac{1}{2}$ mile north of Leckemy post office (entrance at the second pair of white gateposts—ask permission at the farm). Small, oval, drystone building, an Irish version of a Turkish bath, below a little cliff, with a domed roof which has a rectangular aperture in it to allow the steam to escape. The interior is now green with moss. The entrance is very low and not for the obese. Some of these Irish sweat houses were in use until quite recently. They were usually heated with a turf fire for some hours before they were to be used, and the ashes were then removed and rushes put down to protect the bathers' feet.

[396]

Maghera G 660907 (Eire $\frac{1}{2}$″ Map 3)

Four and a half miles west of Ardara. Lonely hamlet of white houses, at the foot of the glen of the Owenree river, on the east side of Slievetooey Mountain. Near it, on the shore road from Ardara, the dark Essaranka waterfall pours over a cliff. Nearby there is a shrine where mass was said in Penal Times. About $\frac{3}{4}$ mile west of Maghera, on the south side of Loughroe Beg Bay, there are three caves in the cliffs. They can be entered at low water. The tide comes in very quickly over the sands. The coast to the westward of Maghera as far as Glencolumbkille (q.v.) is amongst the most impressive and least known stretches on the west coast of Ireland. Between Gull Island, $2\frac{1}{2}$ miles from Maghera, and Tormore Island below Port Hill (both huge off-shore rocks), there are 4 miles of immense cliffs. Marvellous coastal phenomena can also be seen at Sturrall, 2 miles west-south-west of Port, a headland joined to the mainland by a horrible knife-edge ridge with precipices on either side.

At Glen Head, where there are the remains of an old signal tower, a fantastic, smooth precipice falls 745 feet to the water. The 20-mile coastal walk from Teelin Bay over Slieve League and then by way of Malin Beg to Glencolumbkille and Maghera is, as the Murray's *Guide to Ireland* of 1912 says, 'hardly excelled by any locality in the British Isles'.

[397]

The Pass of Glengesh G 688860 (Eire ½″ Map 3)

Four miles south-west of Ardara. From the summit of the Pass the road descends by hairpin bends into the deep glen. Very beautiful in the late afternoon when the green valley is illuminated by the last rays of the sun.

[398]

The Poisoned Glen B 942167 (Eire ½″ Map 1)

One and a half miles south-east of Dunlewy. At the entrance to this strange place stands the roofless 19th century Protestant church of Dunlewy, built of white quartzite, with tall finials on the tower and gaping windows. At the head of the glen, in the interior of the Derryveagh Mountains, sheer cliffs form a huge amphitheatre. The name of this place derives from the poisonous spurge (*genus Euphorbia*) which grows in it. Perhaps because of it, the water in the glen is said to be unsuitable for drinking.

To reach it: from the church follow the rough track, leaving a huge split rock and later, a solitary holly tree, on the immediate left, keeping away from the stream that flows through the glen. The place is a morass in wet weather. From the head of the glen a very rough, steep ascent leads south-east up into the Gap of Ballaghgeeha (1,400 feet), which is hemmed in on either side by great cliffs. From here one can descend to the long glen of the Owenbeagh river. From Owenbeagh Glen, one road goes west-south-west to Doocharry (about 9 miles), another eastwards to Lough Gartan and Church Hill (about 8 miles). Up the glen to the north-east, is the great Glenveagh Deer Forest, one of the few in Ireland.

[399]

The Pullins Surrounding G 942702 (Eire ½″ Map 3)

One and a half miles east of Ballintra, in the demesne of Brown Hall. A remarkable, deep and narrow limestone gorge, choked with debris and trees blown down by

'Hurricane Debby' in 1962. Here the river Blackwater flows through caves, the roofs of which have collapsed in some places, forming enormous holes open to the sky. Very impressive, but difficult to find.

There are two ways of approaching the Pullins—in either case permission must be asked, as the land is private.

(1) By a minor road south-east from Ballintra, which leads to a lodge gate on the west side of the demesne (ask directions here).

(2) By a minor road eastwards of the main Sligo–Ballintra road, ½ mile north of the latter. After 1¾ miles, a ruined lodge is reached on the right. The drive to the house crosses a little bridge over the Blackwater. Just before it, a very overgrown track leads off at a slight angle from the right bank of the river. By following this and crossing a field with a power line running over it, the Pullins can be reached.

[400]

Ray Church B 955327 (Eire ½″ Map 1)

One and a half miles east-north-east of Falcarragh. A track leads to it westwards from the main road, by a shop. In the graveyard of this ruined medieval church near the banks of the river Ray, there is an immense ringed cross made of six flagstones set flat in the ground. At the foot of it is a millstone and there are other ancient millstones hidden in the undergrowth inside the church. This cross is supposed to have been hewn by St Columcille himself on Muckish Mountain, which rises to a height of 2,197 feet 4 miles to the south-east, and to have been intended for a church on Tory Island (q.v.).

[401]

The Reilig at Bruckless G 748775 (Eire ½″ Map 3)

One mile north-west of Dunkineely. A place of pilgrimage in a field immediately east of the bridge which carries the main road to Killybegs over the little Qily river. Small heaps of stones mark the stations among the rushes and bog cotton, which are visited on and after Midsummer Day, June 24, for 9 days. Reilig is the Irish word for cemetery.

[402]

St Columcille's Oratory C 059186 (Eire ½″ Map 1)

At Churchtoen, on the north-west side of Lough Akibbon, 2 miles north-west of Church Hill. Small, ruined oratory and graveyard in a beautiful position on the hillside overlooking Lough Akibbon. In it there is an altar and on it there are offerings left by pilgrims. The oratory is built near the place where the saint is said to have been born in 521, and it is the site of his monastery. Near the road there is a holy well and an ancient stone cross; another old cross is higher up, under the trees. This was the burial place of the O Donnells of Tyrconnell.

The actual place of St Columcille's birth is said to be a flagstone about $\frac{3}{4}$ mile to the south of the oratory on the hillside above Lough Gartan, where a modern cross commemorates the event. Anyone who sleeps a night on this flagstone will henceforward be proof against homesickness. St Columcille is thought to have been baptized at Teampall Douglas (q.v.).

[403]

Slieve League G 545782 (Eire $\frac{1}{2}$″ Map 3)

Two and a half miles west of Carrick. Among the greatest cliffs of the western world, from their highest point falling 1,972 feet to the sea, at an angle of about 45 degrees, though in some places much steeper, and after Croaghaun on Achill Island (q.v.) the summit of which is 2,192 feet above the water, the greatest sea cliffs in Ireland.

The best way to see them is to take the steep mountain road from Teelin on the south-west side of the bay, to Bunglass Point by Lough O Mulligan. The road passes above Carrigan Head where the cliffs are 764 feet high and absolutely sheer. On them, standing on a crazy ledge, there is a watchtower and a ruined coast-watching station.

At Bunglass Point is Amharc Mor (the Great View). There is nothing anywhere in Ireland like these great cliffs, stained many colours by the minerals within them. Bunglass Cliff rises 1,024 feet sheer. From here an active person can climb to the summit by the cliff edge in about an hour, by way of the Eagle's Nest, 1,570 feet to the water, the sheerest place. The going is hard. Just before the summit is One Man's Path, a knife-edged ridge with a fall of 1,800 feet on the seaward side, and a horrible drop to an inland lough on the other.

An easier route to the top is by a track which leads up an interior glen of the mountain from the Carrick–Teelin road. If with a car, leave it near a little lough and walk the rest (about 45 minutes). Great views in clear weather. The cliffs should not be visited at all in bad visibility and high winds, when they are very dangerous.

At the east end of the summit are the remains of an oratory and two wells, the site of a hermitage of Saint Assicus, a metalworker whom St Patrick had put in charge of a church at Elphin in Co. Mayo. He is said to have told a lie by accident and fled here to do penance. After seven years his monks induced him to return, but he died *en route*.

The walk westwards along the cliffs and down to Malin Beg is magnificent. But to see Slieve League to full advantage, go by boat. Bargain at Teelin pier. Fine weather only.

[404]

Teampall Crone B 719104 (Eire ½″ Map 3)

Three and a half miles west-south-west of Dunglow on the Termon Peninsula, about 1 mile north of the village of Maghery. Lonely ruins of an ancient church, abandoned in 1839. Dedicated to the virgin, Croine Beg. A Turas (pilgrimage) takes place here on July 7. The church stands above the rocky, seaweed-covered shore of a creek.

A broad flight of steps leads to the walled graveyard, in which there are tombs of British soldiers and sailors whose bodies were washed ashore here during the war. There is a holy well in the neighbourhood.

The church can be reached by a metalled road from Maghery which is not marked on the ½″ map. After passing some stone walled buildings on either side of this road, continue until you reach a farmhouse set back from it on the right side, at the end of a drive. Teampall Crone is just to the south of this farm.

From Crohy Head, 1½ miles west-south-west of Maghery, where there is a 15th century garrison tower, there are fine views over Aran Island and of the great cliffs of Slievetooey some 14 miles to the south-west. (See Maghera.)

[405]

Teampall Douglas C 090135 (Eire ½″ Map 1)

Near Drumbologe, 2 miles south-east of Church Hill, ½ mile along the secondary road to Kilmacrenan, which runs northwards from the L82, then by a track to the west of it. Very lonely, overgrown and difficult to find ruins in a cemetery. This church is supposed to mark the place where St Columcille was baptized. (See St Columcille's Oratory.)

The gateposts of the cemetery have strange carvings of birds and beasts on them—a swan, and what may be a unicorn.

[406]

Tory Island B 857465 (Eire ½″ Map 1)

Lonely island, 9½ miles north-west of Horn Head. It has the appearance of a great primitive fortress and was known in Irish as torai (full or tors). The high cliffs are impressive. It is 3 miles long and much of its 785 acres are barren. There is a sort of clay on the island which is believed to have heat-resisting properties, and some of it was kept in veneration in one of the churches as a protection against fire and injury. There is a lighthouse on the north-west point of the island. The gunboat, HMS *Wasp*, was wrecked on Rinnsmurreeny Rocks in 1884 while trying to land police and soldiers to collect rents from the inhabitants, or else evict them. All but six of the crew were drowned and because of this fortuitous disaster the islanders did not pay any rent for several years. Still visible are the remains of two churches, one of which was the 'Abbey' of St Ernan, son of St Columcille, the first Christian to arrive. There is also the bottom half of a round tower and two stone crosses, one of which, the Tau Cross, is nearly 7 feet high.

Tory Island was the home of the legendary Fomorians, a race of giants and pirates whose chief was Balor of the Baleful Eye. He had one cyclopean eye which required a wooden beam wielded by several henchmen to prop it open when he went into action. Balor was eventually killed, as predicted by Fate, by his grandson Lugh. Lugh was the only surviving son of Balor's daughter, Eithne. He, together with the rest of her children, Balor wrapped in a cloth and threw into the sea. The others became the ancestors of the seals. Lugh escaped and was brought up by a smith who made weapons for a warrior—the father of Eithne's children in some stories, and the owner of a wonderful cow. Balor stole the cow and killed the warrior, and to avenge these injustices, Lugh pierced the terrible eye with a burning stick or sticks. Balor then asked Lugh to decapitate him and, having done so, to crown himself with his grandfather's bloody head; but Lugh put it on a rock at a safe distance, which split.

There are various rocks named after Balor on Tory, some said to have been aimed at his eye, others to have been placed there deliberately by Balor as obstacles to anyone who tried to carry off his daughter, Eithne, whom he kept in a tower. Dun Bhalair, his fort, is on a promontory at the eastern end of the island with some hut circles in it.

The present population of the island, which has diminished by about a third since the last century, is now about 200. They still continue their traditional way of life. Tory is accessible from Falcarragh, depending on the weather. Day return is not guaranteed.

Section 7

Fermanagh

Tyrone

Londonderry

Antrim

Armagh

Down

[407] H 366315

Aghalurcher Church (N Ireland 1″ Map 7; Eire ½″ Map 8)

One and a half miles south of Lisnakea, by a signposted lane from the by-road to Crockerahoas Bridge, which is west of the main road. An extremely ruined church overshadowed by old yews in a graveyard filled with tombstones all askew, many of them ornamented with skulls and crossbones. Locked up in a dark, barrel-vaulted side chapel there are more tombstones with the same bony ornamentation, and the carved figure of what is thought to be a bishop. Here a member of the Maguire family killed one of his relatives at or on the altar. This may have led to the desertion and ruin of Aghalurcher. Yet in spite of such awful happenings and the macabre embellishments on every side, the atmosphere is very peaceful. Half a mile to the north-west, difficult to arrive at, there is a holy well.

[408] H 096435

The Aghanaglack Grave (N Ireland 1″ Map 7; Eire ½″ Map 7)

Three and a half miles north-north-east of Belcoo. (Marked as 'Cairn' on the 1″ map.) A great neolithic or early Bronze Age gallery grave, otherwise known as a 'horned cairn', standing open to the sky high up on the moorland of Aghanaglack, north of the Belcoo-Boho road. It is known locally as the Giant's Grave. It stands close to a deserted farmhouse and almost in the shade of an ancient, wind-swept ash. When the cairn which covered the grave was excavated in the year before the last war, fragments of ash charcoal—of what were probably the remote ancestors of this tree—were found within it as well as more conventional remains: the cremated bones of a youth, the teeth of animals, neolithic pottery, weapons, etc.

The grave is remarkable for its extent—it is about 80 feet long—and for the size of some of the stones with which it is lined; but what is even more extraordinary is the surrealist debris of a later culture which surrounds and in some places partly fills it—defunct automobiles, broken glass, pieces of rusting farm machinery, plastic detergent bottles, tins and more or less contemporary bones, all of which will provide a field day for archaeologists of the future. As well as all this, the splendid views makes a visit to this place well worthwhile on the rare occasions of good visibility. To reach the grave: follow an unsignposted, surfaced road northwards from the Belcoo–Boho road, 1,000 yards east of the sharp bend in the road known as the 'Devil's S' in the direction of Boho, at a place marked as 'Dooletter' on the 1″ Map. Follow this road uphill until it crosses a cattle grid. Below on the right, until it is obscured from view by conifers which have been newly planted here, Dooletter

Lough can be seen. Fork right after the cattle grid on what is, at the time of writing, a stony road, and then right again. After this the farmhouse, providing that it has not fallen down or been demolished, should be in view.

[409] H 085622

The Boa Island Figures (N Ireland 1″ Map 4; Eire ½″ Map 3)

In Dreena, on Boa Island, Lower Lough Erne. About 1 mile east of the bridge which links the island to the mainland at its western end. Reached by a track south of the road signposted 'Caldragh Cemetery'. In this lonely, overgrown cemetery down near the shore, strange stone figures rise among the bracken and the wild flowers. Two of them are back to back, carved from a single stone—neckless male dwarfs with enormous heads, gaping mouth and pointed chins. Like some of the figures on White Island (q.v.) they have tiny arms crossed high on their bodies. They are powerful, eerie and yet somehow comical. Although they were probably carved in the 7th century they seem to represent something far older than Christianity. A similar effigy is, or was until recently, on Lusty More Island to the east-south-east.

[410] H 127445

The Boho Caves (N Ireland 1″ Map 7; Eire ½″ Map 7)

Immediately north of the village of Boho, by a signposted road. (Marked 'Cave' on the 1″ map.) Here, below a quarry in the limestone, is one of the entrances to some of the most extensive cave systems in Ireland. From the quarry a disagreeably steep path leads down into a deep gorge heavily overgrown with trees full of moss-grown boulders and pieces of rusting quarry machinery. At the head of it, under a fall which is generally dry in summer, there is a deep, dark hole which leads into the depths. Traversing this river bed it is difficult to suppress the feeling that the tap will be turned on and a wall of water will come roaring down and sweep one away. Those who are interested in these caves should consult more specialist publications. The lonely, trackless hills around Boho are riddled with pot-holes and one of them, Noon's Hole, is the deepest hole in Ireland.

[411] H 260431

Castlecoole (N Ireland 1″ Map 7; Eire ½″ Map 8)

Two miles south-east of Enniskillen, east of the main Enniskillen–Dublin road. Magnificent white, classical house of almost perfect proportions, built regardless of cost by the first Earl of Belmore, Armar Lowry-Corry, who exhausted his fortune in the process but at least, unlike some other prodigious spenders of his age, left some-

Boa Island figures, Co. Fermanagh
(*Wonder No.* [illegible])

Stove with classical head, Castlecoole,
Co. Fermanagh (*Wonder No. 411*)

Saint's Tomb,
Bovevagh Church,
Co. Londonderry
(Wonder No. 432)

The Giant's Causeway,
Co. Antrim
(Wonder No. 446)

thing of beauty to be lived in by his descendants and to be admired by posterity. The architect largely responsible both for the exterior and the interior was James Wyatt. Alexander Stewart, Wyatt's deputy, was responsible for the execution of the plan. Belmore himself performed the offices of contractor, arranging for the transportation of the Portland stone from the quarries on Portland Isle in Dorset, which was brought by ship to Ballyshannon in Donegal, thence overland by bullock cart to Enniskillen on Lough Erne, and from there to the site. The account books giving details of the prodigious money and labour expended are exhibited in the house.

William Kane was the stonecutter in chief; the plasterwork is by Joseph Rose who worked for Adam at Syon House, Middlesex, Harewood House, Yorkshire and at Nostell Priory, also in Yorkshire. Rose was alone responsible for the plasterwork on the ceilings of the staircase hall.

The magnificent scagliola pillars were the work of an Italian, Giuseppe Bartoli. The joinery of the mahogany doors, windows and the making of much of the furniture and bookcases was the hardly surpassable work of English joiners working *in situ*. Other furniture was made by Joseph Preston and Son of Dublin.

The effect from the outside is one of supreme elegance, the interior, though now uninhabited and virtually a museum, gives the impression that the owners have gone out for the afternoon and may return at any moment, discarding coats in the hall and shouting for drinks and hot water. On the east side of the house a dark inclined tunnel runs up to the domestic quarters, with enormous store rooms on either side.

Among the great rooms at Castlecoole is the salon opposite the entrance to the great hall, ornamented with grey and white scagliola pilasters with Corinthian capitals made of plaster, and with magnificent stoves with classical heads on them, in niches on either side of the door; another is the lobby on the first floor which is illuminated by a dome. The upper part of the room is surrounded by a gallery, the roof of which is supported by pairs of columns. (National Trust; admission charge.)

On Lough Coole, in the beautiful demesne, is the only breeding colony of grey lag geese in Ireland or England. They were introduced by Colonel James Corry about 1700.

[412] H 365240

Crom Old Castle (N Ireland 1″ Map 7; Eire ½″ Map 8)

Four miles west-south-west of Newtownbutler. In a wonderful situation on a wooded promontory on the shore of Upper Lough Erne in the private demesne of the Earl of Erne. Crom Castle, a late 18th century building, is the present house. Crom Old Castle, a highly picturesque ruin with round towers so overgrown with ivy that they resemble vast trees, was built in 1611 as a Protestant garrison and was accidentally destroyed by fire in 1764. It stands ½ mile from the present Border, and is separated from it by the waters of the lough. In the narrows on Gad Island there is a picturesque tower. The prospect from the Old Castle is arcadian. There is no public access to it, but it is an Ancient Monument and application to visit it can be made at the house.

[413] H 077396

Dabhach Phadraig (N Ireland 1″ Map 7; Eire ½″ Map 7)

At the village of Holywell; by the bridge at the junction of the two roads both of which lead to Garrison. Dabhach Phadraig (St Patrick's Well) much resorted to until recently, is a spring in a little stream on the north side of the bridge. It is now partly overgrown with excellent watercress which is consumed with relish by local people. The water is delicious. Isaac Butler in *A Journey to Lough Derg* published about 1740 described it as 'The best cold bath in the kingdom, relieved numbers in nervous and paralitic disorders . . . after the frost of April and May, 1740, water changed into colour of milk, thought miracle by vulgar who flocked to it, accounted for by priest as marl from channel of spring loosened into water by breaking of frost . . .'

On the other side of the bridge to the left of the road is Templerushin, an ancient ruined church in a graveyard. In it there are penitential stones, two of which are bullauns. Little offerings which include pieces of cheap jewellery, are left inside the church by a stone close to the place where the altar stood. Another stone visited until recently by pilgrims is downstream of the bridge beyond a modern bungalow. This pilgrimage was always made between the last Saturday in July (the day before Garland Sunday) and August 15 and a few older people still carry out this penitence which is probably connected with the Festival of Lughnasa. There is a legend in the country that here St Patrick vanquished a dreadful hound which spurted fire from its eyes, nostrils and mouth, by pushing his staff down its throat up to the handle. After this treatment the animal vanished into Lough Macnean.

[414] H 224469

Devenish Island (N Ireland 1″ Map 7; Eire ½″ Map 8)

Two miles north-north-west of Enniskillen. Otherwise Daimh-Inish (Ox Island). Splendid, melancholy ruins of a monastery originally founded by St Molaise in the 6th century on this green, reed-fringed island in Lower Lough Erne. Down near the shore are two roofless medieval churches, Teampall Mor (the Great Church) and a smaller one, St Molaise's House, an oratory with enormously thick walls which only fell into ruin at the end of the 18th century because the roof was stripped from it. Above them a smooth, conical-capped round tower soars over 80 feet into the sky, like a great space rocket. From the cornice below the cone, four sculptured human heads, three of them bearded, look down on the ruination below as if they were a crew of savants watching the preparations for blast-off.

From a doorway set defensively high above the ground, a series of modern ladders leads to the top of the tower. The four windows over which the heads are set give remarkable but narrow views over the lough and the surrounding country. Round towers, of which this is one of the most splendid in Ireland, served both as belfries and places of refuge from raiding Norsemen.

Uphill, the ruins of St Mary's Abbey or Priory, a rectangular building with a square tower, looms on the skyline. Under the tower there is a stone with a Latin inscription which gives the name of Matthew O Dubagan (or O Dubigan) who built it in 1449 and that of the prior, Bartholomew O Flanagan. A spiral staircase leads to a chamber above the arches which support the tower. A pointed doorway in the north wall of the building has a carving over it of a bird making a meal of leaves. The east window was removed (see Monea Castle). In the churchyard on the south side there are tombs and a high cross with a crucifixion on one side of the head of it and a man's head on the other. St Molaise was a nobleman. Being without a pen and wishing to copy a map, he received in his outstretched hand, literally dropped from heaven, the quill from a goose which was passing overhead, a pleasant and believable miracle. He died in 571. The Reliquary or Shrine of St Molaise, made to hold a copy of the Gospels for Cennfaelad, Prior of Devenish, St Molaise's successor, is in the National Museum, Dublin. The island with its ruins is an unforgettable place. It can be reached by boat from Enniskillen or by a ferry from the end of a long, signposted lane from the main Enniskillen–Kesh road about 3 miles north of Enniskillen. The view of it from the ferry is very fine.

[415] H 427203

The Druids Temple

(N Ireland 1″ Map 7; Eire ½″ Map 8)

In Annaghmore Glebe, 4 miles south of Newtownbutler to the west of the main road which leads to Cavan in Southern Ireland, and less than a mile from the Border.

This extremely difficult to find wonder is on a hill high above the surrounding country to the west of the junction of the main road with the road to Clones. It is a connected circle of truly enormous stones which, together with the trees and bushes which have grown up about it, forms an almost impenetrable fortification. Local inhabitants say that the stone came from the banks of the river Finn close to the point where it joins the now disused Ballyconnell–Ballinamore Canal. Wherever they came from, the labour of getting them to their present site must have been almost superhuman. It is believed locally that a tunnel runs into the hill underneath the circle. For directions to reach it, ask at the post office by the road junction or at the farm opposite on whose property it stands.

[416] H 166542

Inishmacsaint (N Ireland 1″ Map 4; Eire $\frac{1}{2}$″ Map 7)

Eight miles north-west of Enniskillen. Lonely island in Lower Lough Erne, one of many dozens in what is one of the loveliest lakes in Ireland. The ruined church is on a slight eminence above the water. Roofless, it has one long, narrow window. Close to it is a high cross of primitive and powerful form with wide spreading arms. In spring thousands of irises grow in the reedy land about the ruins. The island can be reached by boat from Enniskillen, a journey of about 10 miles, worth making for its own sake. For other excursions by boat to islands in Lower Lough Erne, see also Devenish Island and White Island.

[417] H 207538

The Killadeas Sculptured Stones (N Ireland 1″ Map 4; Eire $\frac{1}{2}$″ Map 7)

At Killadeas, on the west side of the Enniskillen–Kesh road, 7$\frac{1}{4}$ miles north of the former place. Three stones in the churchyard of an unlovely Church of Ireland church, on the east shore of Lower Lough Erne. Two of them are not particularly remarkable —one is a slab with cup marks on one side of it and a cross and an Irish inscription on the other, the second has a Greek cross on it. The third, however, the Bishop's Stone, is very wonderful. The narrow edge of it has a weird, open-mouthed figure on it with an interlaced design instead of a body. On one side with back bent to allow himself to be enclosed within the shape of the stone—there is the even stranger figure of an ecclesiastic with a long pointed nose, a thin mouth and a stylized eye in the form of a curlicue. He carries a quadrangular Irish bell with a long clapper, a crozier, and on his feet he wears pointed shoes. On the back of his robe there is a faint inscription. Perhaps he is the same man who is on the front of the stone. From close to the bishop is not always very visible but he often shows up better from a distance.

[418] H 123358

Killesher Church (N Ireland 1″ Map 7; Eire $\frac{1}{2}$″ Map 7)

Three miles east-south-east of Belcoo on the road to Florencecourt. Ruins of a little medieval church dedicated to St Lasair of Cill Lasrach, on Lough Macnean, one of six holy sisters. It stands in a grove of trees in a circular graveyard, the stone walls of which assume an almost luminous pallor at dusk, which is a nice time to visit the place. Only one window now remains in the roofless nave. The church is surrounded by strange grass-grown vaults that look like barns, and there are many deeply-cut

18th century tombstones (the church was rebuilt for Protestant use in the 17th century). It is a rarely beautiful place.

Near-by, hidden on the side of the hill and not found by us, is said to be St Lasair's Cell, a souterrain with three chambers in it. The site of her holy well, just under the hill to the west of the church, is equally difficult to discover and muddy going. The church, which has now, unfortunately, lost some of its former air of remoteness because of the construction of a modern waterworks, can best be reached by taking the first turning to the left from the Florencecourt–Belcoo road after crossing the Cladagh River in the direction of Belcoo. This bridge is at the entrance to the valley which leads to Marble Arch (q.v.). The church is immediately on the far side of the waterworks, but to get to it, it is necessary to ascend the lane and go around the wire fence which surrounds the works, on foot. If in difficulty the custodian may be able to help.

Florencecourt is a great early 18th century mansion in a splendid situation poised below the Cuilcagh Mountains. (National Trust; admission charge.)

[419] H 122345

The Marble Arch (N Ireland 1″ Map 7; Eire ½″ Map 7)

Three and a half miles east-south-east of Belcoo. An extraordinary natural arch of limestone 30 feet high with a vertical shaft in it. Through both holes the waters of the Cladagh River, which here emerges from a subterranean labyrinth, can be seen. The first person to explore part of the underground river was a Monsieur Martel who penetrated it for 300 yards in a canvas boat in 1897. The Cladagh is formed by three streams which rise on the lonely northern slopes of Cuilcagh, (2,188 feet), the summit ridge of which forms the border between Northern and Southern Ireland and the watershed. The middle one, the Monastir, after rushing down between cliffs 160 feet high, vanishes underground, to reappear fleetingly in caves at Pollnagaple and Cradle Hole.

The Arch can be reached by a recently tourist-furbished track up the deep and wooded gorge of the Cladagh from Cladagh Bridge on the Florencecourt–Belcoo road in about 15 minutes brisk walk. It is too crowded in the summer, except early or late or on the wettest of days, to have much feeling of wonder about it, but the path beyond the Arch leads eventually to the less frequented slopes of Cuilcagh on the upper part of the river.

[420] H 165495

Monea Castle (N Ireland 1″ Map 7; Eire ½″ Map 7)

Five and a half miles north-west of Enniskillen, ½ mile south of Monea village

Reached by a signposted road from the Enniskillen–Belleek road. Small but impressive three-storeyed Plantation castle ruin with two powerful round towers with an arch between them. It was built 11 years after the flight from Ireland of the Earls of Tyrconnell and Tyrone in 1607 by the Scottish Malcolm Hamilton of Portaferry who became Chancellor of Co. Down and later Bishop of Cashel. It stands in the beautiful demesne of Castletown House and is arrived at by a splendid avenue of beech trees, and then by a track past a white farmhouse. Cars should be left at the first green gate near the house.

Castletown House superseded the castle which was burned in 1750. Below the castle, which stands on a slight eminence, there is a small, reedy lough, little more than a pond. In the middle of it there is a circular crannog, the site of a far earlier fortification. On it there is a little grove of trees. It is an enchanting, mysterious place. In the Protestant church at Monea there is a window transported from the abbey on Devenish Island (q.v.).

[421] H 174600

White Island Church (N Ireland 1″ Map 4; Eire ½″ Map 3)

In Castle Archdale Bay, Lower Lough Erne, 1 mile west of Milltown. Can be reached by boat from the caravan site at Castle Archdale, or more slowly but pleasurably from Enniskillen by speedboat in about 1 hour. On this beautiful, wooded island in the lough the ruins of a 12th century church stand in a green meadow. A Romanesque doorway in the south wall leads into the roofless building. A protective covering on the north wall shelters an extraordinary array of sculptures which are amongst the most memorable of their kind in all Ireland. They were only discovered in 1928. Possibly they had been hidden when the earlier church, a wooden structure, was rebuilt in stone, as being too bizarre and pagan to be acceptable to 12th century Christians, for the place where they now hang on the wall is not the place where they were found.

There are seven figures and one sculptured mask. The figure on the extreme left, perhaps the most strange looking, is a small but monstrous creature with a prominent chin, and distended cheeks. Its minute hands rest upon its crossed legs. Next to it there is the figure of a bearded man. He wears a loose-fitting, shift-like garment with a high collar, short sleeves and a wide hem. He holds what might be a book. The third figure, found 30 years later than the others in 1958, embedded upside down in the outer wall at the front of the church, is that of a long-faced, rather dolorous ecclesiastic with downcast eyes. He, too, wears a high-collared robe. In one tiny hand he holds a crozier, in the other a bell. He has been identified as Abbot Constans who lived in the 7th century.

The next figure is the largest: a man with an enormous head and a tonsured pate, like a grotesque mask in a carnival. He carries a staff in his right hand and the other hand points to his mouth which is wide open—this may be St Patrick who fasted in order to bring about the conversion of King Laoghaire to Christianity. The fifth figure from the left is that of a young man with a modish fringe of hair and a surprised expression, possibly because the top of his head is sawn off. He carries a round shield and a sword. This may be Enna, son of King Laoghaire, who expired after eating mutton during St Patrick's fast, but was revived by the saint with the aid of St Michael. The next figure also has a fringe. He holds (by their necks) two strange, bird-like creatures which may not be birds but rams garbed for sacrifice. Possibly this is St Michael. The seventh figure is a rough-hewn block of stone, the outline of a body and a faceless face, abandoned by the sculptor because the stone had a fault in it. The eighth is a human head in relief, with a sort of cap on it, carved on a block of stone. The figures and the expressions on their faces are as enigmatic as the great sculptures on Easter Island in the Pacific. (For other sculptured figures in Fermanagh, see The Boa Island Figures and the Killadeas Sculptured Stones.)

High above the shore on the mainland are the melancholy remains of Castle Archdale House, a splendid 18th century mansion with an enormous disfiguring water tower, a relic of the time when the landing below was a base for flying boats in the second world war.

TYRONE

[422] H 965756

The Arboe Cross (N Ireland 1″ Map 5; Eire $\frac{1}{2}$″ Map 4)

Ten miles east-south-east of Cookstown, on the western shore of Lough Neagh; just over a mile south of Newport French, and reached by side roads from the main lough shore road. Fine, though weathered cross of the 10th century, 18$\frac{1}{2}$ feet high, standing on high ground next to an ancient churchyard overlooking the lough. The great cross, part of its circle broken, is unfortunately enclosed by low iron railings, which seems pointless. Many of the panels, though worn, are easily interpreted as representing Adam and Eve in the Garden of Eden, the Sacrifice of Isaac, the Nativity, the Adoration, and other scenes more open to speculation.

On Arboe Hill (or Ardboe—the Hill of the Cow)—so called because of the rich surrounding grazing land—are the remains of an old ruined church romantically set above the lough. A beech tree in the corner of the graveyard was superstitiously regarded as a 'wishing tree', and its trunk and lower branches are stuck with the pins, nails and coins of the supplicants. Until the 18th century Arboe was the scene of pilgrimages, and the waters of the lough facing the cross were credited with healing properties.

[423] Surrounding H 460538

Ballyness (N Ireland 1″ Map 4; Eire ½″ Map 8)

Five and a half miles north-west of Clogher, to the east of the main Fivemiletown–Fintona road. Great, lonely peat bog, its highest point on Ballyness (958 feet), set in the midst of heather-covered moors. Ridge upon ridge of peat cuttings, bisected by small streams. Narrow, isolated roads encircle it, giving fine views over the desolate, rusty-brown bog, magnificent in autumn, full of bog cotton in spring and summer; and across the valley to the distant Slieve Beagh Mountains to the south. On the lower slopes the Forestry Commission has been at work; go now before the embryo Christmas trees grow up and block the view.

[424] Surrounding H 550900

Barnes Gap (N Ireland 1″ Map 5; Eire ½″ Map 4)

Four and a half miles north-east of Gortin. Dramatic defile between Mullaghbolig and Craignamaddy (1,264 feet), an upper road running above the gorge, and a lower road hemmed in at the bottom of it. The views from the upper road are the more exciting. Wild, remote scene of boulder-strewn mountains, great enveloping slopes covered in heather heaving up all around. It is best traversed from south to north, when the exit from the Gap faces the daunting range of the Sperrin Mountains across the Glenelly river, here very beautiful.

[425] Surrounding H 370830

Baronscourt (N Ireland 1″ Map 4; Eire ½″ Map 4)

Two and a half miles south-west of Newtownstewart at the foot of a mountain called Bessie Bell (1,387 feet), which rises to the east. Splendid demesne of the Duke of Abercorn, whose fine Georgian mansion is hidden on most sides by magnificent trees. The house is not open to the public, but as it stands on a high grassy terrace, it can be viewed without embarrassment from many of the approach paths. The Agent's House, built earlier (about 1690) is charming. In the demesne are three lakes and on one of them, Lough Catherine, is a crannog called Island MacHugh. Surrounded now by reeds and covered with trees, it has more the appearance of a natural island and it adds considerably to the beauty of a very fine scene. The grounds, through which one may wander undisturbed, are sometimes formal (there is an astonishing avenue of giant monkey puzzle trees), and sometimes wild, with a profuse tangle of undergrowth, flowering shrubs, and thick woods. It is a great pleasure to walk among them. (Open every day except Sunday.)

[426] H 684843

Beaghmore Stone Circles (N Ireland 1″ Map 5; Eire ½″ Map 4)

Two miles north of Dunnamore, signposted by a turning from the main Cookstown–Omagh road. The circles are situated to the west of the minor road running towards Broughderg Bridge. An extraordinary complex of three pairs of stone circles of varying sizes, cairns and alignments, all set on flat ground in the middle of a vast and lonely peat bog, which is itself enclosed by a ring of stony outcrops overlooked from the east by Beleevnamore and Oughtmore Mountains (1,261 feet). In addition to the three pairs of circles, there is one isolated circle, very large, and packed solid with stones and big boulders, and having its own cairn and line of pillar stones.

This was the site of a great ceremonial centre of the Early Bronze Age, apparently built over an earlier neolithic settlement. One of the cairns has been excavated and was found to contain a cremation burial. The whole area might easily have had a faintly artificial air because of the quantities of small loose stones strewn thickly everywhere by the authorities to keep back the bog, already seeping through here and there. But it would take more than that to detract from the extraordinary feeling of isolation and wonder that one feels in the presence of so many ancient constructions so improbably sited. To take in the whole complex at a glance, mount the ridges and hillocks of peat, grass-grown on top, that stretch away for mile upon deserted mile.

[427] H 585571

Errigal Keeroge Cross and Church (N Ireland 1″ Map 5; Eire ½″ Map 8)

Three miles west of Ballygawley; 2 miles north-north-east of the village of Augher, by a side road running north-eastwards from the main Ballygawley–Clogher road. A very ruinous old church, overgrown with creepers, standing on a hilltop in the midst of an ancient graveyard with lopsided, sunken gravestones, some with strangely scalloped tops. The primitive cross is outside the ruin, and is curiously thick and stumpy, about 5 feet high, and armless. The boss at its centre on the western side, shows faint traces of carving. The church ruin has no interesting carvings or, indeed, anything of architectural note, but the situation, high and lonely above the village, is beautiful and moving. The view is over the fertile Blackwater valley with Slieve Beagh and its surrounding hills rising to the south.

[428] Surrounding H 495835

Gortin Gap (N Ireland 1″ Map 4; Eire ½″ Map 4)

Two miles south of Gortin. The road runs southwards through a great gorge between the mountains of Mullaghcarn (1,778 feet) and Curraghchosaly (1,372 feet). The area is a National Park and a 'scenic route' has been constructed to take in twin loughs to the east of the road, set among rounded hills covered in heather and bracken, small streams and waterfalls, a wildfowl pond, and a great deal of beautiful mountain scenery. There are some fine walks along signposted tracks.

[429] H 560468

Knockmany Tomb (N Ireland 1″ Map 8; Eire ½″ Map 8)

Two miles south-south-west of Clogher, signposted through the Ministry of Agriculture's plantation at Knockmany, near the junction with the main road and a minor road to Augher. The tomb stands on the top of a 700-foot hill reached by a path through thick woods of ancient gnarled trees, twisted into eerie shapes. The mound, about 50 feet in diameter, comes into sight as you near the summit, bulbous on the skyline. Beneath it was discovered a burial chamber many of whose wall stones were covered in intricate designs of concentric circles, zig-zags, cup markings and snake patterns such as those of the Boyne Valley graves (see Newgrange, Fourknocks and Loughcrew), although in the case of Knockmany, there is no passage entrance. The very fine stones have been somewhat unimaginatively housed in a concrete hut beneath the grass mound, and an iron grille in front effectively bars visitors except at prescribed times—not always as prescribed. If locked, you can peer through the bars and see the stones grouped inside. The view is really magnificent across the mountains to a patchwork of fields stretching in all directions, and the valley of the Blackwater to the east. (Small admission charge; open April–end September, Sats and Suns, 2–7 or thereabouts.)

[430] H 825743

Tullaghoge Fort (N Ireland 1″ Map 5; Eire ½″ Map 4)

Two and a half miles south-south-east of Cookstown, just north of Tullaghoge village. Great hilltop ring fort, the oval sunken inner area 105 feet across, surrounded by a high bank, which is divided from the outer bank by an extraordinarily wide ditch. Both banks are heavily planted with trees grown gnarled and dense, casting a mystic gloom over the encampment. The banks are wide and firm and you can walk on them. Entrance is by a causeway on the north side through gaps in both banks. Tullaghoge (Telach Oc) was, from early times, a pagan sanctuary, and a place of inauguration. In the early 11th century, the O Hagans, sub-chiefs under the powerful

O Neills, occupied the fort, and assisted in the O Neill inauguration ceremonies. The site remained the ceremonial capital of the kings until 1641, when the last ceremony —the inauguration of Sir Phelim O Neill—took place. The way to it is from a signposted, fenced path from the Cookstown road, running up through farmland (often muddy) to the fort.

LONDONDERRY

[431] C 678066

Banagher Old Church (N Ireland 1″ Map 2; Eire ½″ Map 4)

Two miles south-west of Dungiven, on a hill beside a minor road, above farm fields. Ancient ruined church enclosed within a crumbling drystone wall, attributed to an 11th century local saint, Muiredeach O Heney. It is small, with a massive lintelled doorway, square-headed outside, round-arched on the inside, with the door jambs inclining inwards. Beside the church is a diminutive stone building of similar shape with a high pitched stone roof, a string course at its western end, probably to protect the curious, very weathered carved figure beneath it which is thought to represent the saint, whose tomb this is. At all events it is known locally as O Heney's Tomb, and if sand is collected from beneath it by an O Heney, this is supposed to ensure his success in battle or contests of any kind.

[432] C 694136

Bovevagh Church (N Ireland 1″ Map 2; Eire ½″ Map 2)

Two and a half miles north of Dungiven, on a knoll overlooking the river Roe; reached by a signposted lane. Lonely small ruined church in a lovely position high above a bend of the peaty-brown river. Its origins are obscure, but it is thought to occupy the site of a church founded by the local patron, St Ringan. Certainly this is an ancient place—Bovevagh means 'Hut of Maeve', a powerful queen of pagan Ireland (see Maeve's Lump). The church, very ruinous, dates from the 13th century. Beside it is the Saint's Tomb, a small stone construction 9 feet long, 6½ feet broad, and 7½ feet high. It is a tomb similar to that at Banagher (q.v.) though it is older, built in the style of the early Irish oratories.

[433] C 686323

Duncrun Graveyard (N Ireland 1″ Map 1; Eire ½″ Map 2)

Six miles north of Limavady; reached by a narrow turning off the main road which runs northwards up the low-lying Magilligan Peninsula. An ancient church and graveyard on a rocky eminence adjacent to a modern church. In front of the east wall of the very ruinous church, a tall wooden cross marks the tomb of St Aidan of Lindisfarne whose remains were thought to have been brought here by St Colman in the 7th century. The tomb is a humble, very small construction of boulders shaped roughly like the Ark of the Covenant. Above the ruin looms the great mass of Binevenagh (1,260 feet), like a massive oval fortress, its bare, forbidding ramparts dropping sheer into low-lying woodland, and with rifts in them which resemble great caverns. Paths lead up to the summit through rough scrub and bushes. Magnificent views from the top over the flat, green peninsula to Lough Foyle and the Mountains of Donegal to the west, and to the north, the magnificent 7-mile stretch of Magilligan Strand, a raised sandy beach extending from the cliffs below Mussenden Temple (q.v.) to Magilligan Point, the extremity of the eastern arm of Lough Foyle.

[434] C 710075 to H 740980

Dungiven-Draperstown Mountain Road (N Ireland 1″ Map 2; Eire ½″ Map 4)

Mountain route which leaves the main road 2 miles south-east of Dungiven, and joins the Feeny-Draperstown road 3 miles north-west of Draperstown. A narrow road driven through an immense peat bog, running under the brow of White Mountain (1,774 feet) and Mullaghmore (1,825 feet) which rise to the east, and the lesser mass of Crockalougha (1,547 feet) on the west. Vast empty slopes enclosing a few small loughs heave up all round, deserted except for grazing sheep. The great Sperrin range looms to the south-west. Superb views as the road descends to Draperstown.

[435] C 694084

Dungiven Priory (N Ireland 1″ Map 2; Eire ½″ Map 4)

Half a mile south of Dungiven, on a rocky promontory high above the river Roe; reached by a signposted lane. Ruined Augustinian priory, founded in the 12th century by the O Cahans and restored in the late 14th century by the Bishop of Armagh. After the Dissolution it fell into disrepair until, in the 17th century, it was used for Protestant services, the last being held in 1720, after which a new church was built. In the 14th century chancel there is a fine medieval altar tomb beneath an arched canopy carved with delicate stone tracery. The chest is topped by a full length effigy in mail armour with curiously padded headgear, thought to be that of an O Cahan chieftain, Cooey-na-Gall (the Terror of the Stranger). The front side of the chest is decorated with figures wearing swords and what appear to be kilts. (Ask for key at post office.) In the graveyard is an old well, noted for its wart curing properties. To the north of the priory, in a field on high ground, a bulky pillar stone about 5½ feet high and very wide, stands amid trees against the skyline like a sentinel. It can be seen closer to from the back of the adjacent modern churchyard.

[436] C 897042

Dunglady (N Ireland 1″ Map 2; Eire ½″ Map 4)

Three and a half miles north-east of Maghera, reached by a turning off the Maghera–Kilcrea road. Immense, prehistoric ring fort crowning the summit of a hill in the midst of low-lying countryside. It is exceptionally large, with three ramparts, and is one of the best preserved early forts in Northern Ireland. Great drooping trees intertwined thickly with brambles, spread so densely across the banks that the ditches between and the banks themselves are impenetrable. The centre can only be reached by a low-lying causeway, dank and often very muddy and slippery, which cuts across the banks. Once you are through to the middle, you are in a great, grassy circle, edged with hawthorn, hazel and sloe, light and utterly quiet, and mysteriously guarded by the thick and gloomy tangle of the circles of trees outside it. Nothing can be seen from the centre, but outside, there are marvellous panoramic views to mountains which ring the horizon.

In Maghera, 3½ miles to the south-west, are the ruins of an ancient small church on the site of one said to have been founded in the 6th century by St Lurach. Unprepossessingly situated on the edge of the town, it is nonetheless worth visiting for the 11th century doorway which has a semicircular arch on the inside, and is square-headed on the outside, with inclined jambs. The massive stone lintel, 5½ feet long, is beautifully carved with a crucifixion scene. Unfortunately, the carving is in a very dark corner.

[437] C 763364

Mussenden Temple (N Ireland 1″ Map 1; Eire ½″ Map 2)

Six miles north-west of Coleraine; half a mile from Castlerock railway station, on the cliff top. Domed, circular structure with columns, after the style of the temples of Vesta in Tivoli and Rome, probably built by the architect Michael Shanahan for the Earl of Bristol, the eccentric Bishop of Derry. It was completed in 1785 when it was intended to be used as a library. It was dedicated to the Bishop's cousin Mrs Frideswell Mussenden, who died before its completion. It is a lovely, sophisticated small building, its outer columns linked by carved stone swags, and around the dome in letters once covered in gold, is a quotation from Lucretius which Dryden translated as:

Tis pleasant, safely to behold from shore
The rolling ship, and hear the tempest roar –

an undoubted fact, since the temple is poised – though disconcertingly close – on the edge of a great precipitous cliff, below which the surf rolls on the 7-mile-long Magilligan Strand. The unrestored interior, badly damaged by rough weather, is beautifully proportioned. It now houses a miscellaneous collection of heads and other fragments of sculpture unearthed from the ruin of near-by Downhill, the great house built by the Bishop and in which he kept his art treasures. It is now a gaunt shell and a somewhat grim sight squatting on the headland. Mussenden Temple can be reached through the Bishop's Gate on the Limavady–Coleraine coast road, which adjoins a charming lodge; a long walk through fine rambling grounds leads to the edge of the windswept cliff. (National Trust; open most afternoons; admission free.)

[438] C 526113

Ness Waterfall (N Ireland 1″ Map 2; Eire ½″ Map 2)

Three miles north-west of Claudy; ½ mile south of a minor road to Slaghtmanus. Splendid fall formed by the Burntollet river, racing here through a wooded and overhung gorge spiked with great jutting rocks. Paths have been cut to give view points, and descend almost to the valley bed. The river hurtles – heard, but often hidden in the dense undergrowth – over the rocks, finally pitching in a great, brown-streaked peaty fall to the bottom of the gorge. The ground, often muddy in winter, is carpeted with bluebells and other wild flowers in the spring.

[439] H 860828

Springhill (N Ireland 1″ Map 5; Eire ½″ Map 4)

A mile south-east of Moneymore, reached from the Moneymore–Coagh road. Charming 17th century house of great character, in an estate acquired by the Conyngham family in that century. The house was built later, and the wings added in about 1765. Flanking the courtyard in front of the house are a pair of delightful, curiously shaped barns one of which is now used as a family museum of costumes and relics. The great barn (which houses a collection of carriages) is a fortified building with slit windows from which the occupants and workers could defend themselves – as they often needed to – during the unsettled days during which the work of building took place. The interior of the house is made for comfort and good living. There is a splendid oak staircase with a yew-wood balustrade, and some good furniture and paintings. A long and very fine beech avenue almost bisects the grounds and close to the house there is a thicket of great, ghostly yews. (National Trust; admission charge.)

[440] D 125408

Bonamargy Friary (N Ireland 1″ Map 1; Eire ½″ Map 2)

Half a mile east of Ballycastle. Fine and extensive remains of a Franciscan friary founded about 1500 by Rory MacQuillan, on low ground on the south side of the Cushendall road beside the Margy river, Knocklayd (1,695 feet) rising steeply in the background. It was damaged by fire when English troops occupied it towards the end of the 16th century and were attacked by warring MacDonnells and Scots. In spite of this it survived and was in use until 1642. There are substantial remains of the aisleless church, a gatehouse with a high chimney and parts of the claustral buildings. Some good details include carvings of beasts, considerably weathered, and a male and a female head wearing caps. There are tombs of some of the Earls of Antrim and their ladies, and of Francis Stewart, the Roman Catholic Bishop of Down and Connor, who died about 1749. A primitive cross is believed to mark the grave of Julia MacQuillan who, for some reason, was known as 'the black nun'.

[441] J 216925

Browndod Cairn (N Ireland 1″ Map 3; Eire ½″ Map 5)

Five miles north-east of Antrim, a mile south-west of the Ballymena–Doagh road. An 868-foot hill, near whose summit is a long cairn of the Ulster 'horned' variety, oval in shape, the 'horns' partly enclosing the courtyard, behind which are four aligned burial chambers. The outer edge of the tomb is marked out by a broken border of stones. Sunken and somewhat overgrown, and with some of the stones missing, it is nonetheless quite clear and a poignant example of the high and lonely places chosen by neolithic man for his burial grounds.

Up on Browndod, a heathy hill with clumpish grass and great outcrops of rock near the summit, the cairn is not at first easy to find among the other stones and boulders which form part of the contour of the slopes. It is best approached from a farm gate on the road below, then over rough ground to the main summit on which there is an Ordnance Survey pillar and, near it, the topmost of a line of electricity pylons. The cairn is on a slight, subsidiary summit, 300–400 yards to the north of the Ordnance pillar; or a short way east of the summit pylon. Marvellous views of the encircling hills, of Lough Neagh and of Slemish Mountain, a distinctive outline to the north.

[442] D 062450

Carrick-a-Rede Island (N Ireland 1″ Map 1; Eire ½″ Map 2)

Three quarters of a mile north-east of Ballintoy, just off the north shore coast road. A great rock stack ½ mile off-shore, reached by a footpath across a prominent, grassy headland. Between the mainland cliffs and the broken-off stack is a 60-foot-wide chasm. The extraordinary formation of the cliffs is marvellously exposed here, showing layers of chalk and black basalt streaked with colour. In season the salmon swim through the narrow strait and fishermen fix their nets from mainland to island with the help of a rope swing bridge slung alarmingly across the chasm 80 feet above the water. In winter, when the sea beats viciously round the great rocks, the bridge is considered unsafe and is removed. Wonderful views from the headland above the precipice, of Rathlin Island and, far off, the Scottish Isle of Arran. An orientation table on the cliff top gives the legend: Iceland 800 miles north-north-west; Cape Farewell, Greenland, 1,300 miles west-north-west; Goatfell, Arran, 52 miles north-north-east; and other points nearer home. (National Trust; admission charge to bridge, late April–mid September.)

[443] J 057852

Cranfield Church (N Ireland 1″ Map 5; Eire ½″ Map 5)

Four miles south-west of Randalstown, on a grassy eminence above the shore of Lough Neagh. Small, roofless 13th century church of Cranfield (Cream Choill—Wood of Wild Garlic), with a big and most symmetrical hawthorn tree beside it. The west door has an arch pointed on the outside, flattened on the inside. The only sign of an east window is a large, triangular opening. One hundred yards along the shore to the east, in the midst of rough grazing land and clumps of bushes tied with rags left by supplicants, is a holy well—a scene of pilgrimage until well into the 19th century, when stations of the cross were performed round the church and the pilgrims drank the water of the well, and washed in it. Amber coloured stones known as Cranfield pebbles, in reality gypsum crystals, have been found in the well, and were regarded by men as a talisman against drowning, and by women as a safeguard against the dangers of child-birth. Lovely serene views over the lough where, in this quiet corner, a number of wild swans congregate.

[444] C 904414

Dunluce Castle (N Ireland 1″ Map 1; Eire ½″ Map 2)

Three miles east-north-east of Portrush. Magnificent ruin of a great castle built on precipitous rocks detached from the coast by the constant working of the sea. The way to it is by a bridge built across the intervening chasm. Always a defensive site because of its almost impregnable position, evidence has been found of early Christian and Viking occupation. The earliest castle known was built here in the 13th century and, in the 16th, belonged to the MacQuillans, who were afterwards united by marriage with the powerful MacDonnells, Earls of Antrim. It was Sorley Boy MacDonnell who, in 1588, when the Armada galleon *Gerona* was wrecked on the rocks near-by (see Giant's Causeway), salvaged some of the guns and reinforced his castle with them. In 1639 a cliff fall took with it some of the living quarters and many of the servants. But it was only after the 1641 Rising that the Earls of Antrim abandoned it, and the great fortress fell into decay.

The ruins are considerable. Two of the massive drum towers remain and parts of the curtain walls, as well as turrets, high, broken façades, and stumps of masonry, forming an astonishing group of irregular shapes—ruinous, but very powerful. They look particularly impressive and mysterious in silhouette. Spectacular views down the broken, precipitous rock faces to the turbulent sea, along the coast where the cliffs are carved into strange columns and arches, and to the Skerries, a line of spiny rock-islands a mile off-shore. (Admission charge.)

[445] D 180436

Fair Head (N Ireland 1″ Map 1; Eire ½″ Map 2)

Four miles north-east of Ballycastle. Great, thrusting headland, also known as Benmore, rising like the ramparts of a fortress for nearly half its total height of 636 feet in sheer, basaltic cliffs. Magnificent views from the Head to Rathlin Island (q.v.), the lower part of whose cliffs are chalk and edge it like a white frill. Awe-inspiring views of the headland itself and its dark, distinctive profile, from the sea on the way to Rathlin. In these often inhospitable waters—the Sea of Moyle—where the sea works viciously, and in the mouth of the Margy river at Ballycastle, the Children of Lir lived for the second 300 years of their 900-year transformation into swans—a bitter, angry waste in winter. (See Lough Derravaragh and Cross 'Abbey'.)

On top of Fair Head, a few hundred yards back from the cliff edge in the midst of wild, windy moorland, are two small loughs—Lough Doo and Lough Na Cranagh—reached by a minor road from the coast road, followed by a rough, uphill scramble, when the lough comes into view below. Lough Na Cranagh is named for the crannog at its centre, which could date back to neolithic times when the earliest of these artificial islands were constructed as defensive dwellings. Oval in shape and measuring about 120 feet by 90 feet, and faced round its outer edge with drystone walling rising above 5 feet above the water level, it is grass-grown with a few, windswept trees. A lonely, wild, and haunting place.

[446] Surrounding C 950445

The Giant's Causeway (N Ireland 1″ Map 1; Eire ½″ Map 2)

Two miles north of Bushmills, on the western side of Benbane Head. Marvellous and unique rock formations, one of the world's strangest phenomena. According to legend, it was the work of the giant, Finn Mac Coul (see Hill of Allen and Fionn Mac Cumhail's Fingerstone), who intended to walk across the great causeway to Scotland. There are thousands of basalt columns formed by cooling lava and splitting rocks, some hexagonal, others polygonal. Below great cliffs, they stretch seawards in long, irregular tongues, fitting as neatly together as pieces in a Victorian patchwork quilt.

There are three main sections: the Little Causeway, the Middle, or Honeycomb Causeway, and the Grand Causeway. Massed columns, some no more than a few feet high, form pathways; others rise against the cliff face for 20 feet or more, long and thin like organ pipes. Many of the formations have been 'suitably' christened: the Amphitheatre, the Lady's Fan, the Wishing Chair, and so on. Skirting the jagged cove (called Port Na Spaniagh because of the Spaniards washed ashore from the wrecked Armada galleon *Gerona* in 1588), and along the cliff top, are some ten miles of footpaths from which there are wonderful views. But it is from sea level, walking on the tops of the perfectly shaped hexagonal rocks, the waves breaking hugely over far-out clumps of them, that the sense of wonder is strongest. (National Trust.)

[447] Surrounding D 230240

Glenariff (N Ireland 1″ Map 3; Eire ½″ Map 2)

Two miles south of Cushendall, and running inland for 5 miles. Largest and one of the most beautiful of the Nine Glens of Antrim, the river entering the sea between wooded cliffs at Red Bay. This lush valley, densely overhung with great beech and other trees, is protected between high, basaltic rock walls over whose bare face drop long waterfalls. The narrow, shut-in upper valley, to which there is a small admission charge, has been made easier to explore by the discreet construction of paths, bridges, and view-points overlooking more waterfalls—Ess-na-Larach (Fall of the Mares) and and Ess-na-Crub (Fall of the Hoof)—pitching in brown, peaty cascades over crags and boulders. The ground is carpeted thickly with primroses and bluebells in spring. A melancholy, romantic sight in autumn and winter, when the trees drip dankly.

[448] J 485980

The Gobbins (N Ireland 1″ Map 3; Eire ½″ Map 5)

On Islandmagee, 4 miles north of Whitehead. A remarkable section of precipitous cliff, 240 feet high, on the eastern shore of the narrow, curving spit of land formed by the penetration of Lough Larne. It can be explored by means of lanes which run steeply down from the coast road. Paths have been cut at the foot of the cliff face, and run for over a mile; the narrow chasm spanned by bridges, and tunnels hewn out of the rock, was the imaginative planning of a railway engineer, used to such manoeuvres. The cliffs are the haunt of many sea birds. They were also the scene of a particularly nasty act of reprisal by the Scottish garrison at Carrickfergus in 1642, who massacred the Catholic inhabitants and flung them over the cliff top. Accounts as to the number of persons so murdered vary from 30 to as many as 3,000.

At the north-western end of the island, about a mile south-west of Brown's Bay, and seen from the western coast road, is Ballylumford Dolmen (D 420020), improbably situated in front of a house, with a small array of flowers planted round it. It is a single-chambered neolithic tomb with a 6½-foot-high capstone poised on four sturdy supporting pillars.

[449] D 245288

Layde Church (N Ireland 1″ Map 3; Eire ½″ Map 2)

One mile north-north-east of Cushendall. Reached by a well-signposted lane from the main Cushendall–Cushendun coast road. The final approach is down a wide, grassy avenue of great trees. The very ruinous church and some remnants of monastic buildings—all that remains of a 13th century Franciscan foundation—lie in a deep, tranquil hollow on the cliff top among half-buried graves and subsiding tombstones. A small stream runs near, between overhung banks. In one corner, marked by a Celtic cross, are the tombs of the MacDonnells, lords of Antrim. Here, too, is the grave of Dr James MacDonnell, founder of Belfast Medical School. Beyond the graveyard, out towards the cliff edge, are splendid views of the rugged, indented coast. A serene, enchanting place.

[450] D 210276

Ossian's Grave (N Ireland 1″ Map 3; Eire ½″ Map 2)

Two miles west of Cushendall. Approached by a singposted lane through a farm off the Cushendall–Ballycastle road. Segmented gallery grave or Ulster 'horned' cairn, in a field 450 feet up on the slope of Tievebulliagh (1,346 feet), above the enchanting Glenaan river. Two chambers open on to a forecourt bounded by 3-foot-high boulder-like stones. The tomb is dated between 2500 and 2000 BC. In spite of its name, it has no connection with Ossian, the early pre-Christian warrior-poet. In this area were discovered remains of neolithic 'axe factories'—axes and other implements, made from the specially suitable stone found on Tievebulliagh. From the cairn on its lonely mountain spur, there are beautiful views across the chequer-board of distant fields, to the hills and the sea beyond.

[451] Surrounding D 130510

Rathlin Island (N Ireland 1″ Map 1; Eire ½″ Map 2)

Five miles out from Ballycastle. Boomerang-shaped island about 9 miles long, surrounded by high, weathered cliffs most spectacular on the western side, petering out at the eastern end in a ridge of strangely carved, colour-streaked rocks like the spiny tail of a crocodile. A deep base of chalk edges the cliffs like a white pie frill. The cliffs are the haunt of sea birds, at their most profuse in early summer, when up to 200 species have been observed. Except for Church Bay, sheltered on the inner side of the curve, where there is a village, two churches, a school and a pub, and some isolated farms on other parts of the island, it is quite untouched. There are no made up roads, only rough stony tracks, acres of high grassland and heath, with rocky outcrops, and many small, reedy loughs. There are three lighthouses—at the western, the eastern, and the southern extremities. The Vikings came marauding to Rathlin in the 8th century; and in the early 14th century Robert Bruce hid there from the English, in a great sea cavern in the eastern cliffs. Here he is alleged to have watched the spider. Marconi used the island to transmit early radio signals to Ballycastle on the mainland.

Rathlin can be reached by boat in summer from Ballycastle to Church Bay (45 minutes), when the islanders help visitors by arranging trips in tractors (very bumpy ride), or if available, by car. At other times of the year, weather permitting, make arrangements with local boatmen.

[452] J 115880

Shane's Castle (N Ireland 1″ Map 5; Eire ½″ Map 5)

Two miles north-west of Antrim, on the shores of Lough Neagh. The ruins stand at the edge of the lough and are reached by a 2½-mile drive through a fine tangle of great trees and shrubs in the magnificently dilapidated demesne of Shane's Castle Park, property of the Lord O Neill. The present castle, now ruined, replaced an earlier 16th century fortress originally called Edenduffcarrick, settled by James I on Shane McBrian O Neill. In the early 19th century Earl O Neill commissioned Nash to enlarge the house and give it a southern aspect. Only the terrace and the conservatory had been completed when fire destroyed the main block, a calamity attributed to the wrath and vengeance of the resident banshee whose empty room was inconsiderately used for a banquet. The conservatory, a delightful piece of Nash designing,

nluce Castle, Co. Antrim *(Wonder No. 444)*

Ballylumford Dolmen on Islandmagee, Co. Antrim *(see under The Gobbins)* *(Wonder No. 448)*

arlemont Fort, Co. Armagh *(Wonder No. 457)*

The Giant's Ring, Co. Down *(Wonder No. 4*

houses in tangled splendour a fine collection of camellias. The outlook from the terrace is across the waters of the lough, along whose edges water birds shelter.

Few other outstanding features remain, though the place is pleasing. On the east face of the tower nearest to the lake, can be seen, about 20 feet up, a small head carved on a corner stone, and said to be the Black Head of the O Neills. In a thicket beside the drive is a firmly closed stone mausoleum built in 1722 and inscribed 'This vault was built by Shane McShane McBrian McPhelim O Neill Esq., for a burial place to himself and family of Clanaboy.' It is empty now, the coffins having been removed to the family vault at Drummaul parish church. (Admission charge to castle ruins.)

[**453**] D 222053

Slemish Mountain (N Ireland 1″ Map 3; Eire ½″ Map 5)

Seven miles east-north-east of Ballymena; reached by minor roads crossing the mountains to the south of the Braid valley. Great, distinctive mountain (1,437 feet), its bulky head rising clear above the lesser heights surrounding it, and a recognizable and impressive landmark. Here, the young St Patrick was brought as a slave by Milcho (Miliuc) to tend his flocks for 6 years on the then terrifying mountain fastness with its menacing forests. A tall, shapely rock—St Patrick's Chair—stands on the summit close to an Ordnance Survey pillar, which seems like an impertinence. Regarded for centuries as a place of pilgrimage, people still make the ascent, as much now for the superb views. The climb—not a difficult one—is best started from tracks which run up from the northern side of the mountain.

On the north side of the river Braid, on Knockooghran (824 feet), are the remains of Skerry Church, a high ruin visible from the road which traverses the valley, and the traditional site of a church founded by St Patrick himself. According to legend, here was the home of Milcho, St Patrick's master. A hollow in a boulder is called St Patrick's Footmark—the imprint of the saint's foot when he miraculously stepped across the valley from the summit of Slemish. Another version credits the footprint to an angel who visited St Patrick, and who took off from the rock when reascending to heaven.

[**454**] D 234406

Torr Head (N Ireland 1″ Map 1; Eire ½″ Map 2)

Five miles north-north-west of Cushendun. Splendid headland, the nearest point to Scotland (13 miles), with tremendous views across the sea to the Mull of Kintyre and Ailsa Craig—an enormous granite island like a pudding on the horizon. A high, narrow coast road with fuchsia hedges follows the contours of the coast north from Cushendun, veering westwards across Torr Head to Ballycastle on the north coast. It has very steep gradients and sharp hairpin bends and needs care to negotiate, but there are superb views all the way. A mile and a half to the south-west of the Head, close to the summit of Carnanmore (1,253 feet), is Carnanmore passage-grave, with a corbelled chamber whose inner roof stones are decorated with rings and cup markings.

ARMAGH

[455] H 916560

Ardress House (N Ireland 1″ Map 5; Eire ½″ Map 8)

Six miles west-north-west of Portadown, south of the Portadown–Moy road (signposted). Beautiful, small, pink-washed Georgian country house reconstructed by the English architect, George Ensor, about 1775. One of two brothers who worked extensively in Dublin, Ensor lived at Ardress with his wife who was heiress to the place. To the old, steep-pitched, twin-gabled manor house built about 1660, he added two wings, one on the north side, another on the east, preserving the symmetry with curved screen walls embellished with niches and recessed panels on the garden front, and Venetian windows, some of which are fakes. On the garden front, too, there is an urn of Coade stone, an artificial, kiln-burnt stone made at Mrs Coade's works in Lambeth by a process the secret of which has never been divulged.

The chief glory of the interior of Ardress, is the drawing room, originally the kitchen, which was completely remodelled by Ensor and wonderfully decorated by the famous Irish plasterworker, Michael Stapleton, who was also responsible for the splendid decorations at Powerscourt, the frieze in the Examination Hall at Trinity College, Dublin, and many great Dublin houses.

The ceiling of the drawing room is a beautiful conception of circles and parts of circles and segments, delineated by chains of husks and reeding within which there are patterns of urns, from the bases of which burgeon exuberant growths of foliage. The circular plaque in the centre shows Aurora in the Chariot of Dawn. At the four corners of the room there are oval plaques with beautiful, neo-classical figures. The plaques on three walls depict the four seasons and a group, the central figure of which is Pallas Athene and Cupid Bound. The room is a masterpiece. (National Trust; admission charge.)

[456] J 063238

The Ballymacdermot Cairn (N Ireland 1″ Map 8; Eire ½″ Map 9)

Two miles south-west of Newry. Reached by the minor road from Newry to Killevy. The cairn stands by the roadside on the southern slope of Ballymacdermot Mountain. (Ask directions in Newry for the road to Killevy.)

Excavated in 1962, this long, wedge-shaped cairn had already been deprived of its contents by Messrs Bell and Seaver, who dug into it early in the 19th century. There are too many toffee papers in it to satisfy the romantic taste, but in fine weather the view over the green fields in the vale below, to Carlingford Lough which can just be seen, and of the dark mass of Slieve Gullion (q.v.) which lies to the south-west, is memorable.

[457] H 858560

Charlemont Fort (N Ireland 1″ Map 5; Eire ½″ Map 8)

Half a mile south-east of Moy. Interesting, very rare remains of 17th century artillery fortifications on a commanding hill on the right bank of the river Blackwater, above the bridge which leads to the little town of Moy in Tyrone. It was originally built during the English Deputy Lord Mountjoy's campaign against Great Hugh O Neill in 1602. It changed hands several times and was a British post until 1858. The outer earthworks, which have pointed bastions, were thrown up in 1673 to enclose a star-shaped fort built 40 years earlier. They can still be followed, although a modern house makes it impossible to make the entire circuit of them. Good view.

Of the other buildings—the Governor's House and a more modern barracks were burned down by guerillas in 1922—the only one that remains is an 18th century gatehouse surmounted by a belfry with clock faces on it. It has the arms of the Governor, Caulfield, on the outer side. Chains for the drawbridge which spanned the moat, now filled in, can still be seen. The gateway is approached by a noble avenue of trees. The earthworks can be reached by an entry on the south side of the bridge. The gate on the road which leads to the gatehouse is usually locked.

[458] H893168

Corliss Fort (N Ireland 1″ Map 8; Eire ½″ Map 8)

One and a half miles north-west of Crossmaglen. From the town, follow the road to Clarebane Bridge which marks the border with Co. Monaghan in Southern Ireland, and then take the second road to the right. The fort is on the left, just past the junction with another road on the right.

This great rath, probably medieval, is in a splendid situation on a high green hill or drumlin, with very steep ramparts. It stands in a beautiful grove of beech trees and at sunset the place has a truly magical quality. Near the centre of it there is an L-shaped souterrain. Corliss is also known as the Beech Fort, the Black Fort, or Donaghy's Fort, and any of these names will probably be more recognizable to any local person from whom you ask the way to it, than Corliss Fort.

Half a mile to the north-east of Corliss, in Annaghmare, there is an interesting prehistoric grave in a cairn, known locally as the Black Castle, which was excavated in 1963–4 (H 905178). Cremated human remains, bones of wild and domestic animals, a flint javelin head and fourteen scrapers were among the objects found in it. It stands high up on a rock in desolate, marshy country. It has a long gallery in it and remarkable dry-walling work. It can be reached from Corliss by following the road to Crossmaglen for a few yards, and then taking the first turning to the left.

[459] H 950193

The Dorsey (N Ireland 1″ Map 8; Eire ½″ Map 8)

Six miles south of Newtown Hamilton. This difficult to find Wonder (Marked 'Site of Ancient Entrenchment' on the 1″ map, and 'Dorsy Entrenchment' on the ½″ map), is an extraordinary earthwork which encloses an area of 300 acres in the very up and down country south of Newtown Hamilton. It consists of a rampart between ditches, with another rampart outside it, in some places so steep that it is almost impossible to cross it. Where it traversed stretches of bog, the foundations were supported on oak piles. The Dorsey was probably a frontier defence set up by the inhabitants of Navan Fort (Emania), the great hill fort of the Gaelic kings which lies to the west of the city of Armagh, and which currently looks less than wonderful due to elaborate excavation which has destroyed the mystery of the place.

Fine sections of the Dorsey can be seen immediately south-west of the main Newtown Hamilton–Dundalk road at Drummill Bridge on the Dorsey river. Another good section on the southern side, which is the best preserved, can be reached by continuing south along the main road for ½ mile from Drummill Bridge, and then turning first left, following this road turning neither to left nor right until it climbs to nearly its highest point, about 400 feet. Here, on either side of this old coach road, the Dorsey is 120 feet wide and the rampart is very high and steep above the ditch. It shows up well in the sunshine of late afternoon. One-third of a mile northwards, along the coach road, is the northern line of the Dorsey.

[460] H 965413

Gosford Castle (N Ireland 1″ Map 8; Eire ½″ Map 8)

One mile north-north-east of Markethill. This enormous, mock Norman castle (not to be confused with the old castle which is marked in Gothic type on the 1″ map) was begun for the second Earl of Gosford by Thomas Hopper in 1819. How long it took to complete is uncertain, but Lewis's *Topographical Dictionary of Ireland* stated that, at the time the entry was written, 'it has been above 20 years in process of erection, and is not quite completed'. Externally, with its narrow windows on the entrance front, and closely barred door, flanked by drum-shaped towers, it resembles the house of a Citizen Kane—a place of nightmare. Built of granite from the Mullinglass quarries, it is probably indestructible, which may be one of the reasons why it has been used to house documents belonging to the Record Office. It is planned to open it to the public eventually. The demesne, which is extensive and beautiful, was a favourite resort of Dean Swift, who was a frequent visitor to the old castle, erected by Sir A. Acheson in 1617. It was destroyed in the rising of the Old Irish of Ulster in 1641, which was led by Sir Phelim O Neill.

[461] J 041221

The Killevy Churches (N Ireland 1″ Map 8; Eire ½″ Map 9)

Four miles south-west of Newry. (Signposted.) Two ancient, ruined, roofless churches in a graveyard enclosed by beech trees on the east side of Slieve Gullion (q.v.). The situation is very beautiful. The churches stand one behind the other and joined to one another, but now with no other communication. The westernmost church is the older of the two, 9th or 10th century, and the west door has an enormous lintel stone over it. Behind it, in the churchyard, there is an enclosure with slate and carved stone tombs of the McCoys in it.

[462] J 062149

The Kilnasaggart Inscribed Stone (N Ireland 1″ Map 8; Eire ½″ Map 9)

Seven and a half miles south-south-west of Newry, ¼ mile east-south-east of Kilnasaggart railway bridge, behind a farm. Signposted. (Ask permission at the farm.) This rough, slightly pointed 7-foot-high granite pillar, stands on the site of a monastery or hermitage in a little enclosure which was constructed in modern times, probably to prevent cattle rubbing themselves against it and destroying the beautiful, incised crosses of which there are ten on one side, each enclosed in a circle. Some of the crosses have spiral ends on their horizontals.

On the other side of the stone, between a tall, free-standing Latin cross and another in a circle, there is an inscription in Gaelic which reads: 'This place Ternoc, son of Ceran, bequeathed under the protection of Peter the Apostle'. Ternoc died about 714 or 716. This makes the Kilnasaggart stone (Kilnasaggart means 'Church of the Priests') one of the oldest, if not the oldest, Christian monument in Ireland which can be given a date. At the foot of it are several stones also with crosses on them and one that might be a bullaun. The place where the stone stands was the cemetery and in it there were, at one time, two concentric circles of graves lined with slabs, but there is no longer any sign of them. This is a very impressive memorial.

[463] J 058147

Moyry Castle (N Ireland 1″ Map 8; Eire ½″ Map 9)

A quarter of a mile south-west of Kilnasaggart railway bridge, 7½ miles south-south-west of Newry. A beautiful little tower of pale stone with some slight remains of a bawn about it, built on a rock in the Moyra Pass, a little over ¼ mile from the Border. The three-storeyed tower is only 24 feet square and there is little to see except musketry loop-holes, the remains of fireplaces with an unusual chimney, and a machicolation over the entrance door. The situation is good, and if one has made the journey to the Kilnasaggart Inscribed Stone (q.v.) which is close by, it is a pity not to visit it.

The castle was built by a Dutch engineer to command the Moyra Pass during Lord Deputy Mountjoy's campaign of 1600. The Pass—the Gap of the North—was the only way from the South into the then Gaelic-speaking North, apart from the route along the Carlingford coast, and the boggy and thickly wooded country round about, which was called the Fews (from Fiodha—a forest) was the scene of some awful battles. Hugh O Neill defeated the English here in 1595 and held the Pass for nearly six years until Mountjoy dislodged him, but his triumph was short-lived, as a few days later another battle was fought at Ravensdale, a little to the west, in which Mountjoy was severely wounded and the English were forced to retreat to Dundalk.

[464] J 025202

Slieve Gullion (N Ireland 1″ Map 8; Eire ½″ Map 9)

Five and a half miles west-south-west of Newry. On this long, heather-covered mountain, which slopes gradually upwards from north to south, there are two prehistoric graves, one at the north end, the other on the summit at a height of 1,894 feet. They can be reached from a white farmhouse on the roadside on the north flank of the mountain (signposted). There is a small charge for admission to the passage-grave on the summit, payable at the farmhouse. (It is open on Saturdays and Sundays, 2–6 p.m., April–September.) The climb to the ridge takes about half an hour.

The northern cairn is about 50 feet in diameter and 10 feet high. It is surrounded by lumps of rock. Human remains and potsherds were found when it was excavated in 1961. The southern summit cairn, known as Calliagh Birra's House is 100 feet in diameter and has a retaining kerb of stones. Inside it there is an octagonal tomb chamber, reached by a walled and lintelled passage. The tomb has been reinforced with concrete, which is a pity, as it tends to destroy the atmosphere of this lonely, exposed Bronze Age burial place. For non-archaeologists the main point in going to the summit of Slieve Gullion is the view, which is immense in clear weather, and unforgettable, extending 40 miles south to the Loughcrew Hills in Meath (q.v.). Slieve Gullion was the abode of the outlaw Redmond O Hanlon, an Irish Robin Hood, who confined his depredations to the English.

DOWN

[465] J 579761

The Ballycopeland Windmill (N Ireland 1" Map 6; Eire ½" Map 5)

One mile west of Millisle on the road to Newtownards. A fine tower mill 33 feet high to the curb, with stone walls 23 feet in diameter at the base, and 2 feet thick. It is the only complete windmill in Co. Down, in which county there were formerly over 100. It ceased work in 1915. The mill, which has three pairs of stones, stands on a bare hill above the road.

Another fine, but very much neglected and ruined windmill on the Ards Peninsula can be seen in Ballybryan (J 585665), just over a mile south of Grey Abbey on a hill to the east of the road to Kircubbin along the shore of Strangford Lough. It is 19 feet in diameter and the walls are 3¾ feet thick, 34 feet high. One of the stones is, or was until recently, intact.

[466] J 462427

The Ballydugan Flour Mill (N Ireland 1" Map 9; Eire ½" Map 9)

Two miles south-west of Downpatrick. This magnificent flour mill which stands 58 feet and six storeys high, was built in 1792. It is roughcast rubble masonry and has a tiled roof. The walled forecourt has an entrance gateway under the storehouse. Behind the mill there is an engine house which housed a 25 h.p. steam engine, and a tall, tapering brick stack. Huge wooden beams and columns support the upper floors, which are reached by ladders. When there was sufficient water, the power came from Ballydugan Lake on the other side of the road. On a hill behind the mill to the north, there is the ruined stump of a windmill built of the same material as the flour mill. It can be reached by the first turning to the right off the main Downpatrick–Clough road.

[467] J 482404

The Ballynoe Stone Circle (N Ireland 1″ Map 9; Eire ½″ Map 9)

Two and three quarter miles south of Downpatrick. Large and impressive circle of more than 50 stones, some of them 6 feet high with other uprights and outlying monoliths in the field around it. An oval mound inside the circle was excavated shortly before the last war. Two rectangular graves were found with cremated bones. Gathered around the long mound, the stones have a rather human air, as if they had come to wonder at the grave of a dead giant.

The circle can be reached on foot by a lane opposite what was, until recently, the railway station at Ballymoe (now no longer shown as such on the 1″ map.) Ballymoe can be reached by taking the first turning to the right at the Flying Horse, on the road from Downcastle to Killough.

[468] J 573494

Castleward House (N Ireland 1″ map 9; Eire ½″ Map 9)

Six miles east-north-east of Downpatrick; 1 mile west of Strangford. Beautiful mid-18th century house in an arcadian 60-acre demesne on the shore of Strangford Lough. It was begun for Bernard Ward, first Lord Bangor, by an unknown architect about 1765. The demesne has belonged to the family since the 16th century. The front of the house on the south-western, landward side is majestically restrained Palladian, that on the north-east, which faces an inlet of Strangford Lough, is romantic, battlemented, Strawberry Hill Gothic. The two styles here uniquely united in one house was the result of a difference of opinion between Lord Bangor, who wanted the classical decencies to be observed, and his wife, Lady Anne, who wanted the house to be Gothic and up to date.

The interior is equally at variance, one part with another. The entrance hall, staircase, dining and music rooms on the south-west front are Lord Bangor's; those on the north-east are Lady Bangor's. The most remarkable of her rooms is the sitting room, with its fantastic, pendulous stucco vaulting, so distended that it seems about to burst about one's ears. This is one of the most fantastic interiors in Ireland.

Beyond the classical front of the house, in the demesne, there are noble oaks and beeches of great size and antiquity. From the Gothic front the land slopes gently to the lough in a dream of contrived vistas. To the north of the house there is a long, artificial, reed-filled water with a temple above it on a hill and, before one comes to it, a great and noble avenue of limes. (Open April–September; admission charge.)

[469] J 405369

Dundrum Castle (N Ireland 1″ Map 9; Eire ½″ Map 9)

Immediately north of the village of Dundrum. A fine, 12th century Norman castle in a grove of trees on a hill, partly surrounded by a deep, rock-cut ditch. The great cylindrical keep is on the summit. Although very much an Ancient Monument with conveniently placed hand-holds and gratings to walk on, the situation is very beautiful, and the view from the keep over an inlet of Dundrum Bay, the Mourne Mountains, and inland, is truly magnificent.

The castle hill was the site of Dun Rudraige, the habitation of Bricriu of the Poisoned Tongue, who, with the promise of the hero's share of a monster banquet—a cauldron of wine large enough to contain three Ulstermen, a 7-year-old boar, and a cow, both superbly nourished, and 100 wheat cakes with honey—incited the three great heroes of Ulster, Cuchullainn, Conall Cernach the Victorious, and Loegaire the Triumphant, to quarrel among themselves—as recorded in *Leabhar Na H-Uidhre* (*The Book of the Dun Cow*) which was originally written down at Clonmacnoise at the beginning of the 12th century.

[470] J 327677

The Giant's Ring (N Ireland 1″ Map 6; Eire ½″ Map 5)

In Ballynahatty, 1 mile south of Shaw's Bridge, 4 miles south of the centre of Belfast. An extraordinarily impressive prehistoric monument to find so close to the centre of Belfast: a huge, neolithic enclosure—a circular earthwork 600 feet in diameter—it encloses an area of about 7 acres. The bank is about 60 feet wide at the base, and about 12 feet high. In the enclosure to the east of the centre, is a dolmen with five uprights which support a single capstone. Remains of what may have been another, lie below it.

[471] J 237118

Green Castle (N Ireland 1″ Map 9; Eire ½″ Map 9)

Four miles south-west of Kilkeel; east of Greencastle Point. Fine ruin of a 14th century English fortress, in a beautiful, wind-swept situation on a promontory on the shore of Carlingford Lough. The congery of buildings, which includes a more modern farm with bright green lichen on one of its roofs, is very fine. Great views towards the lighthouse and navigational marks in the lough, and to the west over the Carlingford mountains. To the north are the Mountains of Mourne.

[472] J 458821

Helen's Bay Railway Station (N Ireland 1″ Map 6; Eire ½″ Map 5)

In the village of Helen's Bay, north-east of Belfast. This splendid Victorian railway station was built to the specifications of Frederick, first Marquis of Dufferin and Ava, by the Belfast, Holywood and Bangor Railway Company in 1865 when it was extending the railway eastwards to Bangor from Holywood. The station is in the baronial manner and its gables bear the Dufferin and Ava initials and a coronet. A tree-lined avenue, 2½ miles long, connects Clandeboye House, the seat of the Dufferin and Avas, to the shore at Grey Point. It passes under the arch of a bridge specially built to allow it to do so. This bridge also has heraldic embellishments. Beyond it, a flight of covered steps led to a private waiting room in the station so that the marquis and his family could reach their train relatively unobserved. Behind the station there is a fantastic turret, the top part of which has unfortunately been removed.

[473] J 477455

Inch Abbey (N Ireland 1″ Map 9; Eire ½″ Map 9)

Three quarters of a mile north-west of Downpatrick. Beautiful, lonely ruins of a Cistercian abbey, hidden at the foot of a wooded valley on the left bank of the river Quoile. It was built by Norman de Courcy around 1180 as a peace offering to the church, he having destroyed Carrick Abbey close by in Erenagh, and the monks came to it from Carrick. There are three magnificent, tall lancet windows in the east wall of the chancel—very beautiful against the sky on a fine evening. Across the river, Downpatrick Cathedral can be seen on a hill.

[474] J 598457

Kilclief Castle (N Ireland 1″ Map 9; Eire ½″ Map 9)

Two and a half miles south of Strangford on the road to Ardglass. Splendid, four-storeyed tower house standing above a rocky foreshore, with a cottage on one side and a farm on the other. There are projecting turrets, one of which contains latrines at the various levels of the upper storeys, and with a pit which acted as a receptacle at the foot. This is the oldest dateable tower house in Co. Down, and it may be the oldest in all Ireland.

It was built by John Cely who was appointed to the bishopric of Down in 1413 and was deprived of it for living in it with a married woman called Lettice Thomas in 1441. Over a fireplace on the second floor, a 13th century tombstone serves as a lintel stone. Fine views from here over the disused lighthouse at the mouth of Strangford Lough, to Ballyquintin Point on the Ards Peninsula.

[475] J 232154

The Kilfeaghan Dolmen (N Ireland 1″ Map 9; Eire $\frac{1}{2}$″ Map 9)

Four miles west of Kilkeel. At the foot of the Mourne Mountains, this portal dolmen, which has a 35-ton granite capstone supported on a pair of seemingly inadequate portal stones, resembles a fungus sprouting up from the earth, and like a fungus it is not very easy to find. It stands under a hedge in a field about 500 yards north of the Rostrevor–Kilkeel road, and can be reached by an unsignposted lane from the bus stop immediately west of the bridge over the Cassy Water. There is a sign in the lane itself which indicates its whereabouts.

[476] J 289434

The Legananny Tripod Dolmen (N Ireland 1″ Map 9; Eire $\frac{1}{2}$″ Map 9)

Six and a half miles north-west of Castlewellan. (Marked 'Dolmen' by the 'L' of Leganny on the 1″ map.) This rather difficult to find tomb stands in the middle of a labyrinth of small roads, none of which actually leads anywhere. With the exception of The Labby (q.v.), it is probably the most bizarre of all the Irish dolmens, although officially it is said to be the most graceful. It stands on the side of a track opposite a farm, 850 feet up on the rocky slopes of Cratlieve, an outlier of Slieve Croob. The capstone, which is over 10 feet long, is raised above the ground in front by two portal stones and a third, shorter one, supports it at the back. Looking up the track towards it, one has the impression that a gigantic spider is advancing on one. From the back it resembles a huge coffin being carried by three pall bearers. The view from this place is splendid in fine weather over the Mourne Mountains and the sea.

To reach it: leave Castlewellan by the Banbridge road. Take the first turning to the right which presents itself—this road leads through the small village of Leitrim in which there is a church. Continue through the village and take the second turning to the right after just over a mile. Take the second turning on the left after $\frac{3}{4}$ mile, then the first right after $\frac{1}{2}$ mile. The farmhouse where the dolmen is, is at a bend of the road just over $\frac{1}{2}$ mile along this road.

[477] J 425455

The Loughinisland Churches (N Ireland 1″ Map 9; Eire $\frac{1}{2}$″ Map 9)

Four miles west of Downpatrick and immediately to the east of the village of Loughinisland. Signposted from the main Belfast–Newcastle road. Three ruined churches on an island in a lough. The oldest one, which may be 13th century, is in the middle; the two which flank it are probably 16th century, the one on the south side being known as Phelim MacCartan's Chapel (the initials PMC and the date, 1636, are carved at the west door.) The situation is extremely beautiful. A sign among the tombs in the churchyard, one of which has a handle, like that of a drawer, reads: 'No fishing'.

One mile to the south, at Nutgrove, there is a very fine large 18th century corn mill (J 427439). There are three pairs of stones and the machinery is, or was until recently, still in position. The building is very beautiful.

[478] J 370342

Maghera Church and Round Tower (N Ireland 1″ Map 9; Eire ½″ Map 9)

Two miles north of Newcastle, reached by a signposted lane from the road, 1¼ miles south-west of Maghera village. The church, which is reached by a straight drive, is hidden behind the austere but pleasing little 19th century parish church. It is now below the level of the ground and one steps down into it. It is very, very ruined. There is a great gap in the west wall and only it and the north wall are still standing. In the churchyard there is an extraordinary collection of tombstones, many of them at crazy angles. One of the headstones is a broken lid of a 13th century coffin. The round tower, or rather, the stump of it, for now only 18 feet of it remain, is hidden away in a field north-west of the modern church. It was blown down in a great gale about 1714. It fell in one piece and did not break.

[479] J 524636

Nendrum (N Ireland 1″ Map 6; Eire ½″ Map 5)

On Mahee Island, 5¾ miles south-east of Comber. Remains close to the shore of Strangford Lough in what was formerly, until the island was joined to the mainland by causeways, a very lonely place. This primitive monastery may have been founded by St Machaoi (St Mochaoi) in the 5th century. Whether it was or not, the island is named after him. The remains, which were excavated in the 1920s, include three stone ramparts, the innermost one 6 feet thick. They enclose within them a church, partly 12th century, with cross slabs built into it, the lower part of a round tower, a building the purpose of which is conjectural, with a circular roofed pit under it, and a monks' cemetery. There are also ruins of other houses and huts in the outer rings of walls. A bell and other objects found at this fascinating place are in the Ulster Museum, Belfast.

[480] J 237297

Pat Kearney's Big Stone (N Ireland 1″ Map 9; Eire ½″ Map 9)

Two and a half miles east-north-east of Hilltown and ¼ mile south from the Hilltown–Castlewellan road, from which it is signposted; on an old road which runs from the church at Hilltown beyond the bridge over the Leitrim river. Officially known as the Goward Dolmen (some great humorist has changed the 'G' to 'C'), but locally as Pat Kearney's Big Stone or Cloughmore. (Not to be confused with another conglomeration of remains, cairns and court graves which are marked on the 1″ maps as 'Dolmen'.) Unless the run-in is made from the signpost on the road, difficulty will be experienced in finding the Big Stone, which may add to its charm for those of tenacious temperament when they eventually get to it.

It is a dolmen with a really enormous granite capstone which has partly slipped from its original position – not surprising considering that it weighs about 50 tons. It stands by the side of the narrow track, into which the old road from Hilltown has degenerated, beyond a farmhouse, and is modestly concealed from view until one arrives at it, as so many such structures seem to be. Below it, in the dell on the edge of which it lurks, are a number of stones which perhaps formed part of the kerb of the cairn which originally covered it. If going to the Big Stone by car, leave it at the second signpost as there is no turning place, and other seekers after the antique, also car-borne, may be on your heels.

[481] J 247597

St Malachi's Parish Church (N Ireland 1″ Map 6; Eire $\frac{1}{2}$″ Map 5)

At Hillsborough. A charming Gothic church built for William Hill, first Earl of Hillsborough in 1773 by an unknown architect. It is approached through twin lodges up a gently sloping avenue, flanked by splendid trees. The interior, which has had many alterations made to it since it was first built (the electric lights were designed by Sir Albert Richardson), is memorable. The 18th century prayer desk and pulpit are very elegant, and there are box pews.

[482] J 514443

Struel Wells (N Ireland 1″ Map 9; Eire $\frac{1}{2}$″ Map 9)

One and a half miles east of Downpatrick, by a lane from the Ardglass road to the left, immediately after the mental hospital. This strange, slightly oriental place – one might be in Turkey, near the shores of the Bosphorus, rather than in Ireland – with its four bath houses and its ruined church, is in a green hollow among trees close under a rocky hillock. It is more popularly known as St Patrick's Wells. The stream which supplies the wells rises below a place on the hillside where there are four stones, known as St Patrick's Chair. It emerges in the Drinking Well, a small circular stone building with fragments of the ancient church, probably 13th century, which stood here, built into it. The 'new' church, now a ruin, was built in the 18th century. It stands close to the Drinking Well outside the modern wall which encloses the meadow through which the spring flows underground after it leaves the well. This wall has portions of the window of the old church built into it.

The Eye Well, in which the stream next surfaces, is a minute rectangular building with a pyramidical roof in the middle of the meadow. Warning notices everywhere state that the water is unfit for human consumption—a useless admonition as the wells are still visited by great numbers of pilgrims for cures on the night of June 23rd, Midsummer Eve, each year.

The stream again vanishes from view and it, or some tributary, next appears, gurgling merrily in the Men's Bath House, a very solid, 17th century building where it enters a tank. Next to it is the Women's Bath House, now roofless.

St Patrick is supposed to have visited Struel from his habitation at Saul, a little over a mile to the north and the site of his first church in Ireland. It would be more surprising if he had not done so. Well into the 19th century it was believed that the wells overflowed on Midsummer's Eve, and that the sick were cured at this time. A penance was also performed here during which the little hill was ascended barefoot or crawling, the 'Chair' visited, and certain movements performed in it, and the rounds made of a large number of cairns. In earlier times, the wells were also visited the Friday before Lughnasa (Lammas).

[483] J 113551

Waringstown House and Church

(N Ireland 1″ Map 5; Eire ½″ Map 9)

At Waringstown, 3 miles south-south-east of Lurgan. Seventeenth century manor house—it was actually built in 1667—with a pink and grey-washed façade with window frames in the same pale shade of grey. The irregularities of the façade, due to its age, add to its charm. The interior has good panelling and staircases, but it is not open to the public. The house can be seen quite easily from the main road which runs along the foot of the front lawn.

It was designed by James Robb, an apprentice assistant of Inigo Jones, as was the church which is close by—one of the best of the 17th century Plantation churches in Ireland. It was built in 1681. The square brick tower has a slated spire topped by an elaborate weathercock; the chancel, aisle and transept are later additions. The great, black oak roof is supported by two huge, carved timbers decorated with swags of vines, and there is an elaborate pulpit with carved panelling, with a canopy over it.

Waringstown was established as a linen manufactory by William Waring, the original owner of the house in the early part of the 18th century. He visited the Low Countries and had special reels and spinning wheels made for the production of fine cambric. There are a few old thatched weavers' cottages left in the village street, but they are in bad repair and the majority have been swept away.

[484] J 369467

Whitepark (N Ireland 1″ Map 9; Eire ½″ Map 9)

Four miles south of Ballynahinch, on the east side of the Castlewellan road. Impressive, 19th century premises of a linen manufacturer, now used as a farm. They consist of a large, white stuccoed house and two very long, low buildings which were used as store rooms. On the east side of the courtyard which they form, there is a scutch mill with a tall brick stack—all very decayed. The date when they were built is unknown.

Maps

Legend

	Motorway		County Boundary
	Trunk Road		International Boundary
	Main Road		Section Boundary
	Secondary Road	*99	Position of Wonder

Scale

0 10 20 30 40 50 Miles

0 10 20 30 40 50 60 70 80 Kilometres

Key to Sections and Counties

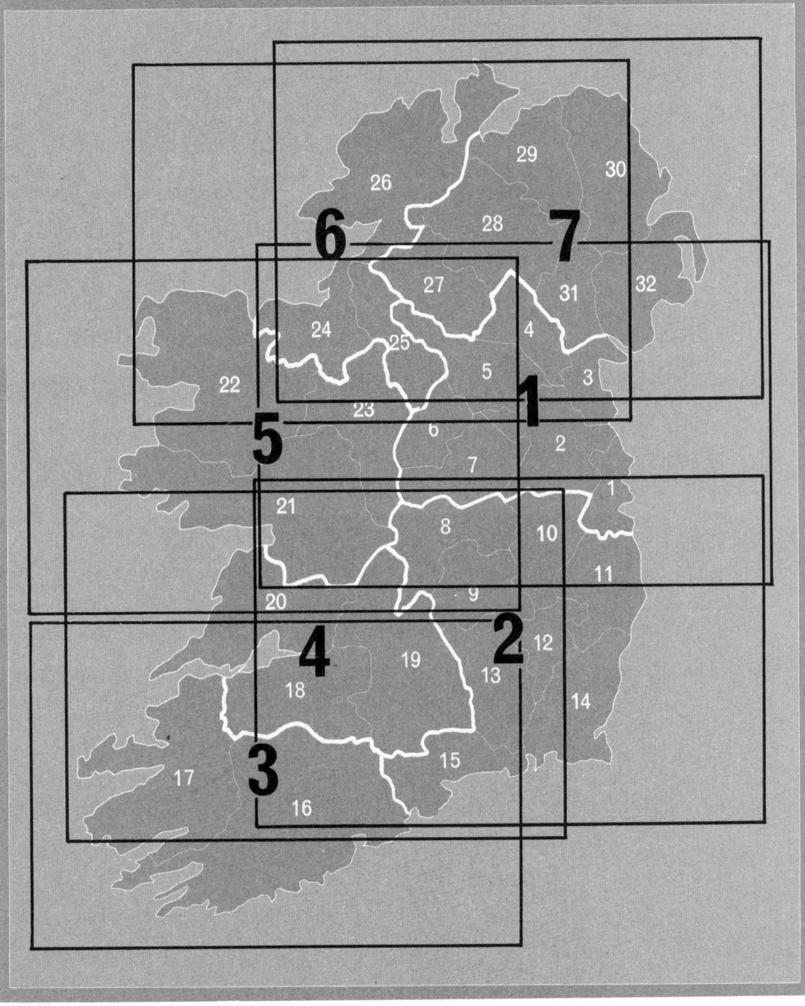

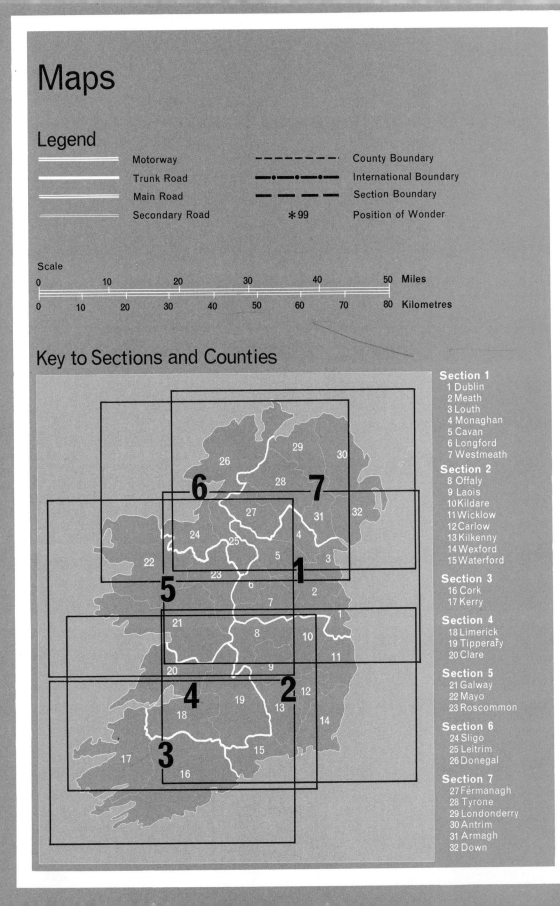

Section 1
1 Dublin
2 Meath
3 Louth
4 Monaghan
5 Cavan
6 Longford
7 Westmeath

Section 2
8 Offaly
9 Laois
10 Kildare
11 Wicklow
12 Carlow
13 Kilkenny
14 Wexford
15 Waterford

Section 3
16 Cork
17 Kerry

Section 4
18 Limerick
19 Tipperary
20 Clare

Section 5
21 Galway
22 Mayo
23 Roscommon

Section 6
24 Sligo
25 Leitrim
26 Donegal

Section 7
27 Fermanagh
28 Tyrone
29 Londonderry
30 Antrim
31 Armagh
32 Down

1

DONEGAL BAY
Ballintra
Coolmore
Ballyshannon
Bundoran
Mullaghmore
INISHMURRAY
Kinlough
L. Melvin
Pettigo
Lack
Ederny
Kesh
Milltown
Irvinestown
Dromore
Fintona
Belleek
Lower Lough Erne
Garrison
Grange
Rossinver
FERMANAGH
Fivemiletown
Carney
L. Glencar
Raghly
Drumcliff
Sligo Bay
Easkey
Dromore West
Skreen
Templeboy
Inishcrone
Sligo
Manorhamilton
Tycloghe
L. Macnean
Belcoo
Blacklion
Enniskillen
Lisbellaw
Brookborough
Maguire's Bridge
Lisnaskea
Boho
L. Gill
Dromahaire
CUILCAGH MTS.
Swanlinbar
Newtownbutler
Collooney
Coolaney
SLIGO
Drumkeeran
LEITRIM
L. Allen
SLIEVE GAMPH MTS.
Lavagh
Ballymote
Ballyfarnan
Arrow
Keadew
Ballyconnell
Belturbet
Milltown
Tobercurry
Ballinafad
Ballinamore
Drumshanbo
Fenagh
Killeshandra
L. Oughter
Curry
Gorteen
Boyle
Arigna
Carrick-on-Shannon
Cavan
Foxford R. Moy
Charlestown
Swinford
Jamestown
Drumsna
Rathallen
Mohill
Arvagh
R. Erne
Ballinagh
Ballaghaderreen
Frenchpark
Ballinamuck
Ballyjamesduff
Kilkelly
Elphin
Dromod
L. Gowna
Drumlish
MAYO
ROSCOMMON
Knock
Ballyhaunis
Castlerea
Tulsk
Strokestown
Ballinalee
Granard
L. Sheelin
Oldcastle
Newtownforbes
Longford
LONGFORD
Edgeworthstown
Claremorris
Cloonfad
Ballymoe
Cloondara
Ballyclare
Lanesborough
Ballindine
Castlepollard
L. Derravaragh
Glinsk
Roscommon
Cafrickboy
Dunmore
Glennamaddy
Creggs
Foxhall
Ballymahon
Ballynacargy
WESTMEATH
Crookedwood
Athleague
Lecarrow
Mullingar
Ballygar
L. Ree
Tuam
Mount Bellow Br.
Glasson
Ballymore
L. Ennell
Castletown Geoghegan
Athlone
Moate
Rochfortbridge
Kilbeggan
R. Shannon
Ballynahown
Clara
Claregalway
GALWAY
Kilconnell
Ballinasloe
Clonmacnoise
Ballycumber
Daingean
Athenry
Tullamore
Oranmore
Shannonbridge
Laurencetown
Kiltormer
OFFALY
Kilcogan
Clonfert
Cloghan
Loughrea
Eyrecourt
Banagher
Kilcormac
Ballyboy
Portarlington
Ardrahan
Kinvarra
Tynagh
Clonaslee
Mountmellick
Portumna
Beagh/Ballyclugga
Gort
Birr
Kinnitty
SLIEVE BLOOM MTS.
L. Cutra
Portlaoise
Tubber
Borrisokane
Mountrath
Stradbally

Stewartstown
Coalisland
Donaghmore
Dungannon
Lisburn
470
Carryduff
Comber
Greyabbey
Ballyhalbert
Strangford Lough
479
Ballygowan
481
Hillsborough
Saintfield
457
455
Moy
Lurgan
483
Dromore
Portadown
Benburb
Ballynahinch
Killyleagh
Portaferry
Crossgar
Strangford
484
477
473
468
474
Tanderagee
Banbridge
Downpatrick
482
BALLYQUINTIN PT.
Armagh
460
476
Clough
466
467
Markethill
Poyntzpass
Leitrim
469
Castlewellan
Ardglass
Killough
Keady
Rathfriland
478
Dundrum
Dundrum Bay
480
Newcastle
Hilltown
Belleek
Newtown Hamilton
Newry
MOURNE MOUNTAINS
461
456
459
464
Castleblayney
Warrenpoint
Rostrevor
475
458
Crossmaglen
462
463
23
Omeath
471
Kilkeel
22
30
27
Greencastle
Ballymascanlan
Carlingford
Carlingford Lough
Donaghmoyne
33
Dundalk
Carrickmacross
Dundalk Bay
Kingscourt
Castlebellingham
26
Ardee
Drumcondra
25
Dunleer
Kildemock
Nobber
31
CLOGHER HEAD
Collon
24
Clogher
29
11
14
28
17
Slane
Drogheda
Kilberry
16
10
R. Boyne
Duleek
Navan
13
Athboy
Balrath
8
12
Balbriggan
9
HILL OF TARA
19
Naul
Skerries
21
Trim
20
Lusk
6
Rush
Laracor
Dunshaughlin
Ashbourne
Castlerickard
Summerhill
Swords
Malahide
2
Dublin Airport
Enfield
IRELAND'S EYE
Clonee
Kilcock
81
Finglas
Howth
1
Maynooth
69
68
Celbridge
DUBLIN
Dublin Bay
Dun Laoghaire
73
Clane
R. Liffey
4
Dalkey
Ballybrack
5
7
Killiney
Prosperous
76
Sallins
3
Allen
74
Naas
75
77
91
Glencree
Bray
Enniskerry
Droichead Nua
80
71
92
Blessington
90
Greystones
KILDARE
Kilcullen
Delgany
72
Hollywood
89
93
Roundwood
Dunlavin
Glendalough
Ashford
88
Ballitore
Lower Castleruddery
85
84
Laragh
Wicklow
Timolin
83
IRISH SEA

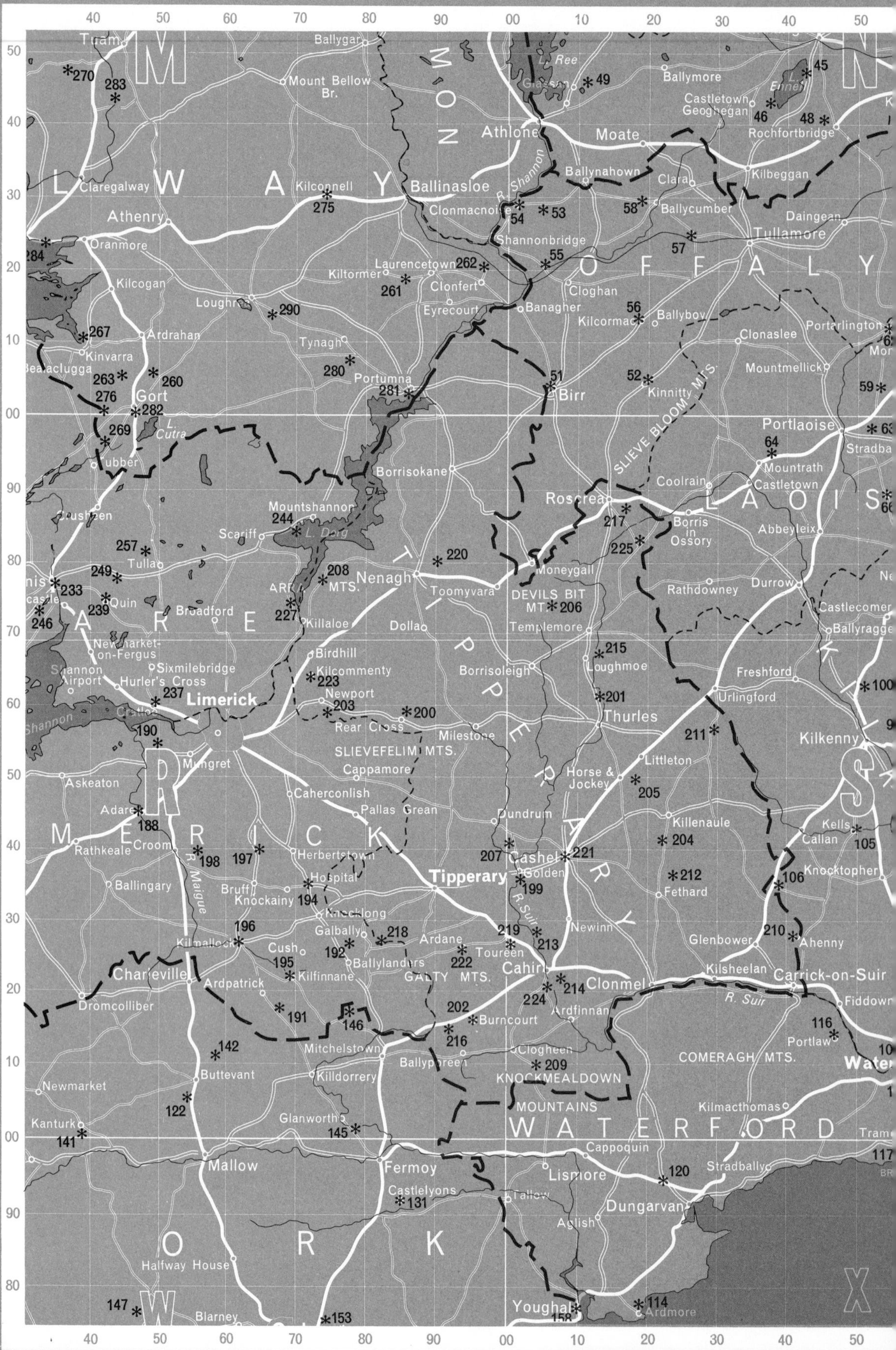

M
W A Y
L
O F F A L Y
T I P P E R A R Y
C L A R E
L I M E R I C K
W A T E R F O R D
C O R K
L A O I S
K I L
MON
N
R
S
W
X
Tuam
*270
283 *
Ballygar
Mount Bellow Br.
L. Ree
Glasson
*49
Ballymore
L. Ennell
*45
Castletown Geoghegan
46
48 *
Athlone
Moate
Rochfortbridge
Kilbeggan
Claregalway
Kilconnell
*275
Ballinasloe
R. Shannon
Ballynahown
Clara
Athenry
Clonmacnoise
*54
*53
58*
Ballycumber
Daingean
Oranmore
*284
Shannonbridge
*55
*57
Tullamore
Kilcogan
Laurencetown
262*
Kiltormer
*261
Clonfert
Cloghan
Loughrea
*290
Eyrecourt
Banagher
Kilcormac
56
Ballyboy
Portarlington
*267
Ardrahan
Tynagh
Clonaslee
Kinvarra
Bealaclugga
263*
*260
*280
Portumna
281
*51
Birr
52*
Kinnitty
Mountmellick
59*
Gort
276
*282
00
SLIEVE BLOOM MTS.
Portlaoise
*63
269
L. Cutra
Tubber
64
Mountrath
Stradbally
Borrisokane
Coolrain
Castletown
Crusheen
Mountshannon
244
L. Derg
Roscrea
217
Borris in Ossory
Abbeyleix
Scariff
*225
257*
*220
Tulla
249*
ARRA MTS.
*208
Nenagh
Toomyvara
Moneygall
Rathdowney
Durrow
Ennis
*233
Newcastle
*239
Quin
DEVILS BIT MT *206
Castlecomer
246
Broadford
227
Killaloe
Dolla
Templemore
Ballyragget
Newmarket-on-Fergus
Birdhill
*215
Sixmilebridge
Shannon Airport
Hurler's Cross
*223
Kilcommenty
Borrisoleigh
Loughmoe
Freshford
*100
*237
Limerick
Newport
*201
Urlingford
*203
*200
Thurles
Rear Cross
Milestone
211*
Kilkenny
190
SLIEVEFELIM MTS.
Mungret
Littleton
Askeaton
Cappamore
Horse & Jockey
*205
Caherconlish
Adare
188
Pallas Grean
Dundrum
Kells
Callan
105
Rathkeale
Croom
*198
197
Herbertstown
207
Cashel
*221
*204
R. Maigue
Hospital
Tipperary
Golden
*212
*106
Knocktopher
Ballingary
Bruff
Knockainy
194
*199
Fethard
R. Suir
Knocklong
196
Galbally
*218
219
*213
Newinn
210
Ahenny
Kilmallock
Cush
192
Ardane
Toureen
*222
Glenbower
195
Ballylanders
Cahir
Kilsheelan
Carrick-on-Suir
Charleville
Ardpatrick
Kilfinnane
GALTY MTS.
224
*214
Clonmel
R. Suir
Fiddown
Dromcolliber
*191
202
*146
Burncourt
Ardfinnan
116
*216
Portlaw
*142
Mitchelstown
Clogheen
COMERAGH MTS.
Waterford
Ballyporeen
*209
Buttevant
Killdorrery
KNOCKMEALDOWN
Newmarket
*122
MOUNTAINS
Kilmacthomas
Glanworth
Kanturk
145*
141*
Tramore
117
Mallow
Fermoy
Cappoquin
Lismore
*120
Stradbally
Castlelyons
*131
Tallow
Dungarvan
Aglish
Halfway House
147*
Blarney
*153
Youghal
158
*114
Ardmore

Ashbourne
Dunshaughlin
Summerhill
Enfield
Kilcock
Maynooth
Celbridge
Swords
Malahide
Dublin Airport
IRELAND'S EYE
Howth
Clonee
Finglas
DUBLIN
Dublin Bay
Dun Laoghaire
Dalkey
Ballybrack
Killiney
Clane
R. Liffey
Sallins
Allen
Naas
Droicead Nua
Kilcullen
Bray
Glencree
Enniskerry
Greystones
Delgany
Blessington
Hollywood
Roundwood
Dunlavin
Glendalough
Laragh
Ashford
Wicklow
Ballitore
Timolin
Lower Castleruddery
Derrynamuck
WICKLOW MTS.
WICKLOW
Baltinglass
Castledermot
Rathdrum
Ballinaclash
R. Slaney
Hacketstown
Aughrim
Avoca
MIZEN HEAD
Woodenbridge
Arklow
Tullow
Leighlinbridge
Bagenalstown
Carnew
Myshall
Gorey
Bunclody
Courtown
MT. LEINSTER
Ferns
CAHORE PT.
Ullard
Killealy
BLACKSTAIR MTS.
CARLOW
WEXFORD
Enniscorthy
Blackwater
New Ross
Ballynabola
Camaross
Wexford
Campile
Wellingtonbridge
Rosslare
Rosslare Harbour
Killinick
GREENORE PT.
Ballyhack
Passage East
Crooke
Bannow
Fethard
FORLORN PT.
Kilmore Quay
Churchtown
CARNSORE PT.
Slade
HOOK HEAD
SALTEE IS.
IRISH SEA
ST. GEORGE'S CHANNEL

3

Q
V
C
L
K E R R Y
Kilkee
Creegh
Liscasey
Killadys
Kilrush
Labash
Carrigaholt
Kilbaha
LOOP HEAD
Tarbert
Glin
Mouth of the Shannon
Ballylongford
Ballybunion
Knockanure
Ballyduff
Listowel
Ballyheigue
BANNA STRAND
Abbeyfeale
Abbeydorney
Ardfert
BRANDON HEAD
Brandon
Tralee Bay
Tralee
Ballybrack
BRANDON MT.
Cloghane
Camp
SLIEVE MISH MTS.
Castleisland
Smerwick
SYBIL POINT
Kilmalkedar
Ballyferriter
Dunquin
Milltown
Dingle
Aglish
Anascaul
Inch
Castlemaine
Farranfore
Ballydesmond
BLASKET ISLANDS
SLEA HEAD
Killorglin
Beaufort
Killarney
Rathmore
Dingle Bay
Glenbeigh
L. Caragh
Gortboy
L. Leane
CARRAUNTUOHILL MT.
Glencar
Acoose
MACGILLYCUDDY'S REEKS
Glenflesk
Cahirciveen
VALENTIA ISLAND
Knightstown
Kenmare
Ballingeary
L. Allua
Inchigeelagh
Waterville
Sneem
SHEEHY MTS
SKELLIG ROCKS
BOLUS HEAD
Caherdaniel
Castlecove
Kenmare River
Lauragh
LAMB'S HEAD
Ardgroom
CAHA MTS
Glengarriff
Coolagh Bay
Adrigole
Trafask
Dunmanway
Bantry
Bantry Bay
Drimoleague
Dunmanus Bay
Skibbereen
Glandore
Castletown
Goleen
Baltimore
MIZEN HEAD
CLEAR I.
SHERKIN I.
FASTNET ROCK
240
245
255
229
248
232
238
168
177
170
180
162
184
186
173
169
166
165
172
164
178
183
167
174
179
182
176
163
157
181
126
140
185
187
171
175
139
124
138
125
132
148
149
133

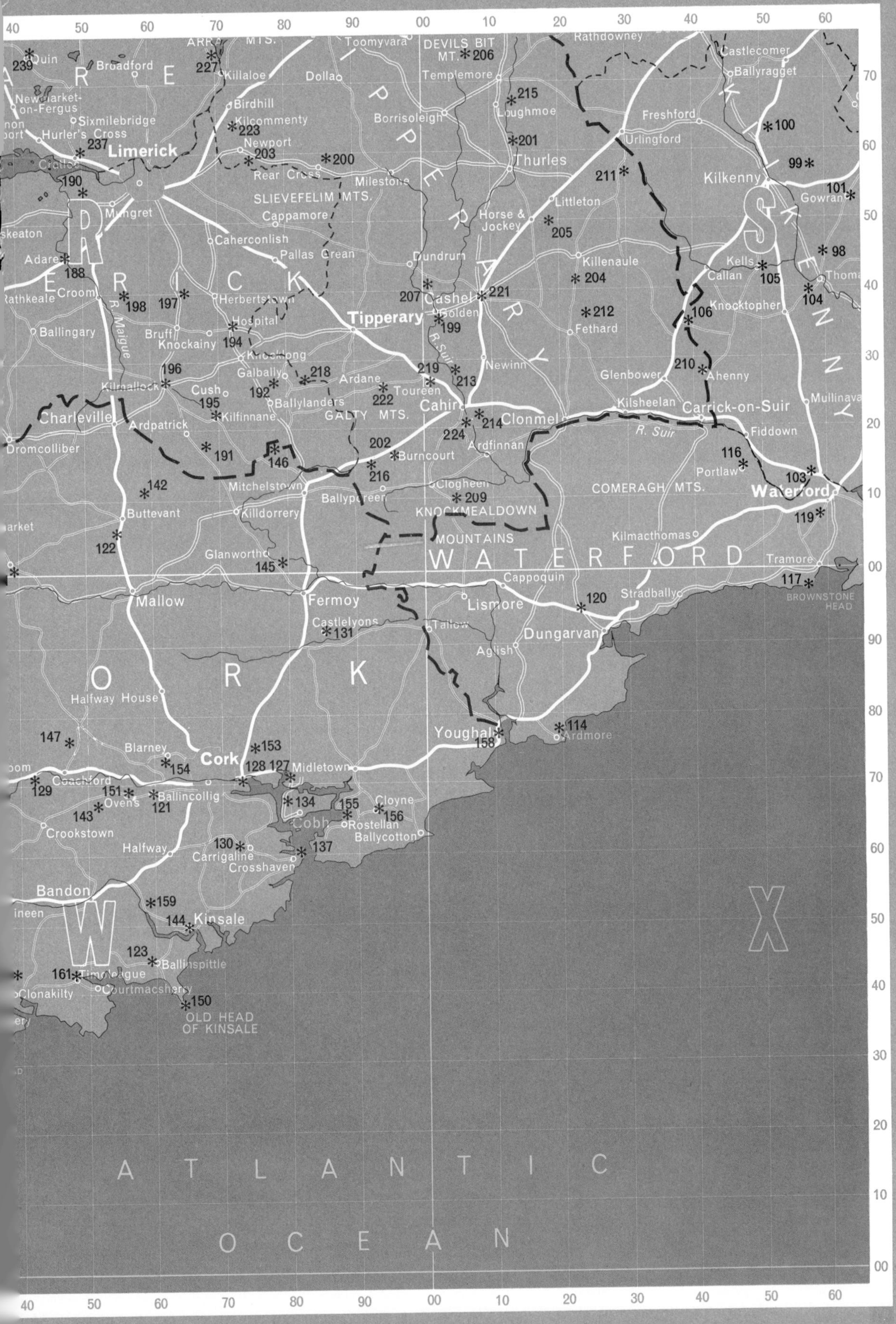
Quin
Broadford
ARRA MTS.
Toomyvara
DEVILS BIT MT.
Rathdowney
Castlecomer
Ballyragget
Killaloe
Dolla
Templemore
Newmarket-on-Fergus
Birdhill
Loughmoe
Freshford
Sixmilebridge
Kilcommenty
Borrisoleigh
Hurler's Cross
Newport
Urlingford
Limerick
Thurles
Rear Cross
Milestone
Kilkenny
SLIEVEFELIM MTS.
Littleton
Gowran
Mungret
Cappamore
Horse & Jockey
Caherconlish
Adare
Pallas Grean
Dundrum
Killenaule
Kells
Callan
Rathkeale
Croom
Herbertstown
Cashel
Golden
Knocktopher
R. Maigue
Hospital
Tipperary
Fethard
Ballingary
Bruff
Knockainy
Knocklong
R. Suir
Newinn
Glenbower
Ahenny
Galbally
Ardane
Toureen
Kilmallock
Cush
Ballylanders
GALTY MTS.
Cahir
Kilsheelan
Carrick-on-Suir
Mullinavat
Charleville
Ardpatrick
Kilfinnane
Clonmel
R. Suir
Fiddown
Dromcolliber
Ardfinnan
Burncourt
Portlaw
Mitchelstown
Clogheen
COMERAGH MTS.
Waterford
Ballyporeen
KNOCKMEALDOWN MOUNTAINS
Buttevant
Killdorrery
Kilmacthomas
Glanworth
WATERFORD
Tramore
Cappoquin
BROWNSTONE HEAD
Mallow
Fermoy
Lismore
Stradbally
Castlelyons
Tallow
Dungarvan
Aglish
CORK
Halfway House
Youghal
Ardmore
Blarney
Cork
Midleton
Coachford
Ovens
Ballincollig
Cloyne
Cobh
Rostellan
Crookstown
Ballycotton
Halfway
Carrigaline
Crosshaven
Bandon
Kinsale
Ballinspittle
Timoleague
Courtmacsherry
Clonakilty
OLD HEAD OF KINSALE
X
W
ATLANTIC OCEAN

Roundstone
Bertraghboy Bay
Mace
Carna
ST. MACDARA'S I.
Screeb
Oughterard
Moycullen
Claregalway
Athenry
Galway
Oranmore
Inveran
North Sound
GALWAY BAY
BLACK HEAD
INISHMORE
ARAN ISLANDS
INISHMAAN
INISHEER
Kilcogan
Ardrahan
Kinvarra
Ballyvaghan
Bellaclugga
Gort
L. Cutra
Lisdoonvarna
CRAB I.
Fisherstreet
CLIFFS OF MOHER
Kilfenora
Tubber
Liscannor
Lahinch
Ennistymon
Corrofin
Inagh
Milltown Malbay
Tulla
Ennis
Clarecastle
Quin
Broadford
Creegh
Liscasey
Newmarket-on-Fergus
Shannon Airport
Sixmilebridge
Hurler's Cross
Kilkee
Killadysert
Kilrush
Labasheeda
R. Shannon
Carrigaholt
Kilbaha
LOOP HEAD
Foynes
Askeaton
Tarbert
Glin
Adare
Croom
Mouth of the Shannon
Ballylongford
Ballybunion
Ardagh
Rathkeale
R. Maigue
Knockanure
Listowel
Ballyduff
Ballingary
Newcastle West
Ballyheigue
BANNA STRAND
Abbeyfeale
Abbeydorney
Ardfert
Charleville
Dromcolliber
BRANDON HEAD
Brandon
Tralee Bay
Tralee
Ballybrack
BRANDON MT.
Cloghane
Camp
SLIEVE MISH MTS.
Castleisland
Kilmalkedar
Ballyferriter
Newmarket
Ballydesmond
Milltown
Dingle
Aglish
Anascaul
Castlemaine
Farranfore
Kanturk
Cloonbannin
Killorglin
L. Caragh
Dingle Bay
Beaufort
Killarney
Rathmore
Glenbeigh
Gortboy
L. Leane
Millstreet
Glencar
CARRAUNTUOHILL MT.
Glenflesk
MACGILLYCUDDY'S REEKS
Halfway House
Cahirciveen
Knightstown
Ballyvourney
Kenmare
Macroom
Coachford
Waterville
Sneem
Ballingeary
L. Allua
L. Lee
Inchigeela
Ovens
G A L W A Y
C L A R E
L I M E R I C K
K E R R Y
C O R K
L M Q R V W
287 278 284 259 243 267 266 235 263 260 258 250 231 253 276 226 230 241 282 236 256 269 234 251 247 228 254 242 257 252 249 233 239 246 240 237 245 190 255 229 232 248 238 168 177 188 198 193 189 170 180 162 184 186 166 173 169 122 178 164 172 141 183 167 174 179 182 176 163 157 147 181 126 129 151 140 143
40 50 60 70 80 90 00 10 20 30 40 50

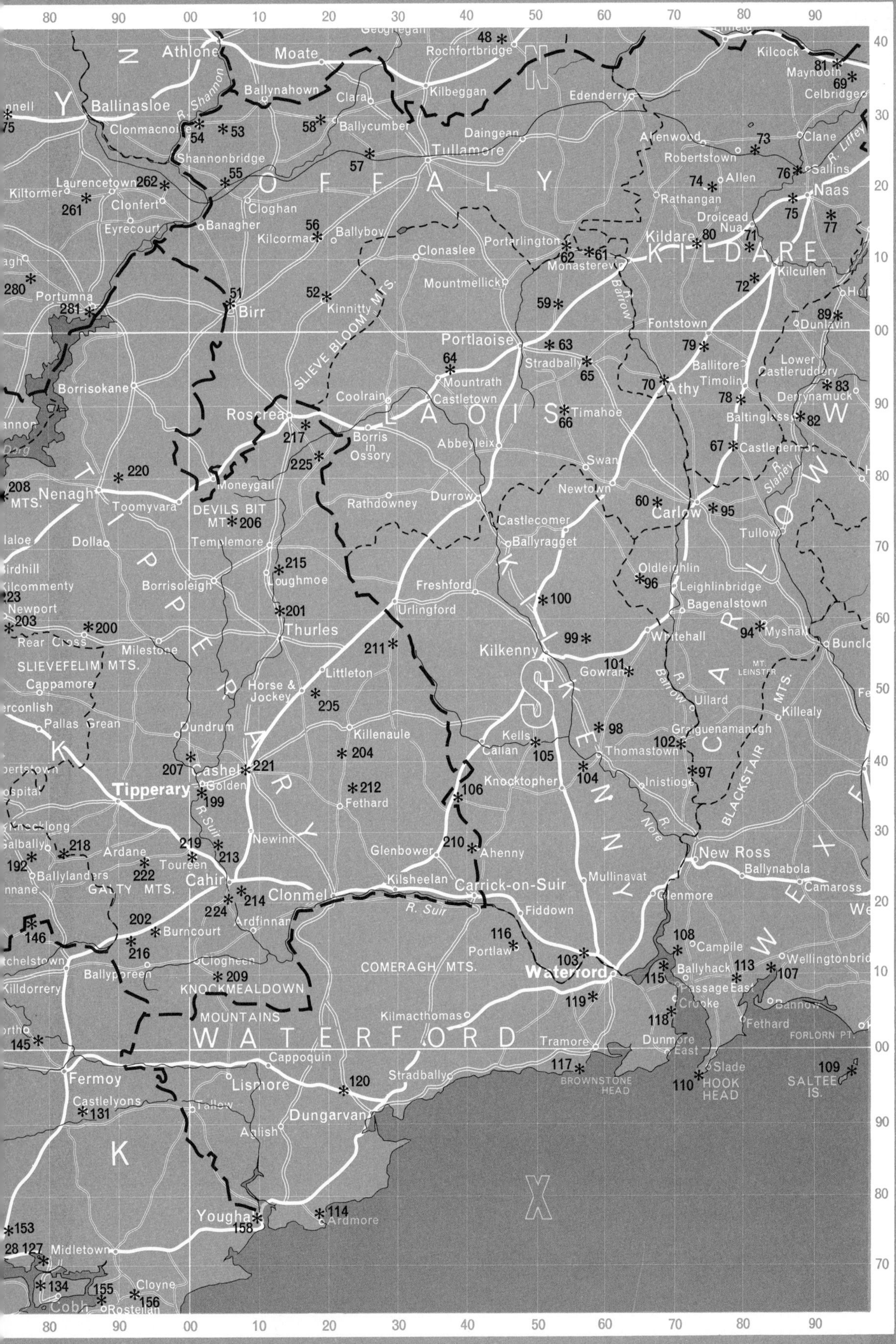

80 90 00 10 20 30 40 50 60 70 80 90
40 30 20 10 00 90 80 70 60 50 40 30 20 10 00 90 80 70
Athlone
Moate
Rochfortbridge
48
Kilbeggan
Edenderry
Kilcock
Maynooth
81
69
Celbridge
Ballinasloe
Ballynahown
Clara
R. Shannon
Clonmacnoise
54
53
58
Ballycumber
Daingean
Tullamore
Allenwood
73
Clane
Robertstown
R. Liffey
Shannonbridge
57
55
76
Sallins
Laurencetown
262
Kiltormer
261
Clonfert
Cloghan
74
Allen
Naas
Rathangan
75
77
Eyrecourt
Banagher
56
Ballyboy
Kilcormac
Portarlington
Droicead Nua
Kildare
80
71
Clonaslee
62
61
Monasterevin
Kilcullen
280
Portumna
281
51
Birr
52
Kinnitty
SLIEVE BLOOM MTS.
Mountmellick
59
R. Barrow
72
Fontstown
89
Dunlavin
Portlaoise
63
79
64
Stradbally
65
Lower Castleruddery
Borrisokane
Mountrath
70
Athy
Ballitore
Timolin
83
Coolrain
Castletown
78
Derrynamuck
Roscrea
217
Borris in Ossory
66
Timahoe
Baltinglass
82
225
Abbeyleix
67
Castledermot
220
Swan
R. Slaney
208
MTS.
Nenagh
Moneygall
Newtown
60
Carlow
95
Toomyvara
DEVILS BIT MT.
206
Rathdowney
Durrow
Castlecomer
Tullow
Dolla
Templemore
Ballyragget
Birdhill
215
Loughmoe
Oldleighlin
96
Leighlinbridge
Kilcommenty
Borrisoleigh
Freshford
100
Newport
203
201
Urlingford
Bagenalstown
200
Thurles
99
94
Myshall
Rear Cross
Milestone
211
Whitehall
Kilkenny
Bunclody
SLIEVEFELIM MTS.
101
Gowran
MT. LEINSTER
Littleton
Cappamore
Horse & Jockey
205
Ullard
Pallas Grean
Dundrum
Killenaule
98
Killealy
Kells
Graiguenamanagh
204
Callan
105
102
Thomastown
207
Cashel
221
104
97
Tipperary
Golden
212
Knocktopher
Inistioge
199
106
Fethard
BLACKSTAIR MTS.
R. Suir
R. Nore
Knocklong
Galbally
218
Ardane
219
213
Newinn
210
Glenbower
Ahenny
New Ross
192
Ballylanders
222
Toureen
Ballynabola
GALTY MTS.
Cahir
214
Clonmel
Kilsheelan
Carrick-on-Suir
Mullinavat
Camaross
224
Glenmore
Ardfinnan
Fiddown
146
202
Burncourt
116
108
Campile
216
Portlaw
Clogheen
103
Wellingtonbridge
Ballyporeen
209
COMERAGH MTS.
Ballyhack
113
107
Killdorrery
Waterford
115
KNOCKMEALDOWN
119
Passage East
Crooke
Bannow
MOUNTAINS
Kilmacthomas
118
Fethard
145
WATERFORD
Tramore
Dunmore East
FORLORN PT.
Cappoquin
117
Slade
109
Fermoy
Lismore
120
Stradbally
BROWNSTONE HEAD
110
HOOK HEAD
SALTEE IS.
Castlelyons
131
Tallow
Dungarvan
Aglish
114
Ardmore
Youghal
158
153
127
Midleton
134
155
Cloyne
Cobh
156
Rostellan
OFFALY
KILDARE
LAOIS
TIPPERARY
KILKENNY
CARLOW
WEXFORD
WATERFORD
N
S
X
K

5

F
M
A
G
A
L
Q
BENWEE HEAD
Portacloy
Porturlin
295
312
294
302
DOWNPATRICK HEAD
Belderg
Ballycastle
301
323
Belmullet
299
306
Glenamoy
Barnatra
Palmerstown
Killala
314
320
Blacksod Bay
Bangor
316
Bellacorrick Br.
Dooleeg
Crossmolina
300
Fallmore
321
DUVILLAUN MORE
ACHILL ISLAND
322
Slievemore
Dugort
ACHILL HEAD
297
Dooagh
Keel
Ballycroy
Castlehill
NEPHIN BEG MTS.
304
Pontoon
311
Dooega
Achill Sound
Mallaranny
Newport
324
Castlebar
CLARE ISLAND
Clew Bay
325
Westport
315
298
Aghagower
Aille
305
292
Louisburgh
307
CROAGH PATRICK
Ballintober
296
313
L. Carra
INISHBOFIN
274
MWEELREA
SHEEFFRY HILLS
317
291
310
Hollymount
Renvyle
289
Leenaun
L. Mask
308
303
Ballinrobe
HIGH I.
279
OMEY I.
Cleggan
Kylemore
277
L. Nafooey
319
309
Neale
318
Letterfrack
THE TWELVE BENS
Clonbur
Cong
Cross
293
Clifden
288
Cur
Maum
272
273
Recess
264
Maam Cross
L. Corrib
Headford
Ballyconneely
286
Roundstone
Oughterard
Bertraghboy Bay
Screeb
Mace
Carna
ST. MACDARA'S I.
287
Galway
Inveran
North Sound
GALWAY BAY
INISHMORE
266
BLACK HEAD
243
ARAN ISLANDS
INISHMAAN
258
INISHEER
Ballyvaghan
250
226
230
236
256
Lisdoonvarna
CRAB I.
Fisherstreet
234
CLIFFS OF MOHER
251
247
228
254
Liscannor
Ennistymon
Lahinch
10
20
30
40
50
60
70
80
90
00

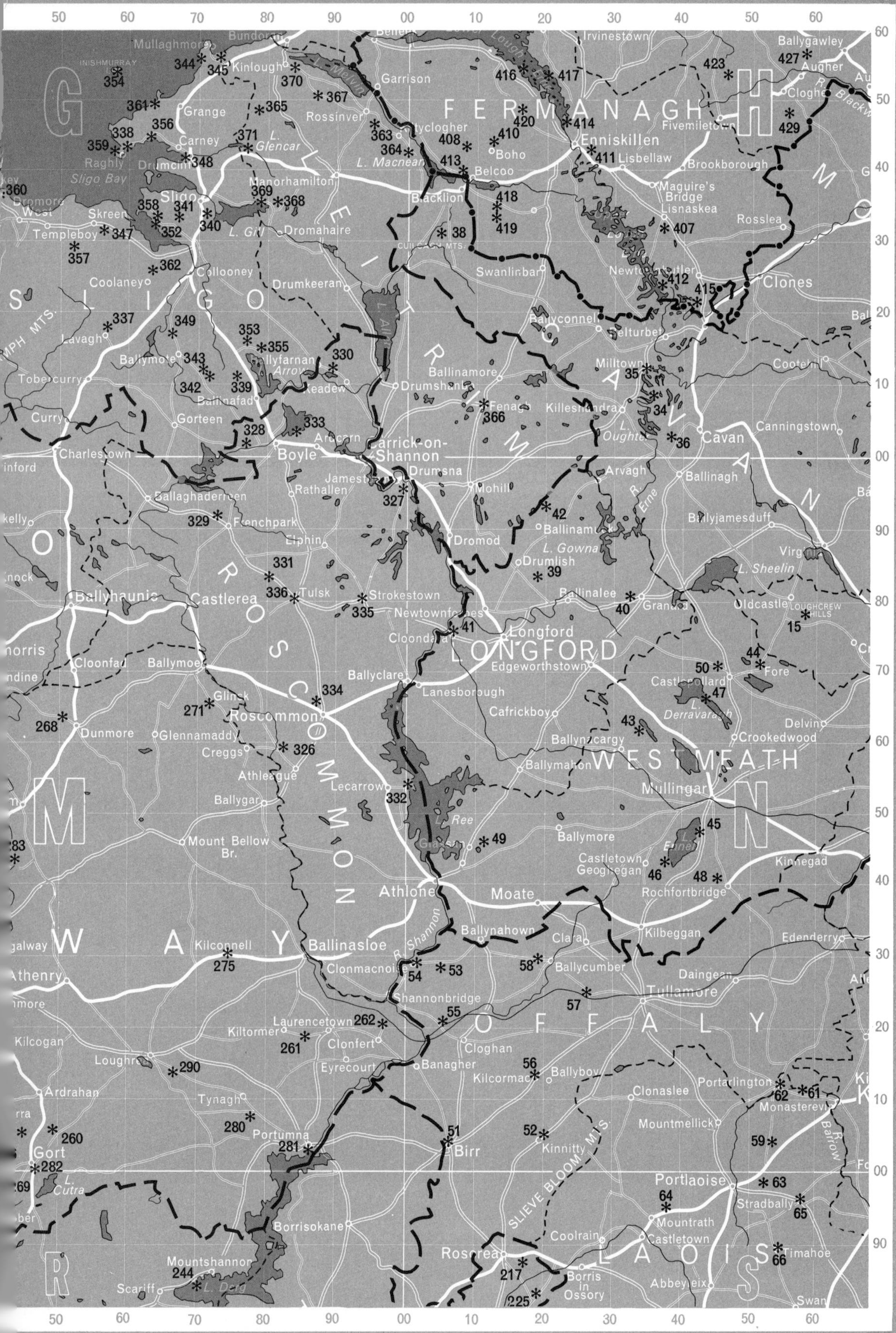

FERMANAGH
LEITRIM
SLIGO
CAVAN
LONGFORD
ROSCOMMON
WESTMEATH
OFFALY
LAOIS
GALWAY
MONAGHAN
G
H
M
N
R
S
Bundoran
Mullaghmore
INISHMURRAY
Kinlough
Grange
Carney
Drumcliff
Raghly
Sligo Bay
Sligo
Dromore West
Skreen
Templeboy
Coolaney
Collooney
L. Gill
Dromahaire
Manorhamilton
L. Glencar
L. Melvin
Garrison
Rossinver
Kiltyclogher
L. Macnean
Blacklion
Belcoo
Boho
CUILCAGH MTS.
Belleek
Lower Lough Erne
Irvinestown
Enniskillen
Lisbellaw
Brookborough
Fivemiletown
Ballygawley
Augher
Clogher
R. Blackwater
Maguire's Bridge
Lisnaskea
Rosslea
Swanlinbar
Newtownbutler
Clones
Ballyconnell
Belturbet
Milltown
Cootehill
Killeshandra
L. Oughter
Cavan
Canningstown
Ballinagh
Arvagh
R. Erne
Ballyjamesduff
Virginia
L. Sheelin
Oldcastle
LOUGHCREW HILLS
Fore
Castlepollard
L. Derravaragh
Crookedwood
Delvin
Mullingar
L. Ennell
Kinnegad
Rochfortbridge
Castletown Geoghegan
Ballymore
Ballymahon
Ballynacargy
Edgeworthstown
Longford
Granard
Ballinalee
Drumlish
L. Gowna
Ballinamuck
Mohill
Dromod
Drumsna
Fenagh
Ballinamore
Drumshanbo
L. Allen
Drumkeeran
Carrick-on-Shannon
Jamestown
Ardcarn
Boyle
Keadew
Ballyfarnan
Arrow
Ballinafad
Ballymote
Gorteen
Tobercurry
Lavagh
OX MTS.
Curry
Charlestown
Ballaghaderreen
Frenchpark
Rathallen
Elphin
Tulsk
Strokestown
Newtownforbes
Cloondara
Lanesborough
Ballyclare
Cafrickboy
Castlerea
Ballyhaunis
Cloonfad
Ballymoe
Glinsk
Roscommon
Dunmore
Glennamaddy
Creggs
Athleague
Lecarrow
L. Ree
Glasson
Ballygar
Mount Bellow Br.
Athlone
Moate
Ballynahown
Clara
Kilbeggan
Edenderry
Daingean
Tullamore
Ballycumber
Clonmacnoise
Shannonbridge
R. Shannon
Ballinasloe
Kilconnell
Athenry
Laurencetown
Kiltormer
Clonfert
Eyrecourt
Banagher
Cloghan
Kilcormac
Ballyboy
Clonaslee
Portarlington
Monasterevin
R. Barrow
Mountmellick
Kinnitty
SLIEVE BLOOM MTS.
Birr
Portumna
Tynagh
Loughrea
Kilcogan
Ardrahan
Gort
L. Cutra
Borrisokane
Mountshannon
Scariff
L. Derg
Roscrea
Coolrain
Borris in Ossory
Mountrath
Castletown
Portlaoise
Stradbally
Timahoe
Abbeyleix
Swan
Charlestown
Kilkelly
Knock
Kilmore
50 60 70 80 90 00 10 20 30 40 50 60
60 50 40 30 20 10 00 90 80 70 60 50 40 30 20 10 00 90

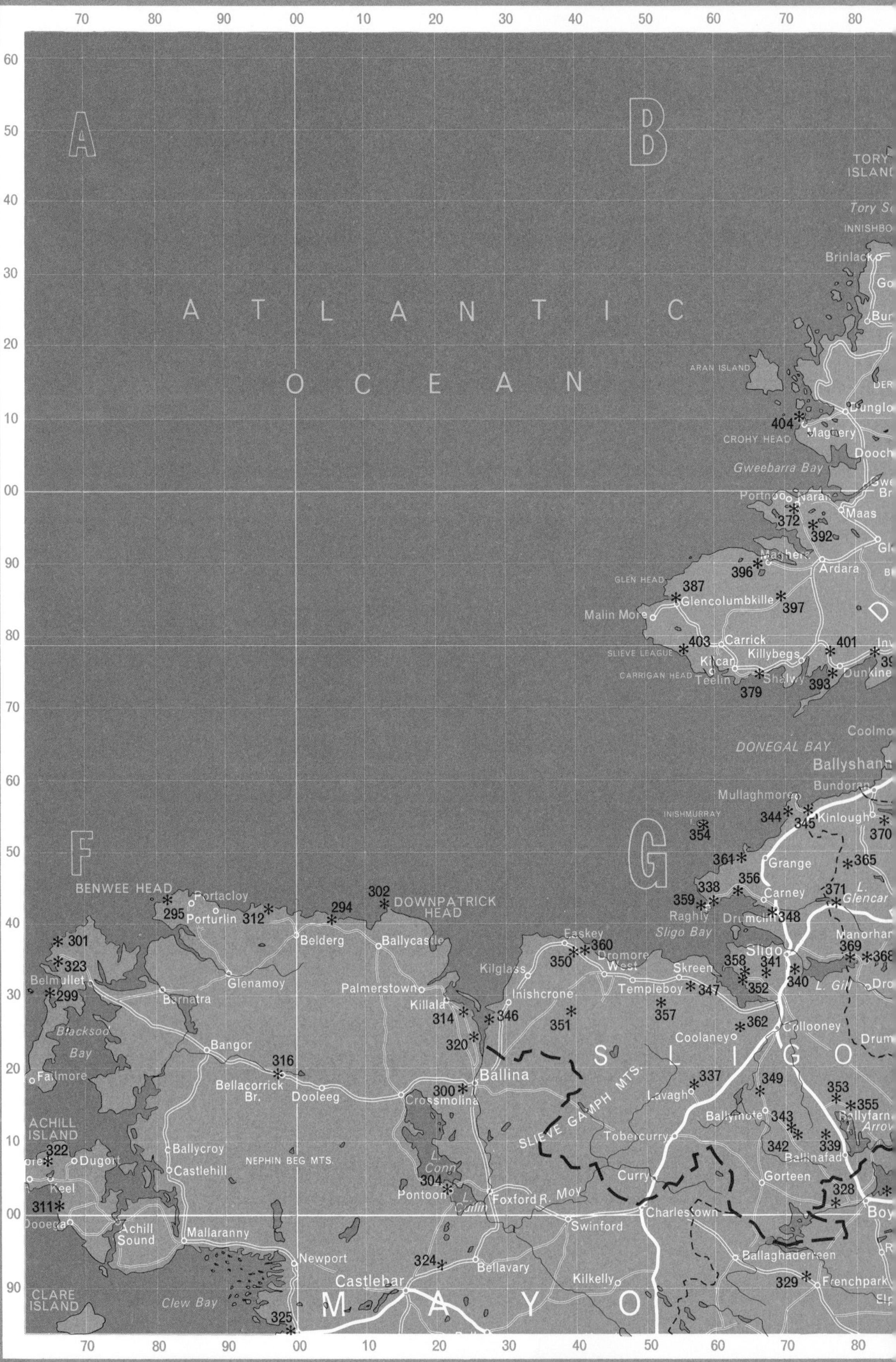
A
B
F
G
ATLANTIC
OCEAN
TORY ISLAND
Tory Sound
INNISHBOFIN
Brinlack
ARAN ISLAND
Dungloe
404
Maghery
CROHY HEAD
Doochary
Gweebarra Bay
Portnoo
Narin
Maas
372
392
Maghera
396
Ardara
GLEN HEAD
387
Glencolumbkille
397
Malin More
403
Carrick
Killybegs
401
SLIEVE LEAGUE
Kilcar
CARRIGAN HEAD
Teelin
Shalwy
379
393
Dunkineely
DONEGAL BAY
Ballyshannon
Bundoran
Mullaghmore
INISHMURRAY
354
344
345
Kinlough
370
361
Grange
365
338
356
359
Carney
371
Raghly
Drumcliff
348
Glencar
Sligo Bay
Manorhamilton
Sligo
358
341
340
369
368
352
L. Gill
BENWEE HEAD
295
Portacloy
Porturlin
312
294
302
DOWNPATRICK HEAD
301
323
Belmullet
299
Belderg
Ballycastle
Glenamoy
Barnatra
Palmerstown
Killala
314
346
Easkey
350
360
Dromore West
Kilglass
Inishcrone
351
Skreen
Templeboy
347
357
362
Coolaney
Collooney
Blacksod Bay
Bangor
320
316
Fallmore
Bellacorrick Br.
Dooleeg
Crossmolina
300
Ballina
S L I G O
SLIEVE GAMPH MTS.
337
Lavagh
349
353
355
Ballymote
343
Tobercurry
342
339
Ballinafad
ACHILL ISLAND
322
Dugort
Ballycroy
NEPHIN BEG MTS.
Castlehill
Keel
L. Conn
304
Pontoon
L. Cullin
Foxford
R. Moy
Curry
Gorteen
328
311
Dooega
Achill Sound
Mallaranny
Swinford
Charlestown
Newport
324
Bellavary
Ballaghaderreen
Castlebar
Kilkelly
329
Frenchpark
CLARE ISLAND
Clew Bay
325
M A Y O

MALIN HEAD
Ballygorman
Malin
Culdaff
Clonmany
Carndonagh
Portsalon
Greencastle
Moville
Rossnakill
Carrickart
Buncrana
Carrowkeel
L. Foyle
Cashel
Rathmullan
Milford
Bridge End
Rathmelton
Kilmacrenan
Church Hill
Newtown Cunningham
St. Johnston
Letterkenny
Pluck
Raphoe
Convoy
Cloghan
Stranorlar
Castlefinn
Ballybofey
Killygordon
Clady
Londonderry
LONDONDERRY
Claudy
Feeny
Dungiven
Dunnamanagh
Ballymagory
SPERRIN MTS.
Strabane
Sion Mills
Plumbridge
Newtownstewart
Gortin
Greencastle
Castlederg
Killeter
Drumguin
Omagh
Carrickmore
Pomeroy
Pettigo
Lack
Kesh
Ederny
Dromore
Fintona
Beragh
Milltown
Irvinestown
Lower Lough Erne
TYRONE
FERMANAGH
Enniskillen
Lisbellaw
Boho
Belcoo
Blacklion
Brookborough
Maguire's Bridge
Lisnaskea
Upper Lough Erne
Swanlinbar
Newtownbutler
Ballyconnell
Belturbet
Clones
Rosslea
Fivemiletown
Clogher
Augher
Ballygawley
Aughnacloy
Benburb
R. Blackwater
Glaslough
Monaghan
MONAGHAN
Clontibret
Ballybay
Cootehill
Castleblayney
Newtown Hamilton
Crossmaglen
Ballymascanlan
Dundalk
Dundalk Bay
Carrickmacross
Donaghmoyne
Shercock
Canningstown
Cavan
CAVAN
Killeshandra
Milltown
L. Oughter
R. Erne
Ballinagh
Arvagh
Bailieborough
Kingscourt
Ballyjamesduff
Virginia
L. Sheelin
Mullagh
Nobber
Drumcondra
Kildemock
Ardee
Castlebellingham
Dunleer
Clogher
CLOGHER HEAD
LOUTH
Ballinamore
Fenagh
Mohill
Dromod
Drumlish
Ballinamuck
L. Gowna
BENBANE HEAD
GIANT'S CAUSEWAY
Portrush
Portstewart
MAGILLIGAN PT.
Downhill
Castlerock
Bushmills
Coleraine
Ballymoney
Ballintoy
Ballycastle
RATHLIN ISLAND
FAIR HEAD
Armoy
Glenariff
Carnlough
Clough Mills
Limavady
Ringsend
Garvagh
Kilcrea
Broughshane
SLEMISH MT.
Ballymena
Kells
Maghera
Tobermore
Draperstown
Magherafelt
Toome
Randalstown
Antrim
ANTRIM
Moneymore
Coagh
Cookstown
Tullahoge
Newport French
Lough Neagh
Crumlin
Glenavy
Stewartstown
Coalisland
Donaghmore
Dungannon
Lisburn
Moy
Portadown
Lurgan
Dromore
Armagh
ARMAGH
Tanderagee
Banbridge
Markethill
Poynzpass
Keady
Rathfriland
Hilltown
Belleek
Newry
MOURNE MTS.
Warrenpoint
Rostrevor
Omeath
Carlingford
Carlingford Lough
DONEGAL
C
D
H
J

ATLANTIC OCEAN
MALIN HEAD
Ballygorman
Malin
B
C
Clonmany
374
Carndonagh
386
406
TORY ISLAND
HORN HEAD
390
Tory Sound
INNISHBOFIN
Dunfanaghy
Portsalon
Rossnakill
Carrickart
Buncrana
400
Brinlack
Falcarragh
376
375
380
Creeslough
Cashel
Gortahork
Rathmullan
Milford
Bunbeg
Bridge End
385
Dunlewy
Kilmacrenan
Rathmelton
ARAN ISLAND
398
402
382
Church Hill
394
373
389
DERRYVEAGH MTS.
Newtown Cunningham
Londonderry
Drumbologe
405
Letterkenny
St. Johnston
Dungloe
404
CROHY HEAD
Maghery
Pluck
438
Doochary
Claudy
Gweebarra Bay
Raphoe
Convoy
Dunnamana
Gweenbarra Bridge
Ballymagory
Portnoo
Narin
Cloghan
Stranorlar
Strabane
372
Maas
392
Castlefinn
Ballybofey
Killygordon
Sion Mills
Glenties
Clady
Ardara
Plumbridge
396
GLEN HEAD
BLUE STACK MTS.
384
387
Glencolumbkille
397
Castlederg
Newtownstewart
Gortin
Malin More
L. Eske
428
425
403
Carrick
Killybegs
401
Inver
381
Killeter
SLIEVE LEAGUE
391
Donegal
Kilcar
CARRIGAN HEAD
Teelin
Shalwy
393
Dunkineely
Laghey
Drumquin
379
Omagh
399
Ballintra
Coolmore
Pettigo
Lack
DONEGAL BAY
Ederny
409
Kesh
Ballyshannon
421
Milltown
Dromore
Belleek
Lower Lough Erne
Fintona
Bundoran
Irvinestown
Mullaghmore
INISHMURRAY
344
345
Kinlough
370
423
354
416
417
G
Garrison
H
361
367
Grange
365
Rossinver
FERMANAGH
356
420
414
Fivemiletown
338
Carney
371
363
Kiltyclogher
408
410
Enniskillen
359
L. Glencar
Boho
Raghly
348
364
411
Lisbellaw
Brookborough
Easkey
Sligo Bay
Drumcliff
L. Macnean
413
Belcoo
350
360
Dromore West
Manorhamilton
Maguire's Bridge
Sligo
369
368
Blacklion
418
Lisnaskea
Skreen
358
341
Rosslea
Inishcrone
Templeboy
347
352
340
L. Gill
Dromahaire
419
407
357
CUILCAGH MTS.
351
362
Collooney
Swanlinbar
Coolaney
Newtownbutler
Drumkeeran
412
415
S L I G O
SLIEVE GAMPH MTS.
337
349
Ballyconnell
Belturbet
Lavagh
353
355
Ballymote
343
330
Milltown
Ballyfarnan
Arrow
Ballinamore
Tobercurry
342
339
Keadew
Drumshanbo
Ballinafad
Curry
Gorteen
366
Killeshandra
Fenagh
R. Moy
328
333
L. Oughter
Cavan
Charlestown
Arigna
Boyle
Carrick-on-Shannon
Swinford

SCOTLAND
NORTH CHANNEL
RATHLIN ISLAND
BENBANE HEAD
GIANT'S CAUSEWAY
FAIR HEAD
TORR HEAD
GARRON PT.
Portrush
Portstewart
Castlerock
Bushmills
Ballintoy
Ballycastle
Coleraine
Armoy
Cushendun
Cushendall
Glenariff
Ballymoney
Ringsend
Clough Mills
Carnlough
Glenarm
Garvagh
DERRY
Kilcrea
Dungiven
Broughshane
SLEMISH MT.
Ballymena
Larne
Portmuck
Gransha
Maghera
Kells
Glenoe
Tobermore
Ballynure
Ballycarry
Draperstown
Whitehead
Magherafelt
Toome
Randalstown
Ballyclare
Antrim
Doagh
Carrickfergus
ANTRIM
Moneymore
Bangor
Donaghadee
Coagh
Cookstown
Newport French
Crumlin
BELFAST
Millisle
Newtownards
Tullaghoge
Pomeroy
Lough Neagh
Glenavy
Dundonald
Stewartstown
Comber
Greyabbey
Coalisland
Lisburn
Carryduff
Ballyhalbert
Donaghmore
Ballygowan
Dungannon
Strangford Lough
Saintfield
Hillsborough
Lurgan
Moy
Benburb
Portadown
Dromore
Ballynahinch
Killyleagh
Crossgar
Portaferry
Strangford
BALLYQUINTIN PT.
Tanderagee
Banbridge
Armagh
Downpatrick
Clough
Leitrim
Markethill
Poyntzpass
Castlewellan
Ardglass
Killough
Dundrum
Rathfriland
Dundrum Bay
Keady
Newcastle
Hilltown
MOURNE MOUNTAINS
Clontibret
Belleek
Newtown Hamilton
Newry
ARMAGH
DOWN
Castleblayney
Warrenpoint
Rostrevor
Crossmaglen
Omeath
Kilkeel
Carlingford Lough
Ballymascanlan
Carlingford
Greencastle
IRISH SEA
Donaghmoyne
Dundalk
Dundalk Bay
Carrickmacross
MONAGHAN
LOUTH
TYRONE
LONDONDERRY
Limavady
Castledawson
Donaghmore
Benburb
Aughnacloy
Monaghan
80 90 00 10 20 30 40 50 60 70 80 90
70 60 50 40 30 20 10 00 90 80 70 60 50 40 30 20 10 00

Reference to Irish National Grid

The Grid is divided into lettered Sub-Zones as shown by the diagram below, and both are superimposed on the maps in this book.
In the text each 'Wonder' has been given its National Grid reference and instructions on finding Grid references are given on all Ordnance Survey sheets.
Reference to these is made by permission of the Ordnance Survey of Ireland, Phoenix Park, Dublin and the Ordnance Survey of Northern Ireland, Belfast.

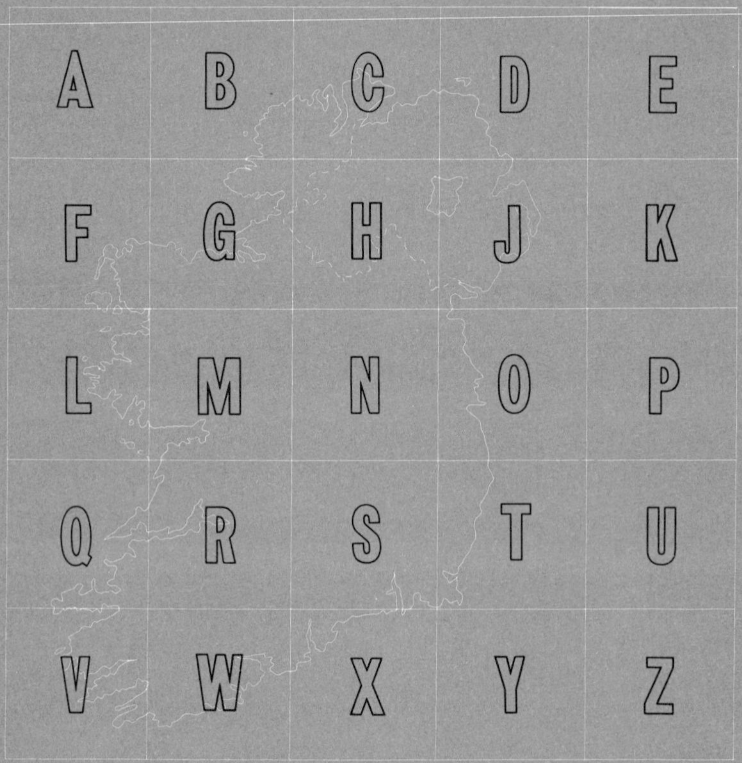